SCIENTISTS SINCE 1660

a Bibliography of Biographies

Scientists since 1660

a Bibliography of Biographies

Leslie Howsam

Ashgate

Published by
Ashgate Publishing Limited
Gower House
Croft Road
Aldershot
Hants GU11 3HR
England

Ashgate Publishing Company
Old Post Road
Brookfield
Vermont 05036–9704
USA

British Library Cataloguing-in-Publication data.

Howsam, Leslie.
    Scientists since 1660: a bibliography of biographies
    1. Science – Bio-bibliography
    I. Title
    016.5'092

Library of Congress Cataloging-in-Publication Data

Howsam, Leslie
    Scientists since 1660: a bibliography of biographies / Leslie Howsam.
    Includes bibliographical references.
    ISBN 1–85928–035–8 (cloth)
    1. Bibliography—Biography—Scientists. I. Title.
Z7401.H66   1997
[Q141]
016.51'092'2—dc20
[B]   96–41789
            CIP

ISBN 1 85928 035 8

Printed on acid-free paper

Typeset in Sabon by Intype London Ltd
Printed in Great Britain at the University Press, Cambridge

Contents

Acknowledgements

I am grateful to Michael Collie for suggesting, to me and to Scolar Press, that a bibliography of biography of scientists would be a worthwhile project. It has proved to be rewarding, and it would not have been possible without the assistance of three researchers: Stephen Connor, Stephanie Wakefield and Laura Gardner. I am grateful for financial assistance from a University of Windsor Research Grant, and for the privilege of being a Visiting Scholar at the Northrop Frye Centre in Victoria University in the University of Toronto.

Librarians at the following libraries provided assistance: the British Library, Cambridge University Library, the Thomas Fisher Rare Book Library and other collections in the University of Toronto Library system, the University of Michigan Library at Ann Arbor, and the Leddy Library at the University of Windsor. Trevor H. Levere and Jane Millgate supported my application for the Visiting Scholarship. Jonathan Topham found me a reference when I needed it. At Ashgate Publishing, Rachel Lynch and Ellen Keeling have been patient and supportive editors, as Sue McNaughton was before them.

Finally I must thank my family, Neil Campbell and Jessica Kamphorst, for the support and security that make my research possible.

LH

Introduction

This book is a work of reference and one of scholarship. It sets out the names of 565 men and women of science whose careers began during or after the burgeoning of modern science around 1660 at the time of the founding of the Royal Society, and whose lives and work have been the subject of one or more biographies. The terms to be defined and limited are science/scientist and biography. For the purposes of the present work, a scientist is someone working in the natural sciences (excluding medical science), and a biography (including autobiography) is a text that focuses on the subject's life since birth and childhood, as well as his or her scientific work.[1] A total of 1,106 book-length biographies, many of them in multiple editions, are recorded in this volume.

Scientists since 1660 is an unconventional bibliography, because life-writing is not often selected as the focus of bibliographical analysis and description. Bibliography is a genre more usually organized around a scholarly interest in a single author, editions of whose books may be owned by public libraries as well as private collectors. A single-author bibliography will reveal textual complexity, unfold the history of an author's relationship with publishers, and provide details of little-known writings. A bibliography organized around practitioners of a single profession will include some well-known authors, but juxtapose them with obscure writers of forgotten books on the same subject that the literary giant happened to choose. Single-author biographies direct collectors and book-dealers to scarce editions and variants. Some of the books listed below are rare and valuable, while others are rare but of no interest to collectors. Many are easily accessible on the shelves of research and public libraries, and some are still in print.

The organization of the bibliography demonstrates how each subject's "life" has emerged into the genre of scientific biography. Within the entry under every scientist's name, all biographies are listed in chronological order of first publication, not according to author. This form of organization is historical: it displays the way in which treatments of each subject have developed over time. The annotations expand upon this development, referring to the occasion for publication when that information is available in preface or introduction, and to the authors' comments upon the quality of previous attempts. These annotations thus provide more information about the text of the book than do many bibliographies. The organization is meant to make standard information available, readily and accurately, but also to reveal information that would otherwise remain concealed. The researcher who wants to pursue the lives of late-Victorian naturalists, for instance, will wish to go beyond the book-length biographies, and trace the subjects through the standard sources that list contributions to periodicals and to biographical dictionaries. Henry Coates's biography of Charles Macintosh of Inver, for example, is not necessarily definitive. But without a bibliography of biographies of scientists, the existence of an obscure volume like *A Perthshire Naturalist* and its appearance in two editions in 1923 and 1924 would be known only through Macintosh's name, and then only to a researcher with access to the catalogues of copyright libraries in Britain. Further details on annotations are provided below in the section on "the organization of an entry".

A bibliography of biographies with extensive publication details alerts the researcher to revisions, corrections and alterations that often appear in variant editions of what appears to be the "same" work and that may affect the historical record. An example may be taken from Bence Jones's 1870 *The life and letters of Faraday* , of which a second edition appeared also in 1870, withdrawing some letters, abbreviating others and correcting errors. In the preface to this book Jones told his readers:

> The most important mistake relates to the loaf of bread which Faraday had weekly when nine years old. I wrongly understood that it came from the temporary help which was given to the working class in London during the famine of 1801. I was too easily led into this error by my wish to show the height of the rise of Faraday by contrasting it with the lowliness of his starting point.

Subsequent writers on Faraday, unaware of the second edition and perhaps equally susceptible to Jones's original assumption that the family was in receipt of poor relief, have perpetuated the error. A juvenile biography by Harry Sootin (NY: Julian Messner; London: Blackie, 1954), not included in the present work, speaks of

> that terrible year, 1801, when the price of corn rose so high that his mother just couldn't make ends meet. That was the year when the Faradays had to ask for public relief . . . And Michael's own portion of the public relief was a loaf of bread which had to last him the whole week.

A bibliography of biographies can trace the making of a myth. For some subjects the myth has been unmade by modern scholarship, and for others the story remains to be rewritten.

Articles in the *Dictionary of Scientific Biography* and other reference works are not recorded in the present work, and nor are the periodical contributions in such publications as the *Biographical Memoirs of Fellows of the Royal Society* . Brief articles, however indispensable as sources of information, do not find a place here because *Scientists since 1660* is not only a contribution to the history of science, but also to the history of the book. It approaches the lives of scientists by indirection, by way of a study of the books, the physical artefacts incorporating literary texts, in which those lives have been published for the use of readers. Over the last two or three years, an exciting scholarly juxtaposition has developed between these two disciplines. Adrian Johns, for example, speaks of "the simultaneous arrival over the last generation of both a new history of the book and a new history of science", and suggests "that a *rapprochement* might be highly beneficial to both camps". He continues:

2

For the historian of science, attention to the history of the book adds a valuable perspective to those detailed considerations of the construction and maintenance of natural knowledge now increasingly prevalent in the field. On the other hand, the history of science offers a way of showing how the culture of books affects apparently the most fundamental and objective aspects of knowledge in our society.[2]

Johns's second point – the demonstration that the culture of books affects the way that knowledge is created and understood in society – is central to my own concern with establishing the history of the book among the historical disciplines. I have argued elsewhere that if mainstream historians are to make the history of the book more central to their professional concerns, scholars who work in the field will have to demonstrate that the study of books as artefacts can contribute to debates and research on issues of importance to the profession.[3] Such a demonstration will incorporate bibliographical analysis and description as a powerful research method through which books yield the evidence of their making and use. Thus prepared, the bibliographer can address the historian's analytical categories of social class, gender, national identity and race/ethnicity, and the historian's interest in recording and analysing the cultural forms within which these multiple and overlapping identities are evidenced. One such form is the book as physical object: texts appear, disappear and reappear in the shapes, sizes and colours, accompanied by the apparatus and even addressing the subjects their readers take for granted. A bibliography of biographies of scientists contributes to the recording and analysis of a changing culture of scientific knowledge by displaying the filiation of biographical and publishing approaches, and it contributes to our understanding of the transitory culture of the printed word by examining the way those approaches were manifested in book form. The present work is offered as a contribution to this interdisciplinary approach. In the spirit of D.F. McKenzie's *Bibliography and the Sociology of Texts* ,[4] I suggest that bibliography is the best way to learn about the history of books, in this case, the history of biography as a literary and scholarly genre, limited to the lives of scientists.

The enduring popularity of biography is well known, to publishers and book-sellers as well as to scholars, and many people in these and other fields have speculated about the apparently inexhaustible market or audience for the genre.[5] What they all recognize is that there is an appealing, and ultimately very satisfying quality about a book in the life-writing tradition – and this quality is evident even when the "life" is not a life of action and event, as is the case with biographies of persons committed primarily to literature, or indeed to laboratory or fieldwork. Readers regard the lives of scientists as sources for gaining an understanding of the history and culture of science, as well as of the subject-matter of particular disciplines. As one biographer has reflected, "the study of individual cases can do something to correct the picture of science and scientists

3

given by those who wish to make generalizations about the subject but have no time or inclination to go back to the sources" (see entry for Gay-Lussac by Maurice Crosland).

Not so well known is the multiplicity and variety of biographical treatments of a single scientist. This remarkable array may be considered from the perspective of publishers and the book trade, or from that of readers and book purchasers, as well as that of biographers and historians of science.

Scientists since 1660 displays in microcosm the variations and development of book form in the English-speaking world. In the case of Boyle, Linnaeus, Newton and other eighteenth-century scientists whose lives have been written and rewritten, the arrangement of the biographies in chronological order of publication, rather than alphabetical order of the author's name, makes these transformations apparent: heavy rag paper printed by hand with eighteenth-century ink and eighteenth-century type, the leaves bound in morocco leather or calfskin, gives way to the few examples of the early experiments with machine-printing of the 1830s and 1840s, and then to a flood of Victorian books, competently machine-printed from a family of conventional typefaces and bound in publisher's cloth, perhaps embellished with a little gilt.[6] Through the nineteenth and twentieth centuries, subtle changes in typography, layout, paper and binding mark each generation's books off from the ones before and after. Even within the same publishing season, the lavishly illustrated coffee-table book is clearly differentiated from the scholarly "definitive" biography, endnotes tucked out of sight in the hope of attracting the general reader while still satisfying the specialist. Publishers and the book trade knew in the past, and know now, what a biography ought to look like, and in a large project like this one the changing design conventions are visible. For the marks of the cultural and commercial nexus from which each book emerged, however, it is necessary to look past publishing format. Researchers may find such evidence in the archival records of publishers and authors, but even when archives have not survived, the book as artefact is a source of evidence. It is necessary to read the messages encoded in printers' and publishers' imprints, and attend to the evidence of publishing circumstances that may survive in prefaces and introductions.

What this evidence demonstrates is that a biography may appear in book form for any number of reasons. If it is published privately, at the expense of the author, or of the subject's family or friends, the considerations of the book trade market-place do not apply. Similarly authors and others can sponsor or commission the production of a biography from a publishing house. Such a book is primarily a memorial, although it is in the nature of such memorials that they set down the subject's character and accomplishments for the sake of preserving his or her memory, and for the benefit of future generations. This kind of memorializing biography was a characteristic of the nineteenth century: lives of several minor figures were published privately. But the impulse to make an eccentric work and publish it independent of either scholarly or commercial constraints, has continued well into the twentieth century. One such book listed below is a study of Sebastian Ziani de Ferranti, published privately with the copyright in the hands of the electrical engineering firm Ferranti Limited, not of the author, who for his part announced his attempt to bridge the "gap between biography and autobiography" by using graphology. Biography published privately can be used to right wrongs (see Boucher's 1924 study of *William Kelly a true history of the so-called Bessemer process* written and published at the request of a widow convinced that her husband's prior claim had been suppressed) or to erect bibliographical tombstones (as recently as 1972, Corinne Miller Simons published *John Uri Lloyd his life and works 1849–1936 with a history of the Lloyd Library* , intending "to preserve and enumerate the authentic facts of his life while they are still fresh in the memories of those who knew him").

When a biography bears the imprint of a commercial or scholarly publisher, however, that imprint may be evidence that a publisher has made the decision that a reading audience exists, and can be persuaded to purchase the work. The question can then be asked, how readers make a market for this particular literary form, and how that market demand has been manifested at different times and places.

The history of markets, or reading audiences, for scientific biography emerges from the chronological organization of all books on each subject. The literary and scholarly conventions and assumptions, within which biographers of scientists – and their publishers – work, have changed with the times along with publishing conventions concerning book form. By tracing the several "treatments" of a major subject, we can see the way in which biographers have responded to the demands of readers, and how publishers have mediated the responses of writers to those readers, not only in terms of book design and presentation, but also in the mere fact of publishing a new treatment. Some "lives" have been recounted numerous times while many others have eluded attention altogether. The list of the largest numbers of biographies appears as Darwin (30); Edison (16); Newton and Einstein (15); Audubon and Huxley (13), Charles Dodgson (11), and ten each for Faraday, Henry Ford and Pascal. Within the scholarly realm of the history of science, the multiplicity of biographies represents debate on how the life is best interpreted; that debate is discussed in the next section. Meanwhile it is important to recognize that this bibliographical profusion is also evidence that publishers have decided, from time to time, that a market could be found for a fresh treatment. A bibliography of biographies reminds us that each biography is a publishing event, as well as the product of a single author's "pen". The "pen" may be scholarly or journalistic or filial, but in almost every case a publisher decided to put his or her imprint on the book, and probably decided to back it financially. In the late nineteenth century and in the twentieth century, with a subject like T.H. Huxley or Michael Faraday, two or more biographies might easily be in print at the same time, one a full-dress scholarly treatment, resulting from years of research and a healthy advance from the publisher, and the other a slim 200-page coverage of the same subject commissioned for a series of "lives" and culled from the pages of the first generation of family memoirs.

It is useful to be aware of the publishers' series in which biographies appeared: some books in series appear because they were commissioned by the publisher, perhaps through the specialist series editor, so that the fact of the series explains the existence of the biography.[7] Series such as "English Men of Science," published 1906–1908 by Dent in Britain and by Dutton in the United States, and the recent "Profiles, pathways, and dreams: autobiographies of American chemists" are in themselves evidence of the cultural preoccupations of publishers, in their attempt to predict and to shape the taste of contemporary readers. The series introduction to the American Chemical Society's "Profiles," as well as the prefaces of many individual texts, demonstrates how series editor Jeffrey I. Seeman is drawing forth books that would never otherwise have been written. A bibliography of biographies, by its arrangement according to subject, highlights the different ways in which the publishers of the English-speaking world have responded to the lives of scientists.

Books in series, as well as individual free-standing texts, express the cultural conventions of their time and place. Authors, biographers, have had to consider the way in which they present their subject's reputation. As Anna Seward noted in her introduction to *Memoirs of the Life of Dr Darwin* (see entry for Erasmus Darwin, 1804),

> Biography of recently departed Eminence is apt to want characteristic truth, since it is generally written either by a near relation . . . or by an highly obliged friend . . . or by an editor who believes it highly conductive to his profits on the writings he publishes, or republishes, to claim for their author the unqualified admiration and reverence of mankind, . . . [Nevertheless] though just biographic record will touch the failings of the good and the eminent with tenderness, it ought not to spread over them the veil of suppression.

Some of Seward's peers in nineteenth-century life-writing have been charged by their successors with suppressing scandalous or unflattering evidence about their subjects. Perhaps the best-known example is that of Charles Darwin, where 12 biographies and editions of the autobiography, and numerous reissues of those books written between 1885 and 1955, appeared before Nora Barlow published the 1958 edition that revealed her grandfather's atheism.

The contrast between Victorian reticence and late twentieth-century approaches to celebrity lives is apparent in several of the entries below. Another case in point is the English nineteenth-century engineer, Isambard Kingdom Brunel. Brunel's first biographer (in 1870, 11 years after his death) was his son, Isambard. But this filial narrative is regarded as being severely limited by the younger Brunel's ignorance of technical matters. There followed four further interpretations between 1938 and 1974, all narratives in the heroic mode. Not until 1991 and railway historian Adrian Vaughan's *Isambard Kingdom Brunel engineering knight-errant* was a more "objective" account published, although by that time numerous other scientists and engineers had been subjected to the scrutiny of a newly critical approach to biography. Vaughan's book, which discussed labour disputes and other evidence unfavourable to Brunel's reputation was reviewed by the *Spectator* as "the *Satanic Verses* of the railway buff's world". As William Scanlan Murphy says of the little-known Victorian English submarine technologist whose memory he resurrected in 1987: "It might well be said that [George Garrett] was no Faraday or Brunel – but, if modern scholarship is to be believed, neither were Faraday and Brunel."

Projects of recovery such as Murphy's appear from the eighteenth to the late twentieth century, rescuing a forgotten or misunderstood life by means of research, perhaps in newly discovered documents. Changing trends in interpretation, however, can be discerned. There are three breaks in the history of biographical interpretation of scientists' lives, one when Freudian thinking began to influence scholarship, and a second when the history of science was transformed by an emphasis on the culture of science, and the sociological milieu in which thinkers worked, rather than the filiation of "great ideas" from one "great man" to the next. A third trend in interpretation is the feminist approach to the writing of history. In addition to these there have been less influential, sometimes eccentric, theories. The attempt to reveal personality through handwriting analysis in the Ferranti biography has already been noted.

The influence of Freud may be detected in the biographical treatments of two mathematicians. One is Charles Lutwidge Dodgson, whose *Alice in Wonderland* books written as Lewis Carroll have generated several biographies. A 1945 treatment by Florence Becker Lennon, entitled *Victoria through the looking glass*, used psychoanalytic theory and generated a debate in the *Times Literary Supplement* in which a reviewer observed that "The sword of Sigmund sits uneasily in the hand of St George". And in 1953 Norbert Wiener, an American mathematician, expressed an interest in psychoanalytic theory in the preface to his autobiography *Ex-prodigy my childhood and youth*. He decided, however, to avoid the temptation "to write an autobiography in the Freudian jargon".

The new approach to the history of science that has been appearing during the 1980s and 1990s had had more of an impact on scientific biography than the Freudian theory of the 1940s and 1950s. The "conceptual revolution" undergone by the historiography of science is succinctly described in an essay by Adrian Wilson:

> This [revolution] has entailed a widening of focus from products (say: Boyle's Law) to their genesis (for instance, in contests); from thought (metaphysics, conceptual methodology) to action (experimental practices, social technologies for securing assent); and from what is taken as science (a lineage through time) to its context (linkages in social space). The central effect of this transformation is that science – or in the early-modern period, natural philosophy – is now seen as a social activity, with implications

for our very conception of the "social". One of its by-products has been that historians of science are becoming increasingly literate in "general" history.[8]

Wilson observes in a note that "an accessible introduction" to this new approach to the history of science is provided by three recent biographies, Cantor's 1991 study of Faraday, Desmond and Moore's 1991 *Darwin* and a life of Lord Kelvin by Smith and Wise, published in 1989. Similarly Lewis Pyenson, in his 1985 study of Einstein, reflected that "an appeal to biographical evidence lies at the base of a search for the environment that encouraged, sustained, or inhibited the thought or actions of a historical figure".

A third intellectual trend is feminist scholarship in biography. The lives of women scientists, such as Mary Somerville, and Ada Byron, Lady Lovelace, were written for the first time in the 1970s and 1980s when the projects were initiated of discovering women's contribution to the history of science, and of writing the history of women's lives. It is worth noting that much of this feminist scholarship has been collective, rather than individual in nature, and does not therefore find a place in *Scientists since 1660* .

Even before the development of women's history in the 1970s and of the new social history of science in the 1980s, "great" men and women were not always fashionable subjects of historical enquiry. The trend to social history, or history from below, to what E.P. Thompson described as "rescuing" working-class subjects "from the enormous condescension of posterity",[9] has mitigated against biography as a discipline. A handful of the studies listed below, however, are projects designed to rescue an individual from obscurity. Examples are Murphy's life of George Garrett, already mentioned, and Henry Coates's book on Charles Macintosh, *A Perthshire Naturalist* , whose life included folk music as well as the study of the fungus of Invershire.

A significant number of scientists (82 of the 565 listed below) have undertaken to rescue themselves from the condescension of posterity by writing their autobiographies. In some cases, such as the astronomer Edwin Frost, writing a memoir of life and work is a project of retirement. In other cases, it has been urged upon the scientist by friends or colleagues, or by publishers. And the autobiographical urge does not always stop with a single text. Six of the scientists listed here have written a second autobiographical work.[10] Carl Djerassi, who was involved in the development of a steroid oral contraceptive, discovered the genre when he was asked to participate in the American Chemical Society's series, "Profiles, pathways, and dreams". His first autobiography, *Steroids made it possible* was published in 1990 with a "coda", written at the request of series editor Jeffrey I. Seeman, which alluded to his "long infatuation with art", his daughter's suicide, his divorces and remarriages. In Djerassi's second and longer autobiography, published in 1992 by Basic Books under the title *The Pill* , *Pygmy chimps* , *and Degas' horse* , he confessed that "this volume is not a conventional scientific autobiography". Rather, it stressed the social context of his participation in producing "the pill" and expanded upon the personal themes first explored in the 1990 "coda".

Long before the new self-consciousness about context among historians of science, however, biographers of scientists had to come to terms with the technical complexity of their subjects' work. In literary biography, the problem is to put the life of a novelist or poet in the context of his or her works, and the author normally assumes that those works are reasonably familiar to the reader. In scientific biography, author after author grapples with the problem of combining the subject's life and his or her science in an appropriate way, and laments the difficulty of explaining technical work to a non-technical readership. A. Vibert Douglas, in his 1956 study of the English astronomer Arthur Stanley Eddington, speaks of the difficulty of providing a dual portrait of a scientist subject, of both personal life and professional importance, so that the biographer aims for what he terms "the stereoscopic merging of the two into one faithful likeness of the great man".

The Organization of an Entry

The Scientist

The list of scientists working since 1660 whose biographies were to be sought, was originally derived from a systematic search through the *Dictionary of Scientific Biography* (*DSB*); all practitioners of the natural sciences, excluding those whose work was primarily in medical science, were selected for a subsequent search in libraries. Further references, for contemporary scientists and for practitioners of technology and engineering, were sought in the *Collins Biographical Dictionary of Scientists* and other reference works.

In some cases it was decided to omit a scientist who had generated a great deal of biographical attention, when that attention was focused almost exclusively on his or her life and accomplishments apart from science. Examples here include Benjamin Franklin, Captain James Cook, and Christopher Wren. On the borderline of this decision about inclusion was Charles Dodgson, Lewis Carroll. He is included because several of the biographies focus on the contrast between the mathematician and the writer of fantasy. Apart from this limitation, every attempt has been made to include all English-language biographies of natural scientists, apart from medical scientists, working since 1660. No major scholar who fits this definition has been passed over, but the rarity of some of the biographies of minor scientists means that those included will to some extent reflect the collecting patterns of the libraries consulted during the research.

A much longer book than the present one could be written about the scientists whose lives have not been the subject of a substantial book-length biography in

English. A rough count of entries in the *DSB* for modern natural scientists for whom no English-language biography was found amounts to 2,000.

The Biographies

As stated above, a biography (including autobiography) is here defined as a text that focuses on the subject's life since birth and childhood, as well as his or her scientific work. Normally it has been written by a single author, and published in one or more volumes of at least 100 pages. The intention here is to capture only substantial book-length texts: it is not possible for the bibliographer to make a judgement of quality about any given biography, but it is possible to set an arbitrary page limit that eliminates most fragmentary treatments.

The list of scientists was used to search library catalogues for entries that looked like biographies. The next step was to examine and describe the books themselves: the libraries used were the University of Toronto libraries initially, then the British Library and Cambridge University Library, and the Library of Congress in Washington, DC, and the library of the University of Michigan in Ann Arbor. In only a handful of cases was at least one copy of the book recorded without having been seen, and in those cases the notation XX is used.

Only full-length biographies published in English, up to 1993, and addressed to adult readers are included. As a result the bibliography is skewed towards subjects from English-speaking countries, although many of the works listed below are translations of biographies that first appeared in other languages. The only exception to the rule of excluding biographical texts published as chapters or sections of books was Samuel Smiles's *Lives of the Engineers* . Not only are these essays classics of Victorian life-writing, but several of them were expanded and republished in one-volume format later on. Biographies written for children were excluded, along with any others that incorporate invented dialogue. Although juvenile biography of scientists has been a flourishing genre, especially from the late nineteenth to the mid-twentieth century, it represents a distinctly different publishing tradition from the memorializing and scholarly works written for adults.[11]

Each entry lists all biographies of a given scientist, in chronological order, giving full information of author, title, place or places of publication and publisher or publishers. The author's name is given as it appears on the title page. The title is recorded in full without punctuation. Places of publication are presented as briefly as possible (e.g. NY not New York, and Cambridge not Cambridge, Cambridgeshire or Cambridge, MA, when the name of the press makes the distinction clear). The name of the publisher is given in full as it appears on the title page. When a book appears simultaneously from two presses, both names are given, separated by a semicolon, with the initiating press named first. If the book appeared in a series, especially if it was a series of biographies of scientists, this fact is noted in square brackets. Reprints and reissues are also noted, as are new editions, when the text reappears with a new setting of type. This is a level of bibliographical precision unusual in biographical reference works, a level that is necessary to demonstrate the way in which publishers and the book trade have treated the lives of scientists, and how that treatment has changed over time.

The bibliographical details conclude with the number of pages in the book, and a note of illustrations, bibliography and index when these elements exist. Pagination of the preliminary part of the book is suppressed. When there are multiple volumes the pagination is given for each, as I:315 II:297. The existence of a single frontispiece is not taken to constitute illustration. The intention here is not to provide a full technical description, but to give the reader an abbreviated clue about what sort of a book the biography is. The presence of illustrations, in books published since the late nineteenth century, may be indicative of a publisher's or author's willingness to invest financially in the production of the book. The absence of an index may indicate the opposite, or it may mean the book is destined for a popular, non-scholarly market. A bibliography may be useful to the reader, and its presence or absence is also tentative evidence of the kind of book one is dealing with.

Finally, most entries provide a brief annotation, in which an attempt is made to "place" the book in the context of other biographies of the same subject. The information is normally taken from a reading of the preface or introduction. The annotation may note the relationship of the author to the subject, or whether the book is written by a scientist, an historian of science, or a professional biographer. The entry may note whether the biographer has used manuscript (MS or MSS) sources, or developed the book from memory or from secondary sources. (Llewellyn Jewitt may safely be taken as an exception: he "scrupulously avoided any reference or allusion" to Josiah Wedgwood's letters and "never sought to see them".) This entry is a report of research, not a judgement of quality. The present work records what the authors of biographies claim about their books, and also what modern commentators have said about the usefulness of earlier attempts. Ultimately, of course, the user will determine for him- or herself how accurate the claims may be.

The Appendices

Appendix A organizes the scientists according to their specialization. Some categories are combined for the sake of simplicity, so that an individual described in the bibliography as "Rubber Technician" appears in the list of Engineers. Appendix B organizes the biographies by publishing houses (firms that produced three or more biographies). Only the publisher from which the book first appeared is listed, even when there was a co-publishing arrangement between a British and American publisher. Appendix C is a list of the series in which biographies of scientists appeared.

Notes

1 For medical scientists, readers should consult *A Bibliography of Medical and Biomedical Biography*, by Leslie T. Morton and Robert J. Moore (Scolar Press, 1989).

2 Adrian Johns, "History, science, and the history of the book: the making of natural philosophy in Early Modern England," *Publishing History* **35** (1994), 5. See also forthcoming work by James Secord and Jonathan Topham.

3 Leslie Howsam, *Victorian Imprint Kegan Paul: Publishers, Books and Cultural History* (Toronto: University of Toronto Press and London: Kegan Paul International, 1997).

4 D.F. McKenzie, *Bibliography and the Sociology of Texts* (London: The British Library, 1985).

5 James L.W. West III, "Book history and biography," *Publishing Research Quarterly* **10** (Fall 1994).

6 The earliest-published books listed here are biographies of Boyle (1744), Boerhaave (1746), Smeaton (1793), Linnaeus (1794) and William Jones and Erasmus Darwin (both 1804).

7 Leslie Howsam, "Sustained literary ventures: the series in Victorian book publishing," *Publishing History* **32** (1992).

8 Adrian Wilson, "A critical portrait of social history," in A. Wilson, ed., *Rethinking Social History: English Society 1570–1920 and its Interpretation* (Manchester: Manchester University Press, 1993), 30.

9 E.P. Thompson, *The Making of the English Working Class* (Harmondsworth: Pelican Books, 1968), 12.

10 Djerassi, Hahn, Infeld, Leakey, Priestley and Wiener.

11 In the course of casting my bibliographical net over the pool of science biography, I discovered the important sub-genre of juvenile biography. From the mid-nineteenth century to the mid-twentieth, a rich market existed for children's books devoted to the lives of scientists. The genre seems to have had its heyday in the 1940s and 1950s, and to have extended until the mid-1960s. In Britain this was the time of series such as Penguin's Puffin Books and Methuen's Story Biographies, as well as Longmans' Lives of Achievement; in the United States there were series like Childhood of Famous Americans, published by Bobbs-Merrill, and Hall of Fame Books (biographies of Americans who had been elected to the Hall of Fame of NY University), published by Prentice-Hall, and the Men of Achievement Series launched in the 1960s by the T.S. Denison & Company, Inc. of Minneapolis.

Abbe, Cleveland (1838–1916), Norwegian meteorologist.

1955 Truman Abbe, *Professor Abbe . . . and the isobars the story of Cleveland Abbe America's first weatherman* (NY: Vantage Press) 259; illus. Author is subject's son; "a picture of the man, not a scientific treatise". Foreword by Ivan R. Tannehill, Asst. Chief, Weather Bureau.

Abel, John Jacob (1857–1938), American biochemist and pharmacologist.

1992 John Parascandola, *The development of American pharmacology John J. Abel and the shaping of a discipline* (Baltimore: Johns Hopkins University Press) 212; illus; bibliog; index. XX

Abel, Niels Henrik (1802–1829), Norwegian mathematician.

1957 Oystein Ore, *Niels Henrik Abel mathematician extraordinary* (Minneapolis: University of Minnesota Press) reprinted 1974 (NY: Chelsea Press Publishing Company) 277; illus; index. Main concern is not Abel's science but "the heart-warming tale of a young man who set out . . . to explore the world of science".

Abragam, Anatole (1914 – –), French physicist.

1989 autobiography, *Time reversal an autobiography* (Oxford: Clarendon Press) 373; illus; index. "A few stories . . . some from my own life, and some which are just stories." Translation (by author) of French edition.

Adams, Roger (1889–1971), American organic chemist.

1981 D. Stanley Tarbell and Ann Tracy Tarbell, *Roger Adams scientist and statesman* (Washington: American Chemical Society) 240; illus; index. Uses MSS.

Agassiz, Alexander (1835–1910), Swiss zoologist; oceanographer.

1913 G.R. Agassiz, ed., *Letters and recollections of Alexander Agassiz with a sketch of his life and work* (London: Constable & Co. Ltd.; Boston and NY: Houghton Mifflin Co.) 454; index; illus. Editor is son; biographical text interspersed with extracts of letters.

Agassiz, Jean Louis Rodolphe (1807–1873), American geologist, palaeontologist, geologist (born Switzerland).

1885 Elizabeth Cary Agassiz, ed., *Louis Agassiz his life and correspondence* (London: Macmillan and Company), seventh edition 1887 (Boston: Houghton Mifflin) 2 vols; 794; illus; index. Editor is subject's wife. Prepared as a memorial; has "neither the fullness of personal narrative, nor the closeness of scientific analysis . . .". Lurie praises its "perception and insight" – but many letters are not reproduced. Marcou says some controversies are suppressed.

1893   Charles Frederick Holder, *Louis Agassiz; his life and work* (NY: Putnam) [Leaders in science] 327; illus; bibliography.

1896   Jules Marcou, *Life letters and works of Louis Agassiz* (NY: Macmillan and Co.) I:302 II:318; bibliog; index. Reprinted in one volume 1972 (Westmead, Farnborough: Gregg International Publishers Ltd.). Spent 20 years collecting material for a "true history"; a European industrialist (a friend) who came to America with Agassiz. Lurie calls it "strange and misleading", dependent on 1885, and in some places unreliable.

1901   Alice Bache Gould, *Louis Agassiz* (Boston: Small, Maynard & Company) [Beacon biographies of Eminent Americans] 154; bibliog. XX

1947   James David Teller, *Louis Agassiz scientist and teacher* (Columbus: The Ohio State University Press) [Education Series, no. 2] 145; index. Seeks to provide information on subject as a teacher. Identifies a need for reading the biographies of all nineteenth-century scientists for a "truer evaluation of the man and his work".

1960   Edward Lurie, *Louis Agassiz a life in science* (Chicago: The University of Chicago Press) 449; illus; bibliog; index. Began as a doctoral dissertation on Agassiz's American career; research in MS sources. He says 1896 is based on 1885 and is "strange and misleading" where it departs from 1885; 1901 is "a short and perceptive appreciation".

Airy, George Biddell (1801–1892), English astronomer.

1896   autobiography, *Autobiography of Sir George Biddell Airy*, (Cambridge: Cambridge University Press) 414; bibliog; index. Editor (Wilfrid Airy) was subject's son; life "essentially that of a hard-working business man". Edition omits many of subject's technical notes.

Alvarez, Luis Walter (1911–1988), American physicist.

1987   autobiography, *Alvarez adventures of a physicist* (NY: Basic Books) 292; illus; index. Published as part of an Alfred P. Sloan Foundation program. XX

Ambartsumyan, Victor Amazapovich (1908 – –), Soviet astrophysicist.

1987   Ashot Arzumanyan, *Envoy of the stars academician Victor Ambartsumyan* (Moscow: Progress Publishers) 232; illus. Translated from Russian by Cynthia Carlile. Uses documentary material and family papers.

Amundsen, Roald Engelbregt Gravning (1872–1928), Norwegian scientific explorer.

1927   autobiography, *Roald Amundsen my life as an explorer* (Garden City, NY: Doubleday, Page & Co., Inc.) 282; illus. XX

1929   Bellamy Partridge, *Amundsen the splendid Norseman* (NY: Frederick A. Stokes Company) 276; illus. Also published 1953 (London: Hale) 206. XX

1935   Charles Turley, *Roald Amundsen explorer* (London: Methuen & Co. Ltd.) 218; illus; index.

Appleton, Edward Victor (1892–1965), English radio physicist.

1971   Ronald Clark, *Sir Edward Appleton GBE KCB FRS* (Oxford: Pergamon Press) 240; illus; index. Commissioned by subject's widow. Uses MSS.

Arbuthnot, John (1667–1735), Scottish mathematician, statistician.

1892   George Aitken, *The life and works of John Arbuthnot* (Oxford: Clarendon Press) reprinted 1968 (NY: Russell & Russell) index. Written "to do tardy justice to the reputation of a good and clever man".

1935   Lester Beattie, *John Arbuthnot mathematician and satirist* (Cambridge: Harvard University Press). Reissued 1962; reissued 1967 (NY: Russell & Russell) [Harvard Studies in English, 16] 432; illus; index. Approach is critical rather than biographical, focusing on subject's work and writings. Indebted to 1892.

Arkwright, Richard (1732–1792), English inventor of spinning technology.

1989   R.S. Fitton, *The Arkwrights spinners of fortune* (Manchester: Manchester University Press) 322; illus; bibliog; index. Foreword by Peter Mathias is obituary of author, an economic historian. Study is "set in the dynastic context" of subject's family.

Armstrong, Edwin Howard (1890–1954), American radio engineer.

1956   Lawrence Lessing, *Man of high fidelity Edwin Howard Armstrong* (Philadelphia: Lippincott). XX

Armstrong, Henry Edward (1848–1937), English chemist and educator.

1958   J. Vargas Eyre, *Henry Edward Armstrong 1848–1937 the doyen of British chemists and pioneer of technical education* (London: Butterworths Scientific Publications) 325; illus; bibliog. Foreword by R.P. Linstead (Rector of Imperial College). Author a student of subject.

Ashmole, Elias (1617–1692), English natural philosopher.

1966   C.H. Josten, *Elias Ashmole 1617–1692 his autobiographical and historical notes his correspondence and other contemporary sources relating to his life and work* Volume 1 *Biographical Introduction* (Oxford: Clarendon Press) 306; illus; bibliog. Uses MS sources; author is editor of the 50-volume works.

Aspinall, John (1926 – –), English zoologist (born India).

1988   Brian Masters, *The passion of John Aspinall* (London: Cape) 360; illus; bibliog; index. Written with co-operation of subject.

Audubon, John James (1785–1851), American naturalist and artist (born Santo Domingo, now Haiti).

1856   [Mrs Horace] St John, *Audubon the naturalist in the new world* (London: Longman, Brown, Green, and Longman) 172. Also published under title *Life of Audubon the naturalist of the new world his adventures and discoveries* (Philadelphia: Lippincott). Revised and corrected edition 1874 (Boston: Crosby and Nichols) 311. Derived from subject's "works, the recollections of his friends, and from fragments published in the United States. The writer's object has been, exclusively, to follow the adventurous American through the episodes of Romance and Discovery which constituted his career as a Naturalist. To the criticisms of Waterton and others, on his Ornithology, all reference has been omitted, to avoid controversy on points of scientific detail". 1874 and subsequent editions have additional material and are illustrated with engravings by J.W. Orr.

1868   Robert Buchanan, ed. *The life and adventures of John James Audubon the naturalist* (London: Sampson Low, Son, & Marston) 366. New edition 1912 (London: J.M. Dent; NY: E.P. Dutton) [Everyman's Library]. Editor a poet and literary critic, who notes that he worked from an overly long MS, mostly journal extracts, "prepared by a friend [the Revd Charles Coffin Adams] of Mrs Audubon's, in NY", whose "literary experience was limited". Preface refers to widow's criticism of his editorial comments. Says he admires subject "hugely" while thinking him vain and selfish. Maria Audubon (1897) says Buchanan used the same journals as she did, and that others are since lost or destroyed. His book "is so mixed up, so interspersed with derogatory remarks of his own, as to be practically useless to the world, and very unpleasant to the Audubon family. Moreover, with few exceptions, everything about birds has been left out. . . . However, if Mr Buchanan had done his work better, there would have been no need for mine; so I forgive him, even though he dwells at unnecessary length on Audubon's vanity and selfishness, of which I find no trace". Peattie (1936) says that Buchanan, the gifted English poet [at 26], regarded this as a hackwork job; he had no feeling for the journals or for American style.

1897   Maria R. Audubon, *Audubon and his journals* (NY: Charles Scribner's Sons; London: J.C. Nimmo, 1898) I:532 II:554; illus; index. Includes zoological and other notes by Elliott Coues. Author is subject's granddaughter. Based on nine journals and about 100 letters. Peattie says there are errors, that the text "smooths out asperities and continues old quarrels".

1902   John Burroughs, *John James Audubon* (Boston: Small, Maynard & Company) [Beacon Biographies of Eminent Americans] 144; bibliog. Based on 1868 and 1897 biographies.

1917   Francis Herbert Herrick, *Audubon the naturalist a history of his life and time* (NY: D. Appleton – Century Company) I:451 II:500; illus; bibliog; index. Second edition 1938, two volumes in one; reprinted 1968 (NY: Dover Publications) [Dover Books on Nature]. Introduction includes comment on the journals and the earlier biographies. Author's research reveals subject's birthdate, place of birth and parentage, and his youth in France. Second edition corrects textual errors in the plates and updates the bibliography.

1929   Edward A. Muschamp, *Audacious Audubon the story of a great pioneer artist naturalist & man* (NY: Brentano's) [American biography] 313; illus. XX

1936   Donald Culross Peattie, *Singing in the wilderness a salute to John James Audubon* (London: George Allen & Unwin Ltd.) 245; bibliog; illus. The author uses the known facts of Audubon's life, especially the early years, to write an imaginative work.

1936   Constance Rourke, *Audubon* (NY: Harcourt, Brace; London: George G. Harrap & Co. Ltd.) 342; illus; index. Popular style; includes suggestion disproved by Herrick that subject was the lost Dauphin of France.

1937   Stanely Clisby Arthur, *Audubon an intimate life of the American woodman* (New Orleans: Harmanson, Publisher) 517; illus; bibliog; index.

1964   Alice Ford, *John James Audubon* (Norman: University of Oklahoma Press) 488; illus; bibliog; index. Published 1988 under title *John James Audubon a biography* (NY: Abbeville Press) 528; illus; bibliog; index. Based on MS sources; aims to "bring the currently idealized life and career of the greatest American delineator of birds into new, more believable, and – I hope – more sympathetic and rather more truthful perspective".

1966   Alexander B. Adams, *John James Audubon a biography* (NY: Putnam; London: Victor Gollancz, 1967) 510; illus; bibliog; index. Popular style; deliberately makes no comment on the mistakes of predecessors.

1978   John Chancellor, *Audubon a biography* (London: Weidenfeld and Nicolson; NY: Viking Press) 224; illus; bibliog; index. Coffee-table book; attempts to portray subject's weaknesses as well as strengths and to note that Audubon the conservationist was not always one.

1987   Claude Chebel, *Audubon the man who loved nature* (London: W.H. Allen) 384; bibliog. Translated by Carys Lewis-Le Disez in collaboration with Jean Yves-Le Disez. No preface or introduction; includes invented dialogue.

Avogadro, Amedeo (1776–1856), Italian chemist.

1984   Mario Morselli, *Amedeo Avogadro a scientific biography* (Dordrecht: D. Reidel Publishing Company) [Chemists and chemistry] 375; illus; bibliog; index. Includes a description of subject's milieu.

Babbage, Charles (1792–1871), English mathematician and pioneer of computing technology.

1864   autobiography, *Passages from the life of a philosopher* (London: Longman, Green, Longman, Roberts, & Green) reprinted 1968 (London: Dawsons of Pall Mall) 496; bibliog. New edition 1994 (New Brunswick, NJ: Rutgers University Press). Does not "aspire to the name of an autobiography;" relates author's "experience amongst various classes of society". 1994 edition has introduction by Martin Campbell-Kelly.

1964   Maboth Moseley, *Irascible genius a life of Charles Babbage inventor* (London: Hutchinson) 288; illus; bibliog; index. Foreword by B.V. Bowden. Uses hitherto unpublished sources and Buxton's unpublished biography. 1988 introduction calls this interpretation "an illegitimate transference of the image of the public polemicist to the private man".

1970   Dan Halacy, *Charles Babbage father of the computer* (NY: Crowell-Collier Press [Macmillan]) 170; index. Popular style.

1982   Anthony Hyman, *Charles Babbage pioneer of the computer* (Oxford: Oxford University Press; Princeton: Princeton University Press) 287; illus; bibliog; index. Based on archival and library research.

1988   H.W. Buxton, *Memoir of the life and labours of the late Charles Babbage Esq FRS* (Cambridge: The MIT Press; Los Angeles: Tomash Publishers) [Charles Babbage Institute Reprint Series for the History of Computing, 13] 401; index; bibliog. Edited and introduction by Anthony Hyman. Author, a barrister, was friend entrusted by subject with the task of a biography but he lacked access to most of the MS material. Written around 1880, the memoir has "many weaknesses and was not really publishable as a biography at the time" but is a useful source document. Introduction correlates memoir with current scholarship.

Bache, Alexander Dallas (1806–1867), American physicist.

1947   Merle M. Odgers, *Alexander Dallas Bache scientist and educator, 1806–1867* (Philadelphia: University of Pennsylvania Press) [Pennsylvania Lives] 223; bibliog; index. Foreword by Leo Otis Colbert. An academic biography.

Bailey, Liberty Hyde (1858–1954), American botanist.

1949   Andrew Denny Rodgers, *Liberty Hyde Bailey a story of American plant sciences* (Princeton: Princeton University Press) 506; illus; index. Uses MSS.

Bailey, Loring Woart (1839–1925), American geologist.

1925   Joseph Whitman Bailey, *Loring Woart Bailey the story of a man of science* (Saint John, NB: J. & A. McMillan Limited) 141; illus; bibliog. Book "relates rather to the experiences of a scientific life than to science itself".

Baird, John Logie (1888–1946), Scottish electrical technologist.

1933   Ronald F. Tiltman, *Baird of television* (London: Seeley Service & Co. Limited) reprinted 1974 (NY: Arno Press) [Telecommunications] 220; illus; index. Foreword by Lord Angus Kennedy. Author stresses the romantic nature of subject's lifestory. McArthur 1986 says that in deference to subject's wishes, this "is full of convenient generalizations and several misleading pointers".

[1952]   Sydney Moseley, *John Baird the romance and tragedy of the pioneer of television* (London: Odhams Press Limited) 256; illus; index. Popular style based on author's reminiscences (see below published 1988).

1973   Margaret Baird, *Television Baird* (Cape Town: Haum) Author is wife of subject. XX

1986   Tom McArthur and Peter Waddell, *The secret life of John Logie Baird* (London: Hutchinson) 274; index. Based on MS research including newly discovered materials.

1988   autobiography, *Sermons soap and television autobiographical notes* (London: Royal Television Society) 147; illus. Introduction by Malcolm Baird, son of subject, and foreword by Paul Fox, who notes that after nearly half a century in MS form this text was published as a contribution to the history of television.

Baird, Spencer Fullerton (1823–1887), English naturalist and zoologist.

1915   William Healey Dall, *Spencer Fullerton Baird a biography including selections from his correspondence with Audubon, Agassiz, Dana, and others* (Philadelphia: J.B. Lippincott Company) 462; illus; index. Author was assistant to subject at Smithsonian; includes transcripts of letters.

1992   E.F. Rivinus and E.M. Youssef, *Spencer Baird of the Smithsonian* (Washington: Smithsonian Institution Press) 228; bibliog; index. Based on MS sources. Seeks to redress "the fadeout of Baird's image into the mists of historical oblivion".

Bakewell, Robert (1725–1795), English agriculturalist.

1957   H. Cecil Pawson, *Robert Bakewell pioneer livestock breeder* (London: Crosby Lockwood & Son Ltd.) 200; illus; index. Based on MS sources; letter texts are included. Foreword by James A. Scott Watson.

Banister, John (1650–1692) American botanist and entomologist (born England).

1970   Joseph Ewan and Nesta Ewan, *John Banister and his natural history of Virginia 1678–1692* (Urbana: University of Illinois Press) 485; illus; bibliog; index. Does not discuss subject's childhood. Uses MSS.

Banks, Joseph (1743–1820), English botanist.

1909   J.H. Maiden, *Sir Joseph Banks the "Father of Australia"* (Sydney: William Applegate Gullick, Government Printer; London: Kegan Paul, Trench, Trübner & Co., Ltd.) 244; illus; index. Purpose is to publicize Banks and solicit donations for a memorial.

1911   Edward Smith, *The life of Sir Joseph Banks president of the Royal Society with some notices of his friends and contemporaries* (London: John Lane, The Bodley Head; NY: John Lane Company) reprinted 1975 (NY: Arno Press) [History, philosophy, and sociology of science]) 348, illus. Purpose is to present an unfamiliar side of the eighteenth century, representing "Science and Public Spirit".

1952   Hector Charles Cameron, *Sir Joseph Banks KB PRS the autocrat of the philosophers* (London: The Batchworth Press) 341; illus; index. Reissued 1966 (Sydney: Angus P. Robertson). Uses MS sources.

1980   Charles Lyte, *Sir Joseph Banks 18th century explorer botanist and entrepreneur* (Newton Abbot: David & Charles) 248; illus; bibliog; index. No introduction; popular style.

1987   Patrick O'Brian, *Joseph Banks a life* (London: Collins Harvill) 328; illus; bibliog; index. Uses MS sources; acknowledges earlier biographies without comment.

1988   Harold B. Carter, *Sir Joseph Banks 1743–1820* (London: British Museum (Natural History)) 671; illus; bibliog; index. Uses MS sources; no explicit acknowledgement of earlier biographies except 1909.

Banneker, Benjamin (1731–1806), American astronomer.

1972   Silvio A. Bedini, *The life of Benjamin Banneker* (NY: Charles Scribner's Sons) 434; illus; bibliog; index. Author is an historian of science and technology. The research is divided into segments including "the problem of evaluating whatever had been written" about the subject – sketches, articles, chapters and juvenile biographies – much of which is focused on interest in an African-American man of science.

Barrow, Isaac (1630–1677), English mathematician and theologian.

1944   Percy H. Osmond, *Isaac Barrow his life and times* (London: Society for Promoting Christian Knowledge) 230; index; illus. An introduction for contemporaries.

Barton, Derek H.R. (1918 – –), English inorganic chemist.

1991   autobiography, *Some recollections of gap jumping* (Washington: American Chemical Society) [Profiles, pathways, and dreams: autobiographies of American chemists] 143; illus; index. Concentrates on scientific theories.

Bartram, John (1699–1777), American botanist.

1940   Ernest Earnest, *John and William Bartram botanists and explorers 1699–1777 1739–1823* (Philadelphia: University of Pennsylvania Press) [Pennsylvania Lives] 187; bibliog; index. Uses MS sources; author "deal[s] most fully with John Bartram."

1982   Edmund Berkeley and Dorothy Smith Berkeley, *The life and travels of John Bartram from Lake Ontario to the River St John* (Tallahassee: University Presses of Florida) 376; illus; bibliog; index. Implies that this is the first "full and adequate biography" of subject; criticizes account by subject's son. Uses MSS.

Bates, Henry Walter (1825–1892) English naturalist.

1969   George Woodcock, *Henry Walter Bates naturalist of the Amazons* (London: Faber and Faber; NY: Barnes & Noble) [Great Travellers] 269; illus; bibliog; index. Focuses on subject's scientific career. Uses MSS.

Beddoes, Thomas (1760–1808), English chemist and physician.

1984   Dorothy A. Stansfield, *Thomas Beddoes MD 1760–1808 chemist physician democrat* (Dordrecht, Holland: D. Reidel Publishing Company) 306; bibliog; index. Calls this the first attempt at a biography (Stock's 1811 account "is truly named 'memoirs'"), but still not an academic project.

Bell, Alexander Graham (1847–1922) Canadian technologist (born Scotland).

1973   Robert V. Bruce, *Bell Alexander Graham Bell and the conquest of solitude* (Boston: Little, Brown and Company; London: Victor Gollancz Ltd.) 564; illus; bibliog; index. Uses papers at the National Geographic Society.

Bell, Eric Temple (1884–1960), American mathematician and science fiction writer.

1993   Constance Reid, *The search for E.T. Bell also known as John Taine* (Washington: Mathematical Association of America) [Spectrum Series] 372; illus; index. Constructed as a report on the genealogical and other research problems; corrects the account in *DSB*.

Bellman, Richard (1920 – –), American mathematician.

1984   autobiography, *Eye of the hurricane an autobiography* (Singapore: World Scientific) 344; index. Written to explore an opportunity to speak freely and personally, and because the author finds biographical works valuable: "Reading about the inertia, stupidity and prejudice faced by others has made me more philosophical."

Bentham, George (1800–1884), English botanist.

1906   B. Daydon Jackson, *George Bentham* (London: J.M. Dent & Co.; NY: E.P. Dutton & Co.) reprinted 1976 (NY: AMS Press) 292; illus; index. Edited by J. Reynolds Green. Uses subject's diary and letters.

Bering, Vitus (1681–1741), Danish geographer.

1969   Peter Lauridsen, *Vitus Bering the discoverer of Bering Strait* (Freeport, NY: Books for Libraries Press) [Select bibliographies reprint series] 223; illus; index. Revised by the author and translated from the Danish by Julius E. Olson, with an introduction to the American edition by Frederick Schwatka. First published 1899. Described by translator as "essentially a defense" of subject, "written especially for the student of history and historical geography, it nevertheless contains chapters of thrilling interest to the general reader". Schwatka notes interest to American readers "desiring an accurate history of a country that has recently come into our possession". Uses MSS.

Berkeley, George (1685–1753), Irish philosopher of science.

1881   A. Campbell Fraser, *Berkeley* (Edinburgh: William Blackwood and Sons) [Philosophical Classics for English Readers] 234. Cheap edition 1901, 228. Edited by William Knight. Subject's philosophic thought "in its organic unity". The 1901 cheap edition was "carefully revised and in part recast", now offered as a biographical introduction to the spiritual philosophy of the universe. Uses the Percival letters and other new material. Luce (1949) describes this as "a mine for biographers . . . but . . . not a work of art, and is hardly even a finished product".

1931   J.M. Hone and M.M. Rossi, *Bishop Berkeley his life writings and philosophy*

(London: Faber & Faber) 286; illus; bibliog; index. Introduction by W.B. Yeats, who praises Hone's knowledge of Berkeley the man, and Rossi's of the philosopher.

1936   John Wild, *George Berkeley a study of his life and philosophy* (Cambridge: Harvard University Press) reprinted 1961 (NY: Russell & Russell) 552; index; bibliography. Integrates the life with an analysis of writings and reproduction of texts (especially sermons); supersedes Fraser's 1871 preface to the *Works* by including the Percival letters.

1949   A.A. Luce, *The life of George Berkeley Bishop of Cloyne* (London: Thomas Nelson and Sons Ltd.) reprinted 1968 (NY: Greenwood Press) reprinted 1992 (London: Routledge/Thoemmes Press) [Seventeenth and Eighteenth Century British Philosophy] 260; index. Includes new MS material; separates the life from the philosophy. Author is co-editor of the *Letters*; book is published uniformly with the nine-volume complete works. 1992 has a new introduction by David Berman, who notes that this "masterful biography [is not] likely to lose its pre-eminent position".

Bernal, John Drummond (1901 – –), English philosopher of science.

1980   Maurice Goldsmith, *Sage a life of J.D. Bernal* (London: Hutchinson) 256; illus; index. Author acquainted with subject.

Berthelot, Pierre Eugène Marcel(l)in (1827–1907), French chemist.

1965   Reino Virtanen, *Marcelin Berthelot a study of a scientist's public role* (University of Nebraska Studies. New Series no. 31) 65. Author is a professor of language; a review from the perspective of intellectual history, not history of chemistry.

Berzelius, Jöns Jacob (1779–1848), Swedish chemist.

1966   Erik Jorpes, *Jac Berzelius his life and work* (Stockholm: Almqvist & Wiksell) 156; illus; index. Reprinted 1970. Based on Söderbaum's 1931 biography in Swedish.

Bessemer, Henry (1813–1898), English inventor of the Bessemer process for steel manufacture.

1905   autobiography, *Sir Henry Bessemer FRS an autobiography* (London: Offices of "Engineering") reprinted 1989 (London: Institute of Metals) 380; illus. Includes concluding chapter by the editor with the assistance of Mr Henry Bessemer.

Bessey, Charles Edwin (1845–1915), American botanist and educator.

1993   Richard A. Overfield, *Science with practice Charles E. Bessey and the maturing of American botany* (Ames: Iowa State University Press) [Iowa State University Press Series in the history of technology and science] 262; illus; bibliog; index. "The perspective of this study tends to be that of a botanist at a land-grant college in the American Midwest." Uses MSS.

Bethe, Hans Albrecht (1906 – –), German theoretical nuclear physicist.

1980   Jeremy Bernstein, *Hans Bethe prophet of energy* (NY: Basic Books Inc., Publishers) 212; bibliog; index. Text originally appeared in *The New Yorker*. Preface observes that "any biography of a scientist which does not focus on his ideas is, in my view, a misspent opportunity".

Bidder, George Parker (1806–1878), English engineer.

1983   E.F. Clark, *George Parker Bidder the calculating boy* (Bedford: KSL Publications) 518; illus; bibliog; index. Author a descendent of subject. Includes an appreciation of subject's calculating ability by Joyce Linfoot. Based on MS sources.

Bjerknes, Vilhelm Friman Koren (1862 – –), Norwegian meteorologist.

1989   Robert Marc Friedman, *Appropriating the weather Vilhelm Bjerknes and the construction of a modern meteorology* (Ithaca: Cornell University Press) 251; illus; bibliog; index. Author is an historian of science; book addressed to a diverse scholarly audience. "Although biographical detail belongs to the narrative, the book does not purport to be a biography of Bjerknes."

Black, Joseph (1728–1799), Scottish chemist and physicist (born France).

1918   William Ramsay, *The Life and Letters of Joseph Black* (London: Constable and Company Ltd.) 148; illus; index. Author a professor of chemistry; includes introduction by F.G. Donnan, "dealing with the life and work of Sir William Ramsay".

Bodenheimer, Friz [Friedrich] Simon (1897–1959), German entomologist and zoologist.

1959   autobiography, *A biologist in Israel a book of reminiscences* (Jerusalem: Biological Studies, Publishers) 492; bibliog; index. Published the year of his death.

Boerhaave, Hermann (1668–1738), Dutch chemist and physician.

1746   Wm. Burton, *An account of the life and writings of Herman Boerhaave doctor of philosophy and medicine professor of the theory and practice of physic and also of botany and chemistry in the University of Leyden president of the Chirurgical College in that city Fellow of the Royal Society in London and of the Royal Academy at Paris in two parts* (London: Printed for Henry Lintot) 236. Second edition. First published 1743; only first part of preface altered. Half of book devoted to subject's writings, including abstracts.

1968   G.A. Lindeboom, *Herman Boerhaave the man and his work* (London: Methuen & Co. Ltd.) 452; illus; bibliog; index. Foreword by E. Ashworth Underwood. Based on MS sources. Author the editor of subject's letters and his bibliographer.

Bohr, Niels Henrik David (1885–1962), Danish atomic and nuclear physicist.

1966   Ruth Moore, *Niels Bohr the man his science & the world they changed* (NY: Alfred A. Knopf; London: Hodder & Stoughton, 1967 under title *Niels Bohr the man and the scientist*) 436; index. Author a science journalist; based on published and MS sources and on interviews, all in English.

1985   Poul Dam, *Niels Bohr (1885–1962) atomic theorist inspirator rallying point* (Copenhagen: Royal Danish Ministry of Foreign Affairs) 102, illus; bibliog. Translated from Danish; author an educator and journalist.

1988   Niels Blaedel, *Harmony and unity the life of Niels Bohr* (Madison, WI: Science Tech Publishers; Berlin: Springer Verlag) [Scientific revolutionaries a biographical series] 323; illus; bibliog; index. Translation of the 1985 Danish edition; "primarily intended [for] those outside the ranks of physicists".

1991   Abraham Pais, *Niels Bohr's times in physics philosophy and polity* (Oxford: Clarendon Press) 565; index. Based on MS sources; uses the life to convey changes in science and its impact on society. Seeks to "counteract the many cheap attempts at popularizing this subject, such as efforts by woolly masters at linking quantum physics to mysticism".

Bok, Bart Jan (1906–1983), American astronomer (born The Netherlands).

1993   David H. Levy, *The man who sold the milky way* (Tucson: The University of Arizona Press) 246; illus; bibliog; index. Author is an amateur astronomer and writer; based on interviews with subject.

Boltzmann, Ludwig Eduard (1844–1906), Austrian physicist.

1983   Engelbert Broda, *Ludwig Boltzmann man physicist philosopher* (Woodbridge: CT: Ox Bow Press) 169; illus; bibliog; index. Translated by Larry Gay and author, from 1955 German edition. Preface by Harold J. Morowitz. Not a definitive biography, but rather an introduction. Based on interviews with subject's circle.

Bond, Claude Courtney J. (1910 – –), Canadian engineer.

1988   autobiography, *An iron in many a fire* (Ottawa: University of Ottawa Press) 266; illus; index. Written as a contribution to the body of "records kept by middle-level persons as secondary historical documents, concerning regions, areas and life-styles".

Bond, William Cranch (1789–1859), American astronomer.

1897   Edward S. Holden, *Memorials of William Cranch Bond Director of the Harvard College Observatory 1840–1859 and his son George Phillips Bond Director of the Harvard College Observatory 1859–1865* (San Francisco: Murdock & Co.; NY City: Lemcke & Buechner) reprinted 1980 (NY: Arno Press) [Three centuries of science in America] 296; illus; index. 1980 reprint has title *Memorials of William Cranch Bond and of his son George Phillips Bond.* Author acquainted with subject; contains extensive reminiscences by family. Uses MSS.

Boole, George (1815–1864), English mathematician.

1985   Desmond MacHale, *George Boole his life and work* (Dublin: Boole Press) [Profiles of genius series] 304; illus; bibliog; index. "[A]ttempts to reconstruct . . . an interesting personality who happened to be a mathematician"; not concerned with subject's work. Quotes extensively from correspondence.

Born, Max (1882–1970), German theoretical physicist.

1978   autobiography, *My life recollections of a Nobel Laureate* (London: Taylor & Francis Ltd.) 308; illus; index. Preface on the scientific work by Nevill Mott.

Borodin, Aleksandr Porfirevich (1833–1887), Russian chemist and composer.

1963   Sergei Dianin, *Borodin* (London: Oxford University Press) 356; illus; index. Translated from 1960 Russian edition by Robert Lord. Seeks to correct a number of details given by earlier biographer; second part devoted to analysis of subject's musical compositions. Focus is on music not science.

1988   N.A. Figurovskii and Yu. I. Solov'ev, *Aleksandr Porfir'evich Borodin a chemist's biography* (Berlin: Springer-Verlag) 171; illus; bibliog; index. Translated from 1950 Russian edition by Charlene Steinberg and George B. Kauffman; foreword by Martin D. Kamen. Examines subject as chemist and educator as well as musician. Written for popular readership in Russia.

Bose, Jagadis Chunder (1858–1937), Indian physicist and comparative physiologist (born Bengal, now Pakistan).

1920   Patrick Geddes, *The life and work of Sir Jagadis C. Bose* (London: Longmans, Green, and Co.) 259; index; illus. An account of Bose as "an Indian pioneer of science", studied "in a sociological way". Author a botanist.

1920   [Jagadisachandra Vasu], *Sir Jagadis Chunder Bose his life and speeches* (Madras: Ganesh & Co.) 271. Biographical memoir (pp. 1–78) followed by documents.

1964   Monoranjon Gupta, *Jagadishchandra Bose a biography* (Bombay: Bharatiya Vidya Bhavan) 134; bibliog. XX

1980   Ashis Nandy, *Alternative sciences creativity and authenticity in two Indian scientists* (New Delhi: Allied) [Man, state and society series] 155; bibliog; index. XX

Bose, Satyendra Nath (1894–1974), Indian theoretical physicist.

1976   Sanitmay Chatterjee and Enakshi Chatterjee, *Satyendra Nath Bose* (New Delhi: National Book Trust) 127; bibliog.

Bougainville, Louis Antoine De (1729–1811), French geographer and mathematician.

1990   Mary Kimbrough, *Louis-Antoine de Bougainville 1729–1811 a study in French naval history and politics* (Lewiston, NY: The Edwin Mellen Press) [Studies in French civilization, 7] 241; illus; bibliog; index. "Focus on the activities of Bougainville's life"; the "primary sources . . . are his own writing". Author is critical of previous attempts because of their lack of documentation; claims they contain "fabricated conversations between Bougainville and eminent personages".

Boulton, Matthew (1728–1809), English technologist.

1865   Samuel Smiles, *Lives of Boulton and Watt* (London: John Murray) 521; illus; index. Published 1874 as vol. 4 *The Steam-engine Boulton and Watt* in the expanded five-volume edition of *Lives of the Engineers* (London: John Murray) 416; illus; index. Author says he initially abandoned work on Watt when Muirhead (1858) began, and returned to it when new documents were discovered in Soho. The two lives are treated "conjointly". Text includes "A history of the invention and introduction of the steam-engine".

1936   H.W. Dickinson, *Matthew Boulton* (Cambridge: Cambridge University Press) 218; illus; index.

Boussingault, Jean Baptiste Joseph Dieudonné (1802–1887), French agricultural chemist.

1984   F.W.J. McCosh, *Boussingault chemist and agriculturalist* (Dordrecht: D. Reidel Publishing Company) [Chemists and chemistry] 280; illus; bibliog; index. Aim is to "lead to a greater understanding of the multifarious interests" of subject.

Boveri, Theodor (1862–1915), German biologist.

1967   Fritz Baltzer, *Theodor Boveri life and work of a great biologist 1862–1915* (Berkeley, University of California Press) 165; illus, bibliog; index. Author was student of and assistant to subject. Translation from 1962 German edition by Dorothea Rudnick deviates from the German text.

Bowditch, Nathaniel (1773–1838), American astronomer.

[1839]   Nathaniel Ingersoll Bowditch, *Memoir of Nathaniel Bowditch* (Boston: Charles C. Little and James Brown) 172. The memoir was originally prefixed to the fourth volume of the subject's *Méchanique Céleste*. Second edition (1840) printed from existing stereotype plates. A "revised edition" was published (Boston: Lee and Shepard, 1869) as *Nat the navigator a life of Nathaniel Bowditch for young persons*. Third edition 1884 (Cambridge: J. Wilson) 178.

1941   Robert Elton Berry, *Yankee stargazer the life of Nathaniel Bowditch* (NY: Whittlesey House McGraw-Hill Book Company, Inc.) 234; illus; bibliog; index. First full-scale biography. Based on memoirs and MS sources.

1969   Paul Rink, *To steer by the stars the story of Nathaniel Bowditch* (Garden City, NY: Doubleday & Company, Inc.) 189. A literary narrative with no notes or paraphernalia.

Bowman, Isaiah (1878–1950), Canadian geographer.

1980   Geoffrey J. Martin, *The life and thought of Isaiah Bowman* (Hamden, CT: Archon Books) 272; illus; bibliog; index. "Geographers are the particular beneficiaries of such studies in their recent history." Uses MS sources.

Boyle, Robert (1627–1691), Irish natural philosopher.

1744   Thomas Birch, *The life of the Honourable Robert Boyle* (London: A. Millar) 458; index. *Life* is 1–318 followed by appendices. This is prefixed to Boyle's *Works* in five volumes from the publisher. Dedication to Thomas Herring, Archbishop of York. Maddison (1969) says author was assisted by the Revd Henry Miles.

1885   Lawrence Saunders, *Robert Boyle inventor and philanthropist* (London: Gilbert Wood & Co.) 104. First appeared in the *Inventor's Record* 1880. Stresses moral lessons to be learned from example of subject as inventor. Includes a chapter on the "advance of sanitary science".

1914   Flora Masson, *Robert Boyle a biography* (London: Constable & Company) 323; index. Based on printed primary sources. More (1944) says it "does not pretend to be more than a pleasing narrative", while Pilkington (1959) says she "pays little attention to his work as a scientist".

1944   Louis Trenchard More, *The life and works of the Honourable Robert Boyle* (NY: Oxford University Press) 313; index. Preface surveys the extant sources. Pilkington (1959) calls this "a full and scholarly account".

1959   Roger Pilkington, *Robert Boyle father of chemistry* (London: John Murray) 179; index. Based on secondary sources; "not intended to be a reference work . . . but rather the story of one among the greatest men of science of all ages".

1969   R.E.W. Maddison, *The life of the Honourable Robert Boyle FRS* (London: Taylor & Francis Ltd.; NY: Barnes & Noble) 332; illus; index. Meant to supplement Birch (no other biographies are mentioned) by dealing with Boyle's publications and influence. Based on MS sources.

Bragg, William Henry (1862–1942) English physicist.

1978   G.M. Caroe, *William Henry Bragg 1862–1942 man and scientist* (Cambridge: Cambridge University Press) 212; illus; index. Author is subject's daughter. "[N]ot especially for scientists." Quotes extensively from correspondence.

Brashear, John Alfred (1840–1920) American astrophysical instrument-maker.

1925   autobiography, *John A. Brashear the autobiography of a man who loved the stars* (Boston: Houghton Mifflin Company) 262; illus; index. Edited by W. Lucien Scaife.

Copyright is held by the American Society of Mechanical Engineers, who urged author to write the text. Left unfinished at his death and completed by Scaife.

1940   Harriet A. Gaul and Ruby Eiseman, *John Alfred Brashear scientist and humanitarian 1840–1920* (Philadelphia: University of Pennsylvania Press) [Pennsylvania Lives] 220; index. "[W]ord of mouth stories about John Brashear comprise the better half of this volume."

Braun, Karl Ferdinand (1850–1918), German physicist.

1981   Friedrich Kurylo and Charles Susskind, *Ferdinand Braun a life of the Nobel prizewinner and inventor of the cathode-ray oscilloscope* (Cambridge: The MIT Press) 289; illus; bibliog; index. Foreword by Bern Dibner. Translated and adapted by Susskind from Kurylo's 1965 German edition. Author a journalist. Translator-adapter an historian of science and technology.

Brewster, David (1781–1868), Scottish physicist (optics).

1869   [Margaret M.] Gordon, *The Home Life of Sir David Brewster.* (Edinburgh: Edmonston and Douglas) 440; illus. Second edition, revised, 1870. Author is subject's daughter; the book is "taken from a home point of view". Professor Tait "revised the allusions to science which have necessarily occurred". Second edition; 482. Described as slightly altered and abbreviated, with some fresh material.

Bridgman, Percy William (1882–1961), American physicist and philosopher of science.

1990   Maila L. Walter, *Science and cultural crisis an intellectual biography of Percy Williams Bridgman 1882–1961* (Stanford: Stanford University Press) 362; illus; bibliog; index. For the general reader as well as for specialists; does not discuss subject's childhood, and makes "extensive use of quotation and close paraphrase". Uses MS sources.

Brindley, James (1716–1772), English engineer.

1861   Samuel Smiles, "Life of James Brindley", *Lives of the Engineers* (London: John Murray) I:5 304–476; illus; index. 1874 edition in five volumes. New edition 1968 based on the 1862 two-volume printing (Newton Abbot: David & Charles Reprints) with introduction by L.T.C. Rolt. The classic "account of some of the principal men by whom the material development of England has been promoted".

1864   Samuel Smiles, *James Brindley and the early engineers* (London: John Murray) 320; illus; index. A "reproduction in a cheaper and more compact form" of Smiles 1861. Sold as a companion to 1864 edition of Smiles 1857 on Stephenson. Includes material on Vermuyden and an appendix on Pierre-Paul Riquet which was prepared for the French edition of *Self Help*.

1956   Laurence Meynell, *James Brindley the pioneer of canals* (London: Werner Laurie) 190; illus. Object is "a short and readable account".

1968   Cyril T.G. Boucher, *James Brindley engineer 1716–1772* (Norwich: Goose and

Son Limited) 130; illus; bibliog; index. Author a university teacher of engineering. Aims to improve on Smiles by stressing technical aspects and comparing subject's work with that of other engineers.

Broom, Robert (1866–1951), South African palaeontologist (born Scotland).

1972   G.H. Findlay, *Dr Robert Broom FRS a palaeontologist and physician 1866–1951 a biography appreciation and bibliography* (Cape Town: A.A. Balkema) [South African biographical and historical studies] 157; index; illus. Introduction by Raymond A. Dart. Uses MS sources.

Brown, Robert (1773–1858), Scottish botanist.

1985   D.J. Mabberley, *Jupiter botanicus Robert Brown of the British Museum* (Braunschweig: J. Cramer; London: British Museum) 500; illus; bibliog; index. First biography, by an Oxford botanist; based on MS letters and papers.

Browne, Thomas (1605–1682), English natural historian.

1905   Edmund Gosse, *Sir Thomas Browne* (London: Macmillan & Co., Limited) [English men of letters] 215; index. American edition (NY: Macmillan & Co., Ltd.) [English men of letters] 214; index.

1950   Jeremiah S. Finch, *Sir Thomas Browne a doctor's life of science and faith* (NY: Henry Schuman) [The Life of science library] 319; illus; bibliog; index. Author says "the sources of biographical information are numerous and scattered". Uses MSS.

1962   Joan Frankau Bennett, *Sir Thomas Browne a man of achievement in literature* (Cambridge: Cambridge University Press) 255; bibliog; index. Focus is on subject's work; an "endeavour . . . to find out what he thought and what the style expresses".

1962   Frank Livingstone Huntley, *Sir Thomas Browne a biographical and critical study* (Ann Arbor: The University of Michigan Press) 283; index. Book is "addressed to the general audience as well as to students and scholars in literature". Emphasizes early life and five main works. Uses MS sources.

Brunel, Isambard Kingdom (1806–1859), English engineer.

1870   Isambard Brunel, *The life of Isambard Kingdom Brunel* (London: Longmans, Green & Company) reprinted 1971 (Newton Abbot: David & Charles Reprints; Rutherford, NJ: Fairleigh Dickinson University Press, 1972) 568; illus; index. 1971 reprint has introduction by L.T.C. Rolt. Chronological narrative ends in 1835; subsequent period discussed in context of ocean steam navigation. Author a barrister, the son of subject; Rolt says he knew little about engineering or writing – but the book is valuable for its extensive quotations.

1938   Celia Brunel Noble, *The Brunels father and son* (London: Cobden-Sanderson) 279; illus; bibliog; index. A "story", based on the standard works but portraying subjects as living characters.

1957   L.T.C. Rolt, *Isambard Kingdom Brunel a biography* (London: Longmans, Green and Co.; NY: St Martin's Press, 1959) 346; illus; bibliog; index. Reissued 1971; Pelican edition 1970, 447. Portrays subject as "artist and visionary", as well as engineer. Based on MS sources.

1973   Peter Hay, *Brunel his achievements in the transport revolution* (London: Osprey Publishing) issued in paperback 1985 with title *Brunel engineering giant* (London: B.T. Basford Ltd.) 134; illus; bibliog; index. Aims to place subject in context of his time and to kill some myths. Acknowledges Brunel and Rolt. Author an economic historian.

1974   John Pudney, *Brunel and his world* (London: Thames and Hudson) 128; illus; bibliog; index. Extensively illustrated.

1991   Adrian Vaughan, *Isambard Kingdom Brunel engineering knight-errant* (London: John Murray) 285; illus; bibliog; index. Paperback issue 1993. A more "objective" account than that of Rolt, stressing labour disputes and other unfavourable evidence. Based on MS sources. Author a railway historian. Reviewed by the *Spectator* as "the *Satanic Verses* of the railway buff's world".

Brunel, Marc Isambard (1769–1849), English engineer (born France).

1862   Richard Beamish, *Memoir of the life of Sir Marc Isambard Brunel* (London: Longman, Green, Longman, and Roberts) 359; illus; index. Second edition revised and corrected: 357; illus; index. Author is friend of subject. Preface to first edition dated March 1862; preface to second edition (dated April 1862) notes revisions.

1970   Paul Clements, *Marc Isambard Brunel* (London: Longmans) 270; illus; index. Foreword by L.T.C. Rolt, who calls this book "the first to assess [the subject's] total engineering achievement". Based on MS sources, patent records etc.

1938   Celia Brunel Noble, see Brunel, Isambard Kingdom.

Byron, August Ada [Countess of Lovelace], English mathematician.

1977   Doris Langley Moore, *Ada Countess of Lovelace Byron's illegitimate daughter* (London: John Murray) 397; illus; index; bibliog. XX

1985   Dorothy Stein, *Ada a life and a legacy* (Cambridge: The MIT Press). 321; illus; index. Interest of biographer stemmed from subject's computer connection; stresses mathematical, scientific and medical issues not covered by Moore 1977.

1986   Joan Baum, *The calculating passion of Ada Byron* (Hamden, CT: Archon Books) 133; illus; bibliog; index. Emphasis is on the analytical engine of Babbage and subject.

Callan, Nicholas (1799–1864), Irish electromagnetician.

1965   P.J. McLaughlin, *Nicholas Callan priest-scientist 1799–1864* (Dublin: Clonmore & Reynolds Ltd.; London: Burns & Oates Ltd.) 128; illus; index. Attempts to portray subject "against the setting of his time".

Calvin, Melvin (1911 – –), American chemist.

1992 autobiography, *Following the trail of light a scientific odyssey* (Washington: American Chemical Society) [Profiles, pathways and dreams: autobiographies of eminent chemists] 175; illus; index.

Carnot, Lazare-Nicolas-Marguerite (1753–1823), French mathematican and engineer.

1940 Huntley Dupré, *Lazare Carnot republican patriot* (Oxford: The Mississippi Valley Press) 343; index; bibliog. Carnot "as a man, as thinker, as public servant, and as patriot".

1954 S.J. Watson, *Carnot* (London: The Bodley Head) 223; index; bibliog. Says Carnot has been neglected by historians, and/or seen in military terms; this biography presents him as "a man of learning with a wide range of interests", but primarily as soldier and politician.

Cartan, Elie (1869–1951) French mathematician.

1993 M.A. Akivis and B.A. Rosenfeld, *Elie Cartan (1869–1951)* (Providence, RI: American Mathematical Society) [Translations of mathematical monographs] 317; illus; bibliog. Authors are geometers. Translated by Simeon Ivanov. Contains some biographical material, but focuses on subject's work and contains mathematical equations.

Casimir, Hendrik Brugt Gerhard (1909 – –), Dutch physicist.

1983 autobiography, *Haphazard reality half a century of science* (NY: Harper & Row Publishers) 356; bibliog; index. Preface acknowledges the support and pressure of the Alfred P. Sloan Foundation, which promotes scientific autobiography.

Catesby, Mark (1683–1749), English natural historian.

1961 George Frederick Frick and Raymond Phineas Stearns, *Mark Catesby the colonial Audubon* (Urbana: University of Illinois Press) 137; illus; bibliog. Combines biographical sketch and scientific evaluation.

Cauchy, Augustin Louis (1789–1857), French mathematician.

1991 Bruno Belhoste, *Augustin-Louis Cauchy a biography* (NY: Springer-Verlag) 380; illus; bibliog; index. Translated by Frank Ragland. Author is an historian; book claims to be more rigorous and scholarly than C.A. Valson's 1868 life.

Cavendish, Henry (1731–1810), English physicist (born France).

1851 George Wilson, *The life of the Honble. Henry Cavendish* (London: Cavendish Society) 478; illus. Subtitle: including abstracts of his more important scientific papers, and a critical inquiry into the claims of all the alleged discoveries of the composition of water. Emphasis is on subject's work in chemistry.

1960   A.J. Berry, *Henry Cavendish his life and scientific work* (London: Hutchinson) 208; illus; bibliog; index. Seeks to redress neglect.

Cayley, George (1773–1857), English aerial navigator.

1961   J. Laurence Pritchard, *Sir George Cayley the inventor of the aeroplane* (London: Max Parrish) 277; illus; index. Foreword by Peter Masefield. Author a mathematician and writer on aeronautics.

1965   Gerard Fairlie and Elizabeth Cayley, *The life of a genius* (London: Hodder and Stoughton) 192. Objective is "to present the character behind the genius". Based on MS sources; incorporates invented dialogue derived from documents.

Chambers, Robert (1802–1871), Scottish biologist and geologist.

1872   William Chambers, *Memoir of Robert Chambers with Autobiographic Reminiscences of William Chambers* (Edinburgh and London: W.& R. Chambers) 336. Seventh edition 1873, revised and expanded; twelfth edition 1883, 402. William Chambers, the scientist's publisher brother, found it "scarcely possible to relate the story of one without frequent reference to the other". 1883 edition has a supplementary chapter added by the publishers.

1959   Milton Millhauser, *Just before Darwin Robert Chambers and Vestiges* (Middletown, CT: Wesleyan University Press) 246; illus; bibliog; index. Revision of dissertation; issued in microfilm 1952 under title "Robert Chambers, evolution, and the early Victorian Mind".

Chandrasekhar, Subrahmanyan (1910 – –), Indian physicist.

1991   Kameshwar C. Wali, *Chandra a biography of S. Chandrasekhar* (Chicago: University of Chicago Press) 341; illus; index. Author a professor of physics. Largely based on interviews with subject and his associates.

Chargaff, Erwin (1905 – –), Czech biochemist.

1978   autobiography, *Heraclitian fire sketches from a life before nature* (NY: The Rockefeller University Press) 252; bibliog; index. Written in the context of a moral crtitique of the destructive power of science.

Châtelet, Gabrielle Emilie le Tonnelier de Breteuil (1706–1749), French writer on science.

[1910]   Frank Hamel, *An eighteenth-century marquise a study of Emilie du Châtelet and her times* (London: Stanley Paul & Co.; NY: J. Pott) 384; index; illus. Written from a broader standpoint than that of her influence on Voltaire's work.

1971   Samuel Edwards [N.B. Gerson], *The divine mistress* (London: Cassell) 275; index; bibliog.

Cherwell. See Lindemann, Frederick Alexander.

Clarke, Edward Daniel (1769–1822), English geologist.

1824   William Otter, *The life and remains of the Rev Edward Daniel Clarke LID professor of mineralogy in the University of Cambridge* (London, 1824) 670. Author is Bishop of Chichester; published by the author under the subscription system.

Clarke, William Branwhite (1798–1878), Australian geologist (born England).

1944   James Jervis, *Rev. W.B. Clarke, MA FRS FGS FRGS The father of Australian geology* (Sydney: Royal Australian Historical Society) 116. Published version of a paper read to the Royal Australian Historical Society. Presents documentary evidence which may be used as "source data" for a later biography.

1982   Elena Grainger, *The Remarkable Reverend Clarke the life and times of the father of Australian geology* (Melbourne: Oxford University Press) 292; illus; bibliog; index. Stresses subject's "personality and his work as a geologist", with minimal attention to his duties as a clergyman.

Clift, William (1775–1849), English anatomist and palaeontologist.

1954   Jessie Dobson, *William Clift* (London: William Heinemann Medical Books Ltd) 144; bibliog; index. Based on MS sources.

Cockcroft, John Douglas (1897–1967), English atomic physicist.

1984   Guy Hartcup and T.E. Allibone, *Cockcroft and the atom* (Bristol: Adam Hilger Ltd) 320; illus; bibliog; index. Allibone a friend and colleague of subject. Hartcup an historian of science and technology. Based on MS sources.

Coghill, George Ellett (1872–1941), American embryologist and anatomist.

1949   C. Judson Herrick, *George Ellett Coghill naturalist and philosopher* (Chicago: The University of Chicago Press) 280; bibliog; index. Depicts "the life of science as it was lived" and "the science itself which he produced", and demonstrates the relationship.

Coke, Thomas William (1752–1842), English agriculturalist.

1908   A.M.W. Stirling, *Coke of Norfolk and his friends* (London: John Lane The Bodley Head; NY: John Lane Company) I:449 II:548; illus; index. One-volume edition published 1912. Subtitle: The life of Thomas William Coke, first Earl of Leicester of Holkham, containing an account of his ancestry, surroundings, public services and private friend-ships, and including many unpublished letters from noted men of his day, English and American.

Colden, Cadwallader (1688–1776), American botanist and physicist (born Scotland).

1906   Alice Mapelsden Keys, *Cadwallader Colden a representative eighteenth century official* (NY: The Columbia University Press; London: Macmillan & Co. Ltd.) 375; index. Based on MS sources. Focus is on eighteenth-century society and politics.

Collie, John Norman (1859–1942), English chemist.

1973   William C. Taylor, *The snows of yesteryear J Norman Collie mountaineer* (Toronto: Holt, Rhinehart and Winston of Canada, Limited) 185; illus; bibliog. Does not discuss subject as a scientist.

Collinson, Peter (1693/94–1768), English natural historian and disseminator of science.

[1925]   Norman G. Brett-James, *The Life of Peter Collinson* (London: Edgar G. Daustan) 287; bibliog; index. Published for the author; stresses Collinson as a Quaker.

Commerson, Philibert (1727–1773), French natural historian.

1909   S. Pasfield Oliver, *The Life of Philibert Commerson D.M., naturaliste du roi An old-world story of French travel and science in the days of Linnaeus* (London: John Murray) 242; index. The book was posthumously completed by G.F. Scott Elliot.

Condorcet, Marie Jean Antoine Nicolas Caritat (1743–1794), French mathematician.

1930   Anne Elizabeth Burlingame, *Condorcet the torchbearer of the French revolution* (Boston: The Stratford Company) 249; bibliog. Author is professor of history in an American college; described as a simple account for readers of English.

Coolidge, William David (1873–1975), American industrial scientist (developed ductile tungsten and the hot-cathode x-ray tube).

1963   John Anderson Miller, *Yankee scientist William David Coolidge* (Schenectady, NY: Mohawk Development Service) 216; bibliog; index. Foreword by Guy Suits.

Cooper, Thomas (1759–1840), English chemist.

1926   Dumas Malone, *The Public life of Thomas Cooper 1783–1839* (New Haven: Yale University Press) reprinted 1961 (Columbia: University of South Carolina Press) [Yale

University Historical Publications] 432; illus. 1961 reprint has new preface and an updated bibliographical note.

Cope, Edward Drinker (1840–1897), American palaeontologist and zoologist.

1931   Henry Fairfield Osborn, *Cope master naturalist the life and letters of Edward Drinker Cope with a bibliography of his writings classified by subject a study of the pioneer and foundation periods of vertebrate palaeontology in America* (Princeton: Princeton University Press) reprinted 1978 (NY: Arno Press) [Biologists and their world] 740; illus; bibliog. Described as a labour of love, designed to do posthumous justice to the subject. Based on MS materials and written with the co-operation of Helen Ann Warren; draws parallel between subject and Lamarck.

1964   Robert Plate, *The Dinosaur hunters Othniel C. Marsh and Edward D. Cope* (NY: D. McKay Company, Inc.); 281; index; bibliog. Author a freelance writer-editor.

Cort, Henry (1740–1800), English industrialist (pioneer of puddling process and use of rollers for iron).

1983   R.A. Mott, *Henry Cort the great finer* (London: The Metals Society) 108; illus; index. Edited by Peter Singer, who eliminated about half the original MS. Occasion is bicentenary of subject's chief patents.

Cottrell, Frederick Gardner (1877–1948), American chemist and engineer.

1952   Frank Cameron, *Cottrell samaritan of science* (Garden City, NY: Doubleday & Company, Inc.) 414; index. Foreword by Ernest O. Lawrence; narrative biography for a popular readership.

Coues, Elliot (1842–1899), American ornithologist

1981   Paul Russell Cutright and Michael J. Brodhead, *Elliott Coues naturalist and frontier historian* (Urbana: University of Illinois Press) 509; illus; bibliog; index. The "purpose in this work is to make more available to the general reader and the professional scientist and historian alike the life story of this colorful and influential American scientist". Uses MSS.

Coulomb, Charles Augustin (1736–1806), French physicist.

1971   C. Stewart Gillmor, *Coulomb and the evolution of physics and engineering in eighteenth-century France* (Princeton: Princeton University Press) 328; illus; bibliog; index. Addressed to engineers and physicists and to historians. First biography.

Coulter, John Merle (1851–1928), American botanist.

1944   Andrew Denny Rodgers, *John Merle Coulter missionary in science* (Princeton:

Princeton University Press) 321; illus; index. Regards biographies as "contributions" by which "the writing of a history of American science must proceed."

Courant, Richard (1888–1972), American mathematician (born Germany).

1976   Constance Reid, *Courant in Göttingen and NY, the story of an improbable mathematician* (NY: Springer-Verlag) 314; illus; index. Published 1986 with author's *Hilbert* in one volume with combined index (NY: Springer-Verlag). Based on interviews.

Cram, Donald James (1919 – –), American organic chemist.

1990   autobiography, *From design to discovery* (Washington: American Chemical Society) [Profiles, pathways, and dreams: profiles of eminent chemists] 146; illus; index. Contains mostly science.

Croll, James (1821–1890), Scottish geologist. 1896

1896   James Campbell Irons, *Autobiographical sketch of James Croll LlD FRS etc with memoir of his life and work* (London: Edward Stanford) 553; bibliog; index. Author records advice of David Masson to leave subject's autobiographical fragment intact (1–41) and add an account of the life and work. Stresses subject's struggles, his intellectual reputation and his religious faith.

Crompton, Rookes Evelyn Bell (1845–1940), English electrical engineer.

1928   autobiography, *Reminiscences* (London: Constable & Co. Ltd) 238; illus; bibliog; index. Preface by Arthur Stanley.

Crompton, Samuel (1753–1827), English technologist (inventor of spinning mule).

1859   Gilbert J. French, *The life and times of Samuel Crompton inventor of the spinning machine called the Mule* (London: Simpkin, Marshall & Co.) 293. Subtitle: being the substance of two papers read to the members of the Bolton Mechanics' Institution. Book is "commended to working men as a subject for serious reflection", both as encouragement and warning.

1927   anon, *Samuel Crompton the inventor of the spinning mule a brief survey of his life and work with which is incorporated a short history of Messrs Dobson & Barlow Limited* (Bolton, Dobson & Barlow. Ltd.) 147; illus. "A tribute to subject's memory, giving the principal events of his life."

Crookes, William (1832–1919), English chemist and physicist.

1923   E.E. Fournier d'Albe, *The life of Sir William Crookes OM FRS* (London: T. Fisher Unwin Ltd.) 413; index. Foreword by Sir Oliver Lodge.

Cunningham, Allan (1791–1839), Australian botanist.

1970   W.G. McMinn, *Allan Cunningham botanist and explorer* (Melbourne: Melbourne University Press) 147; illus; bibliog; index.

Curie, Marie (1867–1934), Polish physicist.

1937   Eve Curie, *Madame Curie a biography* (Garden City, NY: Doubleday, Doran & Company, Inc.) 393; illus. Translated by Vincent Sheean. Author is daughter of subject; claims fidelity to the facts of "this story, so like a myth". Reprints, beginning in 1938, included an index.

1959   Robin McKown, *Marie Curie* (NY: G.P. Putnam's Sons) [Lives to Remember] 128.

1964   Alan Ivimey, *Marie Curie pioneer of the atomic age* (London: Arthur Barker Limited) [Creators of the Modern World] 123; index.

1974   Robert Reid, *Marie Curie* (London: Collins; NY: Saturday Review Press) 349; illus; bibliog; index. Based on MS sources.

1983   Robert Woznicki, *Madame Curie daughter of Poland* (Miami: The American Institute of Polish Culture) [Polish Heritage Series] 175, illus; bibliog. Focuses on subject's Polish background, and reassesses the Curie family's role in modern science.

1986   Françoise Giroud, *Marie Curie a life* (NY: Holmes & Meier) 291; illus; bibliog. Translated by Lydia Davis; popular style.

1989   Rosalynd Pflaum, *Grand obsession Madame Curie and her world* (NY: Doubleday) 496; illus; bibliog; index. Author a professional biographer; popular style.

Curie, Pierre (1859–1906), French physicist.

1923   Marie Curie, *Pierre Curie* (NY: The Macmillan Company) 242; illus. Translated by Charlotte and Vernon Kellogg; introduction by Mrs William Brown Meloney. Author is subject's wife; biography is 151 pages followed by her autobiographical notes (155–242). According to Pflaum, when the book was published outside the USA Curie refused permission to include these notes.

Cuvier, Georges (1769–1832), French comparative anatomist and palaeontologist.

1964   William Coleman, *Georges Cuvier zoologist a study in the history of evolution theory* (Cambridge: Harvard University Press) 212; illus; bibliog; index. Focuses on subject's zoological theories and practice, especially his opposition to evolutionary theory, rather than on his career as an educator and administrator.

1984   Dorinda Outram, *Georges Cuvier vocation science and authority in post-revolutionary France* (Manchester: Manchester University Press) 299; bibliog; index. Written as "a polemical book", revising the biographical tradition by placing the subject in his political context.

D'Alembert, Jean le Rond (1717–1783), French mathematician and philosopher.

1963 Ronald Grimsley, *Jean d'Alembert 1717–83* (Oxford: Clarendon Press) 316; bibliog; index. Revision of 1948 thesis. Hankins calls this the best biography although limited to literary and philosophical activities; says it supersedes Bertrand's 1889 life.

1970 Thomas L. Hankins, *Jean d'Alembert science and the Enlightenment* (Oxford: Clarendon Press) 260; bibliog; index. Intended "as a study of the relations between science and philosophy during the Enlightenment", not a "thoroughgoing biography" but rather "history of science as intellectual history".

Dalton, John (1766–1844), English physicist and chemist.

1854 William Charles Henry, *Memoirs of the life and scientific researches of John Dalton* (London: The Cavendish Society) [Works of the Cavendish Society] 249; bibliog. Author the subject's literary executor. Uses MS sources. Thackray calls it "as unavoidable as it is unsatisfactory".

1856 Robt Angus Smith, *Memoir of John Dalton . . . and history of the atomic theory up to his time* (London: H. Bailliere; Paris: J.B. Bailliere) 298; index. Breaks off biographical narrative when subject first published on atoms; incorporates general history and then returns to life. Does not repeat material covered by Henry. Attempts to avoid dryness (in favour of a "fairy tale of science") by quoting extensively.

1874 Henry Lonsdale, *The worthies of Cumberland John Dalton* (London: George Routledge and Sons) 320; bibliog. Epitomizes the science. Uses MS sources to correct earlier accounts of the subject's personal history. Acknowledges debt to Henry 1854 and Smith 1856: "They wrote for the scientific public; my effort is a much humbler one, aiming more or less to satisfy the wants of a quasi-popular or less instructed class of readers." Thackray says this is more informative than Smith 1856.

1895 Henry E. Roscoe, *John Dalton and the rise of modern chemistry* (London: Cassell and Company Limited) [The Century science series] 216; illus; index. Seeks to write in "a more condensed form" and for "a somewhat larger audience" than earlier biographers and memoirists. According to Thackray, "a thoroughgoing attempt to paint Dalton as the first of the Manchester school of chemistry".

1906 J.P. Millington, *John Dalton* (London: J.M. Dent & Co.; NY: E.P. Dutton & Co.) [English men of science] reprinted 1971 (NY: AMS Press) 225; index; bibliog. Thackray calls this "totally derivative and uninspired".

1966 Frank Greenaway, *John Dalton and the atom* (London: Heinemann [Heinemann books on the history of science]; Ithaca: Cornell University Press) 244; bibliog; index. Occasion is bicentenary; written for both the student first meeting Dalton and the general reader. Thackray says this and 1970 Patterson are popular biographies that "ably review and synthesize the material available".

1970 Elizabeth C. Patterson, *John Dalton and the atomic theory the biography of a natural philosopher* (Garden City, NY: Doubleday) [The Science Study Series] 348; illus; bibliog. According to Thackray, she was able to draw on the insights of the bicentenary conference. XX

1972 Arnold Thackray, *John Dalton critical assessments of his life and science* (Cambridge: Harvard University Press) [Harvard monographs in the history of science]

190; bibliog; index. A series of independent essays interpreting Dalton "not in terms of heroic biography but as a man through whose life we may explore the changing nature of British science at a crucial juncture in its social history".

Dana, James Dwight (1813–1895), American geologist.

1899   Daniel C. Gilman, *The life of James Dwight Dana scientific explorer minerologist geologist zoologist professor in Yale university.* (NY: Harper Brothers Publishers) 409; illus; bibliog; index. Author is the president of Johns Hopkins University. Treatment is "personal rather than scientific" and "the subject of it is his own interpreter".

Darwin, Charles Robert (1809–1882), English naturalist.

1885   Grant Allen, *Charles Darwin* (London: Longmans, Green and Co.; NY: D. Appleton and Company) [English worthies] 206; index. Subject's career "as a moment in a great revolution, in due relation both to those who went before and to those who came after him". "Sanctioned" by Francis Darwin.

1887   G.T. Bettany, *Life of Charles Darwin* (London: Walter Scott Limited) [Great Writers] 175; index; bibliog. Combines "biographical interest with sketches of his most important works"; bibliography is by John P. Anderson.

1887   Francis Darwin, ed., *The life and letters of Charles Darwin including an autobiographical chapter* (London: John Murray; NY: D. Appleton and Company) I:395 II:393 III:418; index; bibliog. Editor wished to illustrate his father's personal character as well as his career; incorporates subject's single-chapter autobiography. 1892 edition entitled *Charles Darwin his life told in an autobiographical chapter and in a selection of his published letters*; reprinted 1958 (NY: Dover Publications Inc.) 265; index. 1929 edition entitled *Autobiography of Charles Darwin with two appendices comprising a chapter of reminiscences and a statement of Charles Darwin's religious views* (London: Watts) [The Thinker's Library] 154. 1950 edition entitled *Charles Darwin's autobiography with his notes and letters depicting the growth of the Origin of Species* (NY: Henry Schuman) 266; index. Editor describes 1892 as "practically an abbreviation of 1887, omitting most purely scientific letters and including the autobiography chapter". 1929 omits some passages in the autobiographical chapter. 1950 has introductory essay by George Gaylord Simpson ("The meaning of Darwin"); includes the autobiography chapter and five more of the 14 chapters of 1892.

1891   Charles Frederick Holder, *Charles Darwin his life and work* (NY: G.P. Putnam's Sons) [Leaders in science] 279; index; illus; bibliog. Proposed to author by the publishers, and adapted to both young and old readers.

1921   Leonard Huxley, *Charles Darwin* (London: Watts & Co.) [Life stories of famous men] 119; illus. This publication issued by Watts for the Rationalist Press Association, Limited.

1927   George A. Dorsey, *The evolution of Charles Darwin* (Garden City, NY: Doubleday, Page & Company [Benefactors of Mankind]; London: George Allen & Unwin Ltd.) 300; bibliog; index. Author a non-scientist; "To understand Darwin is to understand human beings. That must be my justification for this book".

1927   Henshaw Ward, *Charles Darwin the man and his warfare* (Indianapolis: The

Bobbs-Merrill Company; London: John Murray) reprinted 1943 (NY: The New home library) 472; illus; bibliog; index. Popular style. 1943 reprint has title *Charles Darwin and the theory of evolution.*

1934 R.W.G. Hingston, *Darwin* (London: Duckworth) [Great lives] 144; bibliog. Popular style.

1937 Geoffrey West [Geoffrey Harry Wells], *Charles Darwin the fragmentary man* (London: George Routledge & Sons Ltd.) 351; illus; bibliog; index. Also published with title *Charles Darwin a portrait* and author Geoffrey Harry Wells (New Haven: Yale University Press, 1938) 359; illus; bibliog; index. Author is a professional biographer; attempts "to re-live Darwin's life imaginatively"; omits unpublished material.

1955 William Irvine, *Apes angels and Victorians the story of Darwin Huxley and evolution* (NY: McGraw-Hill Book Company, Inc.; London: Weidenfeld and Nicolson) reprinted 1968 (Cleveland: The World Publishing Company) 399; illus; bibliog; index. 1968 reprint has title *Apes angels and Victorians Darwin Huxley and evolution.* Abridged edition 1956 under title *Apes angels and Victorians a joint biography of Darwin and Huxley* (London: Readers Union) 278. Premise is that "Darwin caused history and Huxley made it". London 1955 edition has same title as 1956 abridgement.

1955 Arthur Keith, *Darwin revalued* (London: Watts & Co.) 294; illus; index. Attempts to bring the records together and place them in sequence; tries "to make Darwin tell the story of his life in his own words, while I am merely playing the part of a 'cinema-operator'".

1955 Ruth Moore, *Charles Darwin a great life in brief* (NY: Alfred A. Knopf) [Great lives in brief a new series of biographies] 206; bibliog; index. 1957 edition entitled *Charles Darwin* (London: Hutchinson) [The Stratford Library] 207; bibliog; index. Author an American jouranlist and science writer.

1958 autobiography, *The autobiography of Charles Darwin 1809–1882 with original omissions restored* (London: Collins; NY: W.W. Norton & Company Inc., 1969) [Books that live] 253; index. Edited by Nora Barlow, granddaughter of subject; restores controversial material. See also De Beer, ed. 1974.

1959 Gertrude Himmelfarb, *Darwin and the Darwinian revolution* (Garden City, NY: Doubleday & Company, Inc.) 480; index; bibliog. Also published 1959 (London: Chatto & Windus) 422; index; bibliog. Author an intellectual historian.

1963 Gavin De Beer, *Charles Darwin evolution by natural selection* (London: Thomas Nelson and Sons Ltd. [British men of science]; Garden City, NY: Anchor Books, Doubleday in co-operation with the American Museum of Natural History, 1965) [Natural history library]) 290; index; illus; bibliog. Author is director of the British Museum (Natural History); stresses scientific achievements over private life. Uses MS sources. 1965 edition has title *Charles Darwin a scientific biography*

1964 Alice Dickinson, *Charles Darwin & natural selection* (London: Franklin Watts) [Immortals of mankind] reprinted 1971 (Lewis Reprints Ltd) 212; bibliog; index. Based on secondary sources; series examines subjects who "have made outstanding contributions to the world's human resources".

1964 H.E.L. Mellersh, *Charles Darwin pioneer of the theory of evolution* (London: Weidenfeld & Nicolson (Educational) Ltd.) [Pathfinder biographies] illus; bibliog; index. Author a science writer.

1965 Julian Huxley and H.B.D. Kettlewell, *Charles Darwin and his world* (London:

Thames & Hudson Ltd.; NY: The Viking Press) 144; index; illus. Breaks the life into three phases.

1968   Walter Karp, *Charles Darwin and the origin of species* (NY: American Heritage Publishing Co., Inc.) [Horizon Caravel Books] 153; illus; index. A popular biography in a series produced by the editors of *Horizon* magazine; J.W. Burrow served as consultant.

1973   John Chancellor, *Charles Darwin* (London: Weidenfeld and Nicolson) [Great lives] 231; illus; index; bibliog. Introduction by Elizabeth Longford. Aims "to balance Darwin's public discoveries with his personal life". Written in popular style.

1974   James Bunting, *Charles Darwin* (Folkestone: Bailey Brothers and Swinfen) 126; bibliog; index. Regards most previous biographies (apart from Huxley 1921) as "incredibly dull"; does not claim erudition or accuracy but "to present the man as he really was and to do so without being boring".

1974   Gavin de Beer, ed., *Charles Darwin Thomas Henry Huxley Autobiographies* (London: Oxford University Press [Oxford English memoirs and travels]; paperback edition 1983 [Oxford paperbacks]) 123; illus; index; bibliog.

1980   Arnold C. Brackman, *A delicate arrangement the strange case of Charles Darwin and Alfred Russel Wallace* (NY: Times Books) 370; illus; bibliog. Popular style. Focus is on "the conspiracy against Wallace and its cover-up".

1981   Peter Brent, *Charles Darwin a man of enlarged curiosity* (London: Heinemann) reprinted 1983 (Feltham: Hamlyn) 536; illus; bibliog; index. Claims to be the first biography to use unpublished material; occasion is centenary of subject's death. 1983 reprint has title *Charles Darwin*.

1982   Wilma George, *Darwin* (Glasgow: William Collins Sons & Co. Ltd.) [Fontana Modern Masters] 160. Author a zoologist; occasion is centenary.

1984   Ronald Clark, *The survival of Charles Darwin a biography of a man and an idea* (London: Weidenfeld and Nicolson) 449; illus; index; bibliog. Author a biographer of scientists. Uses MS sources.

1989   L.R. Croft, *The life and death of Charles Darwin* (Chorley, Lancs.: Elmwood Books) 138; bibliog; index. Presents subject as "a man obsessed with himself to a pathological degree", whose confusion over religion made him "the archetypal Jekyll and Hyde character".

1990   John Bowlby, *Charles Darwin a biography* (London: Hutchinson; NY; under title *Charles Darwin a new life* (W.W. Norton, 1991) 511; index; illus; bibliog. Focus is on psychological, medical and psychiatric aspects.

1990   Peter J. Bowler, *Charles Darwin the man and his influence* (Oxford: Basil Blackwell) [Blackwell science biographies] 250; illus; bibliog; index. Not the really detailed biography now possible, but written "for ordinary readers and students".

1991   Adrian Desmond and James Moore, *Darwin* (London: Michael Joseph; NY: Warner Books Inc.) 808; illus; index; bibliog. Aims "to pose the awkward questions", unasked by previous "curiously bloodless" biographies. Uses MS material produced by the Darwin project at Cambridge University Library.

Darwin, Erasmus (1731–1802), English physician, scientist and poet.

1804   Anna Seward, *Memoirs of the life of Dr Darwin chiefly during his residence at Lichfield with anecdotes of his friends and criticisms on his writings* (London: J. Johnson) 430. Preface admits these memoirs "do not form a regular detail of biographical circumstances". Author was friend of subject.

1879   Charles Darwin, "preliminary notice" in Ernest Krause, *The Scientific Works of Erasmus Darwin* (London: John Murray) reprinted 1971 (Farnborough, Hants.: Gregg International Publishers) 127 (of 216-page Krause volume) illus; bibliog. Also included as volume 29 in 1989 edition of *The works of Charles Darwin* (London: Pickering & Chatto) [The Pickering masters].

1930   Hesketh Pearson, *Doctor Darwin* (London: J.M. Dent & Sons) illus; bibliog; index. Author "attempts to combine authority with interest", and claims this is the first full-length biography. King-Hele calls this "an entertaining picture of Darwin and his friends".

1977   Desmond King-Hele, *Doctor of revolution the life and genius of Erasmus Darwin* (London: Faber & Faber) 361; illus; bibliog; index. Relies heavily on Charles Darwin's 1879 life; McNeil says it is too anecdotal and marred by Whiggish interpretations.

1987   Maureen McNeil, *Under the banner of science Erasmus Darwin and his age* (Manchester: Manchester University Press) 307; index; bibliog. Revision of Cambridge University PhD thesis; not a conventional biography, it situates the subject "in his full historical context", as part of a project to identify the social and political aspects of scientific knowledge.

David, Tannat William Edgeworth (1858–1934), Welsh polar explorer and geologist.

1937   M.E. David, *Professor David the life of Sir Edgeworth David KBE DSO FRS MA DSc LLD* (London: Edward Arnold & Co.) 320; illus; index. Author is daughter of subject: "tells of the man rather than the scientist".

Davy, Humphry (1778–1829), English chemist.

1831   John Ayrton Paris, *The Life of Sir Humphry Davy* (London: Henry Colburn and Richard Bentley) I:416 II:456; bibliog. A "contemporaneous biography", solicited from the author (who had published an obituary sketch) by "the leading publishers of the day" and by the subject's widow. Thorpe calls this inaccurate, disingenuous, extravagant and insincere.

1836   John Davy, *Memoirs of the Life of Sir Humphry Davy* (London: Longman) 2 vols. Abridged edition published 1839, forming first volume of subject's collected works (London: Smith, Elder and Co.). Author is subject's brother. Thorpe calls this partial, albeit candid, sober and direct, and says it frequently contradicts Paris.

1858   John Davy, ed., *Fragementary remains literary and scientific of Sir Humphry Davy bart late president of the Royal Society etc with a sketch of his life and selections from his correspondence* (London: John Churchill) 330; index. "The title of this work sufficiently indicates its character."

1896   T.E. Thorpe, *Humphry Davy poet and philosopher* (London: Cassell and Company

Limited) [The Century science series] 240; index. Uses memoirs and biographies of subject's contemporaries as well as printed and MS sources.

1954   James Kendall, *Humphry Davy "pilot" of Penzance* (London: Faber and Faber) 165; index. Object is "a character study of Davy as boy and man". "Intended primarily – on the instructions of my publishers – for the younger generation", but addressed also to adults.

1963   Anne Treneer, *The mercurial chemist a life of Sir Humphry Davy* (London: Methuen & Co. Ltd.) 264; illus; bibliog; index. Based on printed sources and some MS material.

1966   Harold Hartley, *Humphry Davy* (London: Nelson) [British Men of Science] 160; illus; bibliog; index. Contains "more chemistry than anecdotes", and attempts "to give a rather more intimate picture [than earlier lives] of the run of Davy's mind with its cross-currents of the artist and the scientist".

1967   Elba O. Carrier, *Humphrey Davy and Chemical Discovery* (London: Chatto & Windus) [Immortals of science] 161; index.

1992   David Knight, *Humphry Davy science & power* (Oxford: Blackwell) [Blackwell science biographies] 218; illus; bibliog; index. Places life and science in context of contemporary society.

Dawson, George Mercer (1849–1901), Canadian geologist.

1962   Lois Winslow-Spragge, *The life of George Mercer Dawson Dsc LLD ARSM FGS FRSC FRS CMG etc* (place unknown: Privately published) 199. Author is niece of subject. Compiled from MS and printed sources. Not primarily scientific, but rather "with the idea of preserving the nature of this early Canadian".

Dawson, John William (1820–1899), Canadian geologist.

1971   Charles F. O'Brien, *Sir William Dawson a life in science and religion* (Philadelphia: American Philosophical Society) [Memoirs of the American Philosophical Society, 84] 207; bibliog; index. Uses MS sources.

Deam, Charles Clemon (1865–1953), American botanist.

1987   Robert C. Kriebel, *Plain Ol' Charlie Deam pioneer hoosier botanist* (West Lafayette, IN: Purdue University Press) 183; index. Based on MS and printed sources.

De Forest, Lee (1873–1961), American electronic engineer.

1930   Georgette Carneal, *A conqueror of space an authorized biography of the life and work of Lee de Forest* (NY: Horace Liveright) 296; illus. Based on subject's diaries and notebooks and on W. Arvin's article published 1924 in *Radio News*; a narrative style, lacking notes or index.

1950   autobiography, *Father of radio the autobiography of Lee de Forest* (Chicago:

Wilcox & Follett Co.) 502; illus; index. A record of radio and television history combined with personal details; hopes frank revelation of experience will encourage others.

1964   I.E. Levine, *Electronics pioneer Lee de Forest* (NY: Julian Messner, Inc.) 191. Author a journalist and biographer, well known for biographies for young people.

1992   James A. Hijiya, *Lee de Forest and the fatherhood of radio* (Bethlehem, PA: Lehigh University Press; London: Associated University Presses) 182; illus; bibliog; index.

De Havilland, Geoffrey (1882–1965), English aeronautical engineer.

1979   autobiography, *Sky Fever* (Shrewsbury: Airlife) 240; illus; index.

Delbrück, Max (1906–1981), American molecular biologist (born Germany).

1988   Ernst Peter Fischer and Carol Lipson, *Thinking about science Max Delbrück and the origins of molecular biology* (NY: W.W. Norton & Company) 334; illus; bibliog; index. Preface describes the development of the text, from a dissertation in the history of science (abandoned), through an autobiography planned as a record of information (cut short by subject's death), to a biography by one of his students and a collaborator.

De Morgan, Augustus (1806–1871), English mathematician (born India).

1882   Sophia Elizabeth De Morgan, *Memoir of Augustus De Morgan* (London: Longmans, Green, and Co.) 422, index. Author is subject's widow: "I have not attempted a scientific memoir. My object has been to supply that part of my husband's life the material for which would not be within the reach of another biographer." Uses MS sources.

Dewar, Michael James Steuart, (1918 – –) English chemist (born India).

1992   autobiography, *A semiempirical life* (Washington: American Chemical Society) [Profiles, pathways, and dreams: autobiographies of eminent chemists] 215; illus; index.

Dick, Robert (1811–1866), Scottish naturalist.

1878   Samuel Smiles, *Robert Dick baker of Thurso geologist and botanist* (London: John Murray) 436; illus; index. Subject is presented as an exemplar of self-help. Based on MS sources.

Diderot, Denis (1713–1784), French encyclopaedist.

1878   John Morley, *Diderot and the Encyclopaedists* (London: Chapman and Hall) I:338 II:358. Second edition 1886 (London: Macmillan and Co.) I:365 II:351. The last of author's series of studies on the literary preparation for the French revolution.

1955   Lester G. Crocker, *The embattled philosopher a biography of Denis Diderot* (London: Neville Spearman) 442; index. 1966 edition under title *Diderot the embattled philosopher* (NY: The Free Press; London: Collier-Macmillan Limited) 420. Popular style; includes invented dialogue.

1957   Arthur M. Wilson, *Diderot the testing years* (NY: Oxford University Press) 417; bibliog; index. New edition 1972 see below. Written for the general reader and the specialist; emphasis on the contents of the *Encyclopédie*. Author an academic.

1972   Arthur M. Wilson, *Diderot* (NY: Oxford University Press) 917; bibliog; index. Reprint of 1957 Wilson as Part I followed by Part II, "The appeal to posterity", which stresses the subject's "concern for the good opinion of posterity".

1974   Carol Blum, *Diderot the virtue of a philosopher* (NY: The Viking Press) 182; bibliog; index. Follows "the meanings which the concept of virtue held for Diderot as they were expressed in his personal letters and works". Organization is biographical.

1992   P.N. Furbank, *Diderot a critical biography* (London: Secker & Warburg; London: Minerva [paperback], 1993) 524; illus; bibliog; index. Purpose is to "help a little towards connecting up the different ideas suggested by Diderot's name". Acknowledges Wilson, but indicates this is a critical biography interspersing narrative with criticism.

Diesel, Rudolf (1858–1913), German engineer (born France).

1965   W. Robert Nitske and Charles Morrow Wilson, *Rudolf Diesel pioneer of the age of power* (Norman: University of Oklahoma Press) 318; illus; bibliog; index. Thomas says this and Grossen are "in part paraphrase of [subject's son] Eugene Diesel's biography and not based on original research in German archives".

1978   Morton Grosser, *Diesel the man and the engine* (NY: Atheneum) 166; illus; index; bibliog. XX

1987   Donald E. Thomas Jr, *Diesel technology and society in industrial Germany* (Tuscaloosa: University of Alabama Press) 279; illus; bibliog; index. Examines life and work "as a case study in the interrelationship of scientific, technological, social, and economic trends in . . . Germany". Author an historian.

Dirac, Paul Adrian Maurice (1902–1984), English physicist.

1990   Helge Kragh, *Dirac a scientific biography* (Cambridge: Cambridge University Press) 389; illus; bibliog; index. Aims to provide "a more comprehensive and coherent account" than earlier memoirs. Emphasis is on scientific work. Based on MS sources.

Djerassi, Carl (1920 – –), American chemist.

1990   autobiography, *Steroids made it possible* (Washington: American Chemical Society) [Profiles, pathways, and dreams: autobiographies of eminent chemists] 205; illus; index. Includes a personal "coda", written at the request of series editor Jeffrey I. Seeman, which alludes to the author's "long infatuation with art", his daughter's suicide, his divorces and remarriages.

1992   autobiography, *The Pill Pygmy chimps and Degas' horse* (NY: Basic Books) 319; illus; index. "This volume is not a conventional scientific autobiography." It stresses the social context of the author's participation in producing a steroid oral contraceptive and expands upon the personal themes first explored in the 1990 "coda".

Dodgson, Charles Lutwidge [Lewis Carroll] (1832–1898), English mathematician.

1898   Stuart Dodgson Collingwood, *The life and letters of Lewis Carroll Rev C.L. Dodgson* (London: T. Fisher Unwin; Toronto: George N. Morang, [1899?]) 448; illus; bibliog; index. Author is nephew of subject; includes excerpts from journal and letters, but later biographers indicate he suppressed controversial material.

1910   Belle Moses, *Lewis Carroll in wonderland and at home the story of his life* (NY: D. Appleton and Company) 296. Popular style

1932   Langford Reed, *The life of Lewis Carroll* (London: W. & G. Foyle, Ltd.) 142; illus. Occasion is centenary. Reference to Life and Letters about 1902 by relative of the family [i.e. Collingwood]; little attention to Dodgson and mathematics. Green calls it inaccurate and inclined to develop "theories", i.e. of the dual personality of Dodgson and Carroll.

1945   Florence Becker Lennon, *Victoria through the looking glass the life of Lewis Carroll* (NY: Simon & Schuster; London: Cassell & Co. Ltd., 1947 under title *Lewis Carroll*) 358; bibliog; index. Substantially revised edition 1962 under title *The life of Lewis Carroll* (NY: Collier Books) 448; index. Third revised edition 1972 (NY: Dover Publications, under title *The life of Lewis Carroll Victoria through the looking glass*) 448. Uses psychoanalytic theory; comments on the *Times Literary Supplement* debate about Freudian aspects, "The sword of Sigmund sits uneasily in the hand of St. George". British Library copy is inscribed by the author to the British Museum with love. Green 1949 says this book's "industrious author has collected an amazing amount of material – rather as a vacuum cleaner collects dust – without any very clear idea of how to sift or arrange it. Some of her conclusions are startling, and she scarcely begins to understand Dodgson's character, being quite unable to look at the Victorian period from within."

1949   Roger Lancelyn Green, *The story of Lewis Carroll* (London: Methuen & Co. Ltd.) [Story biographies] 179; bibliog; illus. Claims to accept Dodgson as he was and tell a plain story; comments on earlier biographies.

1952   Alexander L. Taylor, *The white knight a study of C.L. Dodgson Lewis Carroll* (Edinburgh: Oliver & Boyd) reprinted 1963 (Philadelphia: Dufour Editions) 209; bibliog; index. Stresses "the man" and "the truth" over "the myth" and "the fairy tale". Uses unpublished diaries.

1954   Derek Hudson, *Lewis Carroll* (London: Constable) 354; index. Second edition 1976 under title *Lewis Carroll an illustrated biography* 272; illus; bibliog; index. First biography to appear after 1954 publication of the *Diaries*; also uses unpublished letters. Preface to second edition stresses author's wish to avoid as much as possible the psychoanalytic interpretation. Text corrects errors and introduces additional material.

1966   James Playsted Wood, *The Snark was a Boojum a life of Lewis Carroll* (NY: Pantheon Books) 184; illus; bibliog. Illustrations by David Levine. Popular style.

1976   John Pudney, *Lewis Carroll and his world* (London: Thames & Hudson) 127; illus; bibliog; index. Popular style; heavily illustrated.

1979   Anne Clark, *Lewis Carroll a biography* (London: Dent & Sons Ltd.) 284; illus; bibliog; index. No preface or introduction; popular style.

1990   Richard Wallace, *The agony of Lewis Carroll* (Melrose, MA: Gemini Press) 298; bibliog; index. A psychoanalytic interpretation of subject's rage and pain.

Doran, Paul H. (1907 – –), Israeli engineer (born Rumania).

1993   autobiography, *Development the eventful life and travels of an engineer* (Jerusalem: Gefen Publishing House) 372. Originally published as a limited edition for a birthday celebration.

Doubleday, Henry (1808–1875), English naturalist.

1978   Robert Mays, *Henry Doubleday the Epping naturalist* (Marlow, Bucks.: Precision Press) 118; illus. Foreword by William Addison.

Douglas, David (1799–1834), Scottish naturalist.

1973   William Morwood, *Traveller in a vanished landscape* (London: Gentry Books) 244; illus; bibliog; index.

Draper, John William (1811–1882), English chemist.

1950   Donald Fleming, *John William Draper and the religion of science* (Philadelphia: University of Pennsylvania Press; London: Oxford University Press) reprinted 1972 (NY: Octagon Books) 205; bibliog; index. Published for the American Historical Association. Originated as a dissertation. Uses MS sources.

Duhem, Pierre Maurice Marie (1861–1916), French physicist and philosopher of science.

1984   Stanley L. Jaki, *Uneasy genius the life and work of Pierre Duhem* (The Hague: Martinus Nijhoff Publishers) [International archives of the history of ideas, 100] 472; illus; index. Includes material from Helen Duhem. Argues for greater recognition of subject and his contributions and influence on later physicists.

1991   R.N.D. Martin, *Pierre Duhem philosophy and history in the work of a believing physicist* (La Salle, IL: Open Court) 274; bibliog; index. Attempt to "understand the implications of Duhem's Catholicism in its historical context".

Du Toit, Alexander Logie (1878–1948), South African geologist.

[1950]   Wilhelm Traugott Gevers, *The life and work of Dr Alex L. du Toit* (Johannesburg: Geological Society of South Africa, The South African Association for the Advancement of Science and The South African Geographical Society) 109; illus. Published simultaneously with memorial lectures on subject.

Dyson, Frank Watson (1868–1939), English astronomer.

1951   Margaret Dyson, *Ninth astronomer royal the life of Frank Watson Dyson* (Cambridge: Published for the Dyson family by W. Heffer & Sons Ltd.) 294; illus. Author is daughter of subject: "does not set out to give a detailed account of his astronomical work" but "to explain why his influence in scientific circles went far beyond his published work".

Eads, James Buchanan (1820–1887), American hydraulic engineer.

1900   Louis How, *James B. Eads* (Boston: Houghton, Mifflin and Company) [The Riverside Biographical Series] reprinted 1970 (Freeport, NY: Books for Libraries Press) 120. XX

1970   Arthur Orrmont, *James Buchanan Eads the man who mastered the Mississippi* (Englewood Cliffs, NJ: Prentice-Hall) [Hall of Fame Books] 143; illus; bibliog. XX

Eaton, Amos (1776–1842), American geologist and educator.

1941   Ethel M. McAllister, *Amos Eaton scientist and educator 1776–1842* (Philadelphia: University of Pennsylvania Press; London: Humphrey Milford, Oxford University Press) 587; illus; bibliog; index. Based on a PhD dissertation; first writing on Eaton's life to deal with his imprisonment for forgery, an event suppressed by his immediate descendents; includes numerous documents.

Eddington, Arthur Stanley (1882–1944), English astronomer and theorist of relativity.

1956   A. Vibert Douglas, *The life of Arthur Stanley Eddington* (London: Thomas Nelson and Sons Ltd.) 207; illus; bibliog; index. Endeavours "to provide both [personal and professional] portraits and the stereoscopic merging of the two into one faithful likeness of the great man". Uses MS sources.

Edgeworth, Richard Lovell (1744–1817), Irish inventor and educationist.

1820   Maria Edgeworth, *Memoirs of Richard Lovell Edgeworth Esq.* (London: R. Hunter and Baldwin, Cradock, and Joy) reprinted 1969 (Shannon: Irish University Press) I:392 II:498; bibliog. Text is begun by subject and "concluded" by author, his daughter. 1969 reprint has introduction by Desmond Clarke.

1896   Beatrix L. Tollemache, *Richard Lovell Edgeworth a selection from his 1820 memoirs* (London: Rivington, Percival & Co.) 163, Extracted from 1820

1965   Desmond Clarke, *The ingenious Mr Edgeworth* (London: Oldbourne) 256; illus; bibliog; index.

Edison, Thomas Alva (1847–1931), American technologist.

1894   W.K.L. Dickson and Antonia Dickson, *The life & inventions of Thomas Alva*

Edison (London: Chatto & Windus) 362; illus. Claims to be written in response to public demand; authors are friends and business associates of subject.

1907   Francis Arthur Jones, *Thomas Alva Edison sixty years of an inventor's life* (London: Hodder & Stoughton) 375; illus. Revised edition [1924] published as *Thomas Alva Edison an intimate record* 399; illus; index. Written with input from subject, friends and family. Author a journalist with a strong personal admiration who calls this "a tribute of admiration and friendship". The 1924 edition is entirely reset with revisions and additional chapters.

1910   Frank Lewis Dyer and Thomas Commerford Martin, *Edison his life and inventions* (NY: Harper & Brothers Publishers) 2 vols, 989; illus; index. "Prior to this, no complete, authentic, and authorized record of the work of Mr. Edison . . . has been given to the world." Written with co-operation of subject.

1915   Francis Rolt-Wheeler, *Thomas Alva Edison* (NY: The Macmillan Company) [True stories of great Americans] 201.

1926   George S. Bryan, *Edison the man and his work* (London and NY: Alfred A. Knopf) 350; illus; bibliog; index. Another edition published 1926 as *Edison the man and his works* (Garden City, NY: Garden City Publishing Company, Inc.) [Star series] 350; bibliog; index. Claims to correct the superficial, inaccurate and misleading material available and to make the subject accessible. Uses material from 1910.

1931   Francis Trevelyan Miller, *Thomas A. Edison benefactor of mankind the romantic life story of the world's greatest inventor* ([NY]: John C. Winston Co.) 320; index; illus. Published 1932 as *Thomas A. Edison the authentic life story of the world's greatest inventor* (London: Stanley Paul & Co. Ltd.) 287; index; illus. Abridged and simplified edition 1952 by M.E. Carter for a series of supplementary reading books for students of English overseas (London: Longmans, Green and Co.) [Lives of achievement] 132. "The first standard life . . . with an historian's estimate of [Edison's] *completed* labours. . . ." Author is related to subject's second wife Mina Miller.

1934   Mary Childs Nerney, *Thomas A. Edison a modern olympian* (NY: Harrison Smith and Robert Haas) 334; index; illus. Author worked as archivist and librarian to organize subject's papers for the firm of Edison industries. She was hired for research on a book which was published shortly after Edison's death [Miller's?]. This work is meant to supply human interest.

1934   William Adams Simonds, *Edison his life his work his genius* (Indianapolis and NY: The Bobbs-Merrill Company) 364; index; bibliog. Much attention to subject's forebears.

1958   Henry Thomas, *Thomas Alva Edison* (NY: G.P. Putnam's Sons; Toronto: Longmans, Green and Company) [Lives to Remember] 128.

1959   Matthew Josephson, *Edison* (NY: McGraw-Hill Book Company, Inc.) reprinted [1986?] (Norwalk, CT: Easton Press) reprinted 1992 (NY: J. Wiley) 511; illus; index. Attempts to remove "veils of myth" and "false legends". Uses MS sources. 1992 reprint has new preface. Describes 1910 as the "most useful" of early biographies.

1969   Lawrence A. Frost, *The Edison album a pictorial biography of Thomas Alva Edison* (Seattle: Superior Publishing Co.) 175; illus; bibliog. XX

1971   Byron M. Vanderbilt, *Thomas Edison chemist* (Washington: American Chemical Society) 373; illus; index. Main sources are subject's journal articles and patents. Focus on his "major contributions in the field of applied chemistry and chemical engineering . . . directed towards the general reader".

1977   Ronald W. Clark, *Edison the man who made the future* (London: Macdonald and Jane's; NY: Putnam) 256; illus; bibliog; index.

1979   Robert Conot, *A streak of luck* (NY: Seaview Books) reprinted 1979 (NY: Da Capo Press) [Da Capo Series in Science] 565; illus; index. A "search for the missing scenes and hidden personality" of the subject and his life. Uses MS sources and new material.

1981   Wyn Wachhorst, *Thomas Alva Edison an American myth* (Cambridge: The MIT Press) 328; illus; bibliog; index. "This book is not a biography. It chronicles the stages in the evolution of a cultural hero . . . its final concern is with the myth rather than the man, the image rather than the reality."

1990   André Millard, *Edison and the business of innovation* (Baltimore: The Johns Hopkins University Press) [Johns Hopkins studies in the history of technology] 387; illus; index. "[N]ot . . . the definitive history of Edison" but "an interpretation of Edison's work that covers the entirety of his business career". Uses MS sources.

Edward, Thomas (1814–1886), Scottish naturalist.

1876   Samuel Smiles, *Life of a Scotch Naturalist Thomas Edward Associate of the Linnean Society* (London: John Murray) 446; illus. New edition 1882: 392; illus; index. Subject is presented as an exemplar of self-help, a shoemaker who "lived *for* science, not *by* science". 1882 reports on transformation of subject's life since initial publication.

Ehrenfest, Paul (1880–1933), Austrian physicist.

1970   Martin J. Klein, *Paul Ehrenfest* (Amsterdam: North-Holland Publishing Company) 330; illus; index. Written with co-operation of subject's widow. Uses all MS sources available.

Ehret, Georg Dionysius (1708–1770), German botanist.

1977   Gerta Calmann, *Ehret flower painter extraordinary an illustrated biography* (Oxford: Phaidon) 160; illus; bibliog; index. Contains reproductions of some of subject's drawings. Uses MS sources.

Einstein, Albert (1879–1955), German physicist.

1931   Anton Reiser [Rudolf Kayser], *Albert Einstein a biographical portrait* (London: Thornton Butterworth Limited) 223; index. Author is son-in-law of subject; Foreword by Einstein, saying Reiser knows him intimately ("in bedroom slippers") but not stating relationship.

1944   Dimitri Marianoff and Palma Wayne, *Einstein an intimate study of a great man* (Garden City NY: Doubleday, Doran and Co.) 211. XX

1947   Philipp Frank, *Einstein his life and times* (NY: Alfred A. Knopf; London: Jonathan Cape, 1948) 367; index. New edition 1965 [A Borzoi book] 298; illus; index. Reprinted 1988 (Norwalk, CT: Easton Press) and 1989 (NY: Da Capo Press) [Da Capo Series in Science]. Translated from German MS by George Rosen. Edited and revised by Shuichi

Kusaka. Makes partial use of earlier biographies; aims to "bridge the gap" between books written for specialists and for the public. Author was acquainted with subject.

1954   Antonia Vallentin, *Einstein a biography* (London: Weidenfeld and Nicolson) 219. Translated from French by Moura Budberg.

1956   Carl Seelig, *Albert Einstein a documentary biography*. (London: Staples Press, Limited) 240; index. Translated by Mervyn Savill. First published in Switzerland; written from personal experience, in the first person.

1959   Arthur Beckhard, *Albert Einstein* (NY: G.P. Putnam's Sons) 126; illus.

1962   Peter Michelmore, *Einstein profile of the man* (NY: Dodd, Mead) 269. Also published 1963 (London: Frederick Muller Limited) 241; index.

1965   Hilaire Cuny, *Albert Einstein the man and his theories* (NY: P.S. Eriksson) [A Profile in science] 175; illus; bibliog; index. Translated by Mervyn Savyll. Contains excerpts from subject's MS; written as a tribute rather than an objective biography.

1965   Boris Kuznetsov, *Einstein* (Moscow: Progress Publishers) reprinted 1970 (NY: Phaedra) 377; illus. XX.

1971   Ronald W. Clark, *Einstein the life and times* (NY: The World Publishing Company) 718; illus; bibliog; index. Paperback edition 1971 (NY: Avon Books). Published 1973 (London: Hodder and Stoughton) 670; illus; bibliog; index. Abridged edition published 1984 (NY: H.N. Abrams) 368; illus; bibliog; index. London edition 1973 "contains material not available when the American edition was published"; also slightly different because of copyright restrictions. Abridgement 1984 has title *Einstein the life and times an illustrated biography*. Uses MS sources.

1973   Jeremy Bernstein, *Einstein* (London: Fontana/Collins) [Fontana modern masters] 202; bibliog. Also published (NY: The Viking Press) [Modern Masters] reprinted 1976 (NY: Penguin Books) [Penguin Modern Masters] 242; bibliog; index. Material appeared originally in the *New Yorker*. Author was acquainted with subject. Book not organized chronologically but rather around subject's three central theories; discusses both life and work; includes anecdotal material.

1974   Lewis S. Feuer, *Einstein and the generations of science* (NY: Basic Books, Inc.) 1982 edition (New Brunswick, NJ: Transaction Books) 374; illus; index. Second edition includes new material in prologue. Concerned "with the conflict of generations as a universal historical theme, with the character of intellectuals, and with the psychological sources of the scientific temperament".

1982   Abraham Pais, *"Subtle is the lord ..." the science and life of Albert Einstein* (Oxford: Clarendon Press) 552; index. Aims "to present a scientific biography" of subject, "an essay in open history". Based on MS sources in Einstein archives at Princeton.

1985   Lewis Pyenson, *The young Einstein the advent of relativity* (Bristol: Adam Hilger Ltd.) 255; illus; bibliog; index. Focuses "on the social circumstances of Einstein's formative years, as well as on the intellectual climate in Germany".

1993   Michael White and John Gribbin, *Einstein a life in science* (London: Simon & Schuster) 279; bibliog; index. XX

Eliel, Ernest Ludwig (1921 – –), German chemist.

1990   autobiography, *From Cologne to Chapel Hill* (Washington: American Chemical Society) [Profiles, pathways, and dreams] 138; illus; bibliog; index. XX.

Ellis, William (1828–1916), English meteorologist and astronomer.

1889   Edmund Kell Blyth, *Life of William Ellis founder of the Birkbeck Schools with some account of his labours for the improvement and extension of education* (London: Kegan Paul, Trench, Trubner & Co.) 365. XX

Ericsson, John (1803–1899), American engineer (born Sweden).

1906   William Conant Church, *The life of John Ericsson* (NY: Charles Scribner's Sons) I:303 II:357; illus; index. Reissued two volumes in one, 1911.

Evans, Lewis (1700–1756), Welsh geographer and geologist.

1939   Lawrence Henry Gipson, *Lewis Evans* (Philadelphia: The Historical Society of Pennsylvania) 246; index. First 83 pages is biography; remainder is documents and maps.

Evans, Oliver (1755–1819), American engineer.

1935   Greville Bathe and Dorothy Bathe, *Oliver Evans a chronicle of early American engineering* (Philadelphia: The Historical Society of Pennsylvania) 362; illus; bibliog; index. Greville Bathe is an engineer. Seeks to correct past misconceptions and record facts. Based on MS sources.

Evelyn, John (1620–1706), English horticulturist.

1968   Florence Higham, *John Evelyn esquire an Anglican layman of the seventeenth century* (London: SCM Press Ltd.) 128; bibliog.

1970   Beatrice Saunders, *John Evelyn and his times* (Oxford: Pergamon Press) 203; index; bibliog; illus. Written to give the subject "his due" as more than just a diarist.

1981   John Bowle, *John Evelyn and his world a biography* (London: Routledge & Kegan Paul) 277; index. Depends on De Beer's 1956 definitive edition of the *Diary*; not new research or interpretation, but to "recreate the personality . . . in the context of his times".

Ewing, William Maurice (1906–1974), American geologist.

1974   William Wertenbaker, *The floor of the sea Maurice Ewing and the search to understand the earth* (Boston: Little, Brown and Company) 275; illus; bibliog; index. Based on interviews with associates of subject.

Fabre, Jean Henri (1823–1915), French entomologist.

1913   C. [*sic*] V. Legros, *Fabre poet of science* (London: T. Fisher Unwin) 352; index. French-language edition (by G.V. Legros) published 1910; new edition 1913; described as "an act of pious homage". Preface by J.H. Fabre. Translated by Bernard Miall.

[1921]   Augustin Fabre, *The life of Jean Henri Fabre the entomologist* (London: Hodder and Stoughton Limited) 299. Translated by Bernard Miall. Author's preface dated 1910; a relative of subject; translator's preface refers to abridgement due to post-war conditions.

Fairbairn, William (1789–1874), English engineer.

1877   William Pole, ed., *The life of Sir William Fairbairn Bart* (London: Longmans Green and Company) reprinted 1970 (Newton Abbot: David & Charles Reprints) 507; bibliog; index. Abridged edition 1878 (London: Longmans, Green, and Co.) 170. Started as an autobiography; edited and completed by Pole. 1878 abridgement issued at a low price to suit working men; personal narrative is retained and scientific and technical portions reduced. 1970 reprint has introduction by A.E. Musson.

Faraday, Michael (1791–1867), English chemist and physicist.

1870   Bence Jones, *The life and letters of Faraday* (London: Longmans, Green, and Co.) I:427 II:499; index. Second edition, revised 1870 withdraws some letters, abbreviates others and corrects errors. Author was Secretary of the Royal Institution and student and colleague of subject. Arranges materials "in the simplest order, with the least connecting matter".

1872   J.H. Gladstone, *Michael Faraday* (London: Macmillan and Co.; NY: Harper & Bros.) 176; index. Second edition 1873. Author is PhD and FRS; calls this personal reminiscences for those "who venerate his noble character without being able to follow his scientific researches". 1873 edition is reset, with a portrait and "further particulars".

[1893]   Walter Jerrold, *Michael Faraday man of science* (London: S.W. Partridge & Co.) [Popular Biographies] 160.

1898   Silvanus P. Thompson, *Michael Faraday his life and work* (London: Cassell and Company, Limited [The Century Science Series]; NY: Macmillan) 308; index. Preface notes that earlier accounts are out of print.

1924   Wilfrid L. Randell, *Michael Faradey (1791–1867)* (London: Leonard Parsons; Boston: Small, Maynard and Company) [The Roadmaker Series] 192; bibliog; index. For non-scientists, using freshly available records.

1931   [E.W. Ashcroft], *Faraday* (London: The British Electrical and Allied Manufacturers Association) 133. Occasion is centenary of the publisher.

1955   James Kendall, *Michael Faraday man of simplicity* (London: Faber and Faber; NY: Roy Publishers) 196; illus; index. Author is professor of chemistry at Edinburgh.

1962   David Gunston, *Michael Faraday father of electricity* (London: Weidenfeld & Nicholson (Educational) Ltd.) [Pathfinder Biographies] 128; illus; index.

1965   L. Pearce Williams, *Michael Faraday a biography* (London: Chapman and Hall; NY: Basic Books) 531; illus; index. Author an historian of science. Attempts first full exploitation of MS and printed sources, "to place him more accurately in the mainstream of the history of science".

1991   Geoffrey Cantor, *Michael Faraday Sandemanian and scientist a study of science and religion in the nineteenth century* (London: Macmillan; NY: St Martin's Press) 359; illus; bibliog; index. Seeks to dispel mythology of scientist as hero, villain or alienated intellectual by analysing "the complex components which link the personality and career of the individual scientist".

Featherstonhaugh, George William (1780–1866), American geologist.

1988   Edmund Berkeley and Dorothy Smith Berkeley, *George William Featherstonhaugh the first US government geologist* (Tuscaloosa: The University of Alabama Press) [History of American science and technology series] 357; illus; bibliog; index. First book-length biography. Uses MSS.

Ferguson, James (1710–1776), Scottish astronomer and instrument-maker

1867   E. Henderson, *Life of James Ferguson FRS in a brief autobiographical account and further extended memoir* (Edinburgh: A. Fullarton & Co.) 503; illus; index. Second edition 1870 "with additions", i.e. 22 additional pages inserted before the main text; includes corrections. Author discovered the subject's autobiographical memoir and then devoted 40 years to research.

1988   John R. Millburn and Henry C. King, *Wheelwright of the heavens the life and work of James Ferguson FRS* (London: The Vade-Medcum Press) 328; illus; bibliog; index. Corrects errors and omissions in Henderson's account.

Fermi, Enrico (1901–1954), Italian physicist.

1954   Laura Fermi, *Atoms in the family my life with Enrico Fermi designer of the first atomic pile* (Chicago: University of Chicago Press; London: George Allen & Unwin Ltd., 1955) reprinted 1982 (Albuquerque: University of New Mexico Press); reprinted 1987 (Los Angeles: Tomash Publishers) [History of Modern Physics] 284. First published in Italian. Author is subject's wife. 1987 reprint has new introduction by Emilio Segre.

1964   Pierre de Latil, *Enrico Fermi the man and his theories* (London: Souvenir Press; NY: P.S. Eriksson, 1966) [Profiles in Science] 178; index; bibliog; illus. Translated from 1963 Paris edition by Len Ortzen.

1970   Emilio Segre, *Enrico Fermi physicist* (Chicago: University of Chicago Press) 276; illus; bibliog. XX

Ferranti, Sebastian Ziani De (1864–1930), English electrical engineer.

1934   Gertrude Ziani de Ferranti and Richard Ince, *The life and letters of Sebastian Ziani de Ferranti* (London: Williams & Norgate Ltd.) 240; illus; index. Foreword by Caroline Haslett. Author is wife of subject. Personal memoir.

1970   Noel Currer-Briggs, *Doctor Ferranti the life and work of Sebastian Ziani de*

Ferranti FRS 1864–1930 (London: published privately) 324; illus; bibliog; index. Attempts to bridge the "gap between biography and autobiography" by using graphology. Copyright is Ferranti Limited.

1988   J.F. Wilson, *Ferranti and the British electrical industry 1864–1930* (Manchester: Manchester University Press) [Business and Society] 165; bibliog; index. XX

Fessenden, Reginald Aubrey (1866–1932), Canadian radio engineer.

1940   Helen M. Fessenden, *Fessenden builder of tomorrows* (NY: Coward-McCann, Inc.) reprinted 1974 (NY: Arno Press) 362; bibliog. Author is wife of subject; stress on his legal difficulties. 1974 reprint has index by Ormond Raby and illustrations.

1970   Ormond Raby, *Radio's first voice the story of Reginald Fessenden* (Toronto: Macmillan of Canada) 161; bibliog. XX

Feynman, Richard Phillips (1918–1988), American theoretical physicist.

1992   James Gleick, *Genius the life and science of Richard Feynman* (NY: Pantheon Books) 632; illus; bibliog; index. Author a science writer. Based on MS and published sources.

Fisher, Ronald Aylmer (1890–1962), English statistician and geneticist.

1978   Joan Fisher Box, *R.A. Fisher the life of a scientist* (NY: John Wiley & Sons) [Wiley series in probability and mathematical statistics] 512; illus; index. Written by subject's daughter.

Fitzroy, Robert (1805–1865), English hydrographer and meteorologist.

1968   H.E.L. Mellersh, *Fitzroy of the Beatle* (London: Rupert Hart-Davis) 307; illus; bibliog; index. Foreword by Nora Barlow. Stresses subject's career apart from his association with Darwin.

Flamsteed, John (1646–1719), English astronomer.

1835–37   Francis Baily, *An account of the Revd John Flamsteed the first Astronomer-Royal* (London: The Lords Commissioners of the Admiralty) reprinted 1966 (London: Dawsons of Pall Mall) 759; bibliog; index.

Fleming, John Ambrose (1849–1945), English electrical engineer.

[1934]   autobiography, *Memories of a scientific life* (London: Marshall, Morgan & Scott Ltd.) 244. Foreword is a letter to the author by Sir Oliver Lodge comparing their two careers.

[1954]   J.T. MacGregor-Morris, *The inventor of the valve a biography of Sir Ambrose*

Fleming. Foreword by E.W. Marchant (London: The Television Society) 141; index. Author professor emeritus of electrical engineering. First written for the British Council for a series "Science in Britain", but unpublished because of spending cuts. The occasion of this expanded version is fiftieth anniversary of invention of thermionic valve.

Flower, William Henry (1831–1899), English zoologist.

1904   Charles J. Cornish, *Sir William Henry Flower . . . a personal memoir* (London: Macmillan and Co.) 274; bibliog; index. Author a zoologist; first two chapters written by subject's son Victor A. Flower. Emphasis is on personal life.

1906   R. Lydekker, *Sir William Flower* (London: J.M. Dent & Co.; NY: E.P. Dutton & Co.) [English men of science] 191; bibliog. Author was aware of Cornish's work in progress and decided to stress the scientific aspect.

Folin, Otto (1867–1934), American biochemist (born Sweden).

1989   Samuel Meites, *Otto Folin America's first clinical biochemist* (Washington, DC: American Association for Clinical Chemistry, Inc.) 428; illus; bibliog. Includes "synopses of many of his published scientific papers" as well as his "life and the significant contributions he made to science".

Forbes, James David (1809–1868), Scottish physicist and geologist.

1873   John Campbell Shairp, Peter Guthrie Tait and A. Adams-Reilly, *Life and letters of James David Forbes F.R.S.* (London: Macmillan and Co.) 577; bibliog. Preface says three authors worked independently, Tait (of University of Edinburgh) on science, Adams-Reilly on Alpine exploration and adventure and Shairp on professoriate and university reform. They acknowledge the editorial work of Mrs Forbes.

Ford, Henry (1863–1947), American automobile engineer.

1922   autobiography, *My life and work* (Garden City, NY: Doubleday, Page & Company) reprinted 1973 (NY: Arno Press) [Big business: economic power in a free society] 289; index. Written in collaboration with Samuel Crowther. Burlingame (1955) calls it a "mine of misinformation".

1923   Allan Louis Benson, *The new Henry Ford* (NY: Funk & Wagnalls Company) 360; illus. Based on interviews; stresses transition from the subject in 1914 to his personality in 1922, when he "pays high wages and shares profits as a matter of routine and habit", and "is primarily concerned with order".

1937   Upton Sinclair, *The flivver king a story of Ford-America* (Pasadena: published by the author) 256. Contains invented dialogue. Burlingame (1955) says it has been described as "a socialistic tract, thinly disguised as a biography".

1943   William Adams Simonds, *Henry Ford his life his work his genius* (Indianapolis: The Bobbs-Merrill Company Publishers) 365; illus; bibliog; index. Occasion is eightieth birthday of subject, who is referred to throughout as "Mr. Ford". Burlingame (1955) says most of the information is "probably correct though undocumented".

1948   Keith Sward, *The legend of Henry Ford* (NY, Rinehart & Company Inc.) 550; bibliog; index. According to Burlingame (1955) the author was a public relations counsel for a competing company; nevertheless "the most complete and documented biography".

1954   Allan Nevins, *Ford* Volume 1: *The times the man the company 1863–1915*; Volume 2: *Expansion and challenge 1915–1933*; Volume 3: *Decline and rebirth 1933–1962* (NY: Charles Scribner's Sons) reprinted 1976 (NY: Arno Press) [Companies and Men] 688; illus; bibliog; index. Written with the collaboration of Frank Ernest Hill.

1955   Roger Burlingame, *Henry Ford a great life in brief* (NY: Alfred A. Knopf, Inc.) 194; index. New edition 1956 (NY: New American Library/Signet Key Books) 143; index. The only life of subject written for the popular market that has used company archives. Author a biographer and historian.

1969   Booton Herndon, *Ford an unconventional biography of the men and their times* (NY: Weybright and Talley) 408; illus; bibliog; index. Characterizes Henry Ford I and Henry Ford II as "men of paradox", "men of industry", "men of social conscience", and "men who love life".

1970   Anne Jardim, *The first Henry Ford a study in personality and business leadership* (Cambridge: The MIT Press) 278; index. Foreword by Abraham Zaleznik says author "goes well beyond narrative biography into [psychoanalytic] analysis and explanation".

1981   Carol Gelderman, *Henry Ford the wayward capitalist* (NY: The Dial Press) 463; illus; index. Aimed at a general reading public; context is the depression of author's contemporary Detroit.

Foucroy, Antoine François de (1755–1809), French chemist.

1962   W.A. Smeaton, *Foucroy chemist and revolutionary 1755–1809* (Cambridge: W. Heffer & Sons Ltd.) 288; index; bibliog. Printed for the author; originally a PhD thesis, University of London, 1958. The life, for general readers, plus an analysis of his contributions to science and a bibliography.

Fourier, Jean Baptiste Joseph (1768–1830), French mathematician.

1975   John Herivel, *Joseph Fourier the man and the physicist* (Oxford: Clarendon Press) 350; illus; index; bibliog. Deals with the problem of mixing the "biographico-scientific content" by dividing text into two parts, the man and the physicist. Based on MS sources.

Frankland, Edward (1825–1899), English chemist.

1986   Colin A. Russell, *Lancastrian chemist the early years of Sir Edward Frankland* (Milton Keynes: Open University Press) 187; illus; index. Uses MS sources.

Friedmann, Aleksandr Aleksandrovich (1888–1925), Russian mathematician and physicist.

1993   Eduard A. Tropp, Viktor Ya. Frenkel and Artur D. Chernin, *Alexander A Friedmann the man who made the universe expand* (Cambridge: Cambridge University Press) 267; illus; bibliog; index. Translated by Alexander Dron and Michael Burov. Occasion of 1988 Russian edition was centenary of subject's birth. "Popular science." Uses MS sources.

Friese-Greene, William (1855–1921), English pioneer of cinematography.

1948   Ray Allister, *Friese-Greene close-up of an inventor* (London: Marsland Publications) reprinted 1972 (NY: Arno Press) [The Arno Press Cinema Program] 192; illus; index. A "true story", but author reports conversations because scenes described in interviews "set themselves in my mind in dialogue".

Frisch, Karl Ritter Von (1886–1982), Austrian zoologist.

1967   autobiography, *A biologist remembers* (Oxford: Pergamon Press) [International series of monographs in history and philosophy of science] 200; illus; bibliog; index. Translated by Lisbeth Gombrich from the 1957 German edition. Occasion was request of the Austrian Academy of Sciences for a written account of members' lives.

Frisch, Otto Robert (1904–1979), Austrian physicist.

1979   autobiography, *What little I remember* (Cambridge: Cambridge University Press) 227; illus; index. Written after seventieth birthday. Ends about 1947.

Frohawk, Frederick William (1861–1946), English naturalist.

1987   June Chatfield, *F.W. Frohawk his life and work* (Marlborough, Wilts.: The Crowood Press) 184; illus; bibliog; index. Foreword by Paul Whalley observes that this "evaluates both Frohawk's artistic and scientific work, and elegantly weaves his work and his association with many eminent Victorian and later naturalists into the story of his life".

Frost, Edwin Brant (1866–1935), American astronomer.

1933   autobiography, *An Astronomer's life* (Boston: Houghton Mifflin Company; Cambridge: The Riverside Press) 300; illus; index. First drafted as a family memoir; later considered "as a record of life in an academic community ... and as an account of scientific work in astronomy in a Midwestern setting".

Fulton, Robert (1765–1815), American engineer (pioneer of steamboats)

1891   Robert H. Thurston, *Robert Fulton his life and its results* (NY: Dodd, Mead, and Company) [Makers of America] 194; illus; index.

1908   Peyton F. Miller, *The story of Robert Fulton* (NY: The Knickerbocker Press) 113; illus; index. Based on earlier biographies.

1913   Henry W. Dickinson, *Robert Fulton engineer and artist his life and works* (London: John Lane) reprinted 1971 (Freeport, NY: Books for Libraries Press) 333; illus; index. Aims to be fair and impartial, unlike earlier biographies. Based on MS sources.

1977   John S. Morgan, *Robert Fulton* (NY: Mason/Charter) 235; illus; bibliog; index. Focus is on subject as technologist.

1981   Wallace Hutcheon Jr, *Robert Fulton pioneer of undersea warfare* (Annapolis: Naval Institute Press) 191; illus; bibliog; index. Author is naval officer and historian. Focus is on subject's work in naval warfare.

1985   Cynthia Owen Philip, *Robert Fulton a biography* (NY: Franklin Watts) 371; illus; bibliog; index.

Funk, Casimir (1884–1967), Polish biochemist.

1955   Benjamin Harrow, *Casimir Funk pioneer in vitamins and hormones* (NY: Dodd, Mead) 209; illus. XX

Galton, Francis (1822–1911), English statistician and psychologist.

1908   autobiography, *Memories of my life* (London: Methuen & Co.) reprinted 1974 (NY: AMS Press) 339; illus; bibliog; index. Arrangement is only partly chronological.

1914–30   Karl Pearson, *The life letters and labours of Francis Galton* (Cambridge: Cambridge University Press) I:242 II:425 III:657; illus; index. Originally intended as a "permanent memorial". Publication interrupted by First World War. Later volumes provide a résumé of subject's writings and other material.

1974   D.W. Forrest, *Francis Galton the life and work of a Victorian genius* (NY: Taplinger Publishing Co.; London: Elek) 340; illus; bibliog; index. XX

Garden, Alexander (1730–1791), American naturalist (born Scotland).

1969   Edmund Berkeley and Dorothy Smith Berekely, *Dr Alexander Garden of Charles Town* (Chapel Hill: University of North Carolina Press) 379; illus; bibliog; index. Based on MS sources.

Garrett, George William Littler (1852–1902), English submarine technologist.

1987   William Scanlan Murphy, *Father of the submarine the life of the Reverend George Garrett Pasha* (London: William Kimber) 254; illus; bibliog; index. Author calls subject "one of the great lost figures of the Victorian age . . . It might well be said that he was no Faraday or Brunel – but, if modern scholarship is to be believed, neither were Faraday and Brunel". Based on MS sources.

Garrod, Archibald Edward (1857–1936), English molecular biologist.

1993 Alexander G. Bearn, *Archibald Garrod and the individuality of man* (Oxford: Clarendon Press) 227; illus; bibliog; index. Foreword by Joseph L. Goldstein and Michael S. Brown, who call this an "incisive biography" by "a disciple" of subject. Based on MS sources.

Gauss, Karl Friederich (1777–1855), German mathematician, astronomer and physicist.

1970 Tord Hall, *Carl Friedrich Gauss a biography* (Cambridge: The MIT Press) 176; index; bibliog. Translated by Albert Froderberg. Deals with the problem of technicality "by formulating the problems, saying something about their origin, and illustrating them with concrete examples".

1981 W.K. Bühler, *Gauss a biographical study* (NY: Springer-Verlag) 208; illus; bibliog; index. Contains passages from subject's writings. Preface quotes Nicolaus von Fuss: "To describe the life of a great man who distinguishes his century by a considerable degree of enlightenment is to eulogize the human mind."

Gay-Lussac, Joseph Louis (1778–1850), French chemist and physicist.

1978 Maurice Crosland, *Gay-Lussac scientist and bourgeois* (Cambridge: Cambridge University Press) 333; bibliog; index. "The study of individual cases can do something to correct the picture of science and scientists given by those who wish to make generalizations about the subject but have no time or inclination to go back to the sources." Author an historian of science.

Geikie, Archibald (1835–1924), Scottish geologist.

1924 autobiography, *A long life's work* (London: Macmillan & Co., Limited) 426. XX

Geikie, James (1839–1915), Scottish geologist.

1917 Marion I. Newbigin and J.S. Flett, *James Geikie the man and the geologist* (Edinburgh: Oliver and Boyd) 227; index; bibliog; illus. Newbigin is editor of the Scottish Geographical Magazine; Flett is of the Geological Survey of Scotland. Based on letters, papers and diaries; wartime conditions limited authors' access to continental geologists.

Gibbs, Josiah Willard (1839–1903), American chemist.

1942 Muriel Rukeyser, *Willard Gibbs* (Garden City, NY: Doubleday, Doran & Company, Inc.) 465; bibliog; index. First full-length treatment, "the story of an imagination which has had a powerful effect on our lives, and which at the same time is an emblem of pure imagination . . .". Admits there is undiscovered evidence. "Not an authorized biography", because relatives are still living.

1963   Benedict A. Leerburger Jr, *Josiah W. Gibbs American theoretical physicist* (NY: Franklin Watts Inc.) 118; illus; index. [Immortals of science] Popular biography; author a science writer.

1951   Lynde Phelps Wheeler, *Josiah Willard Gibbs the history of a great mind* (New Haven: Yale University Press; London: Geoffrey Cumberledge. Oxford University Press) 264; illus; index; bibliog. Revised edition 1952 270; illus; bibliog; index. Paperback edition 1962 with foreword by A. Whitney Griswold, xiii, 270, illus. Author a former student; invited in 1944 by the family and a professional colleague: "Both of them were concerned about the scarcity of available biographical material of a personal nature, and about the use which had been made in recently published biographies of such as did exist." The biography "illustrates the application of his theory to the subsequent development of the physical sciences". Revised edition incorporates material which appeared after the first edition; it all appears in a new Appendix VIII; otherwise only errors and misprints are corrected.

Gilbert, Grove Karl (1843–1918), American geologist and geomorphologist.

1980   Stephen J. Pyne, *Grove Karl Gilbert a great engine of research* (Austin: University of Texas Press) 306; illus; bibliog; index. Uses earlier text by Davies; attempts to modernize subject's biography and to "show how Gilbert's education, temperament, perception, modes of expression and science all intersect". Uses MSS.

Gill, David (1843–1914), Scottish astronomer.

1916   George Forbes, *David Gill man and astronomer memories of Sir David Gill KCB H M astronomer (1879–1907) at the Cape of Good Hope* (London: John Murray) 418; illus; bibliog; index. Subject's science is mentioned "only as throwing light upon his character". Author an electrical engineer and friend of subject.

Goddard, Robert Hutchings (1882–1945), American physicist.

1963   Milton Lehman, *This high man the life of Robert H. Goddard* Preface by Charles A. Lindbergh. (NY: Farrar, Straus and Company) 430; illus; bibliog. Paperback edition 1988 entitled *Robert H. Goddard pioneer of space research*, with new introduction by Frederick C. Durant III (NY: Da Capo Press) [Da Capo series in science]. Title derives from Browning, *A Grammarian's Funeral*. Research includes interviews with contemporaries as well as unpublished papers including an MS autobiography; author does not care for footnotes.

Gödel, Kurt (1906–1978), American mathematician (born Austria).

1987   Hao Wang, *Reflections on Kurt Gödel* (Cambridge: The MIT Press) 336; illus; index. Aims to render subject accessible to non-specialists "without refraining from considerations of new ideas on a level that is challenging to the experts".

Goldschmidt, Richard Benedict (1878–1958), German zoologist.

1960   autobiography, *In and out of the ivory tower* (Seattle: University of Washington Press) 352; illus; bibliog. XX

Goldschmidt, Victor Moritz (1888–1947), Swiss chemist and minerologist.

1992   Brian Mason, *Victor Moritz Goldschmidt father of modern geochemistry* (San Antonio: The Geochemical Society) [Special publication no. 4] 184; illus; index. Addressed to "geologists, chemists, and geochemists; historians of science; and the layman interested in science". Uses MS sources.

Goodyear, Charles (1800–1860), American rubber technician.

1866   Bradford K. Peirce, *Trials of an inventor life and discoveries of Charles Goodyear* (NY: Carlton & Porter) 224; illus. Published for the Sunday School Union. Based on MS sources and family interviews. Refers to subject's short autobiography, "one copy of which was printed upon gum elastic paper, and bound in hard rubber, elegantly carved".

1940   P.W. Barker, *Charles Goodyear Connecticut Yankee and rubber pioneer a biography* (Boston: privately printed) 109; illus.

1941   Adolph C. Regli, *Rubber's Goodyear the story of a man's perseverance* (NY: J. Messner, Inc.) 248; illus; bibliog. XX

Gosse, Philip Henry (1810–1888), English naturalist.

1890   Edmund Gosse, *The life of Philip Henry Gosse FRS* (London: Kegan Paul, Trench, Trübner & Co. Ltd.) 387; index. Reprinted 1896 with title *The naturalist of the seashore* (London: William Heinemann) [Great Lives and Events]. Author is son of subject. Based on MS sources.

Gould, John (1804–1881), English ornithologist.

1991   Isabella Tree, *The ruling passion of John Gould a biography of the bird man* (London: Barrie & Jenkins) 250; illus; bibliog; index. Based on MS sources.

Gray, Asa (1810–1888), American botanist (plant taxonomy).

1959   A. Hunter Dupree, *Asa Gray 1810–1888* (Cambridge: The Belknap Press of Harvard University Press) reprinted in paperback 1988 (Baltimore and London: The Johns Hopkins University Press) 505; index; illus. Begun as a doctoral dissertation at Harvard; includes research in MSS and interviews. "The life . . . includes in the personal story much that belongs also to the history of science." Paperback has a new preface and title *Asa Gray American botanist friend of Darwin*.

Green, George (1793–1841), English mathematician.

1993   D.M. Cannell, *George Green mathematical physicist 1793–1841 the background to his life and work* (London: The Athlone Press) 265; illus; bibliog; index. "First major biography" of subject, "written to interest the lay reader as much as the scientific specialist". Uses MS sources. Foreword by Lawrie Challis.

Haast, Johann Franz Julius von (1822–1887), German geologist.

1948   H.F. von Haast, *The life and times of Sir Julius von Haast . . . explorer geologist museum builder* (Wellington, NZ, published privately, 1948) index; bibliog. Published by the author, who is son of subject.

Haber, Fritz (1868–1934), German chemist.

1967   Morris Goran, *The story of Fritz Haber* (Norman: University of Oklahoma Press) 212; illus; bibliog; index.

Haeckel, Ernst Heinrich Philipp August (1834–1919), German zoologist.

[1906]   Wilhelm Bölsche, *Haeckel his life and work* (London: T. Fisher Unwin) 336; illus; bibliog; index. Revised edition 1901 (London: Watts) 128; illus. Translated by Joseph McCabe, who provides an introduction and supplementary chapter. Author a former pupil of subject, a biologist.

Hahn, Otto (1879–1968), German radiochemist.

1966   autobiography, *Otto Hahn a scientific autobiography* (NY: Charles Scribner's Sons) 296; illus; index. Translated and edited by W. Ley; introduction by Glenn T. Seaborg.

1970   autobiography, *My life* (London: Macdonald & Co; NY: Herder and Herder with title *My life the autobiography of a scientist*) 240. Translated by Ernst Kaiser and Eithne Wilkins. XX

Haldane, John Burdon Sanderson (1892–1964), English physiologist and biochemist.

1968   Ronald Clark, *JBS the life and work of J.B.S. Haldane* (London: Hodder and Stoughton) reprinted paperback 1984 (Oxford: Oxford University Press) 286; illus; index. Also published 1969 (NY: Coward-McCann) 326; illus. Preface by Sir Peter Medewar. Author a biographer of scientists.

1985   Krishna R. Dronamraju, *Haldane the life and work of J.B.S. Haldane with special reference to India* (Aberdeen: Aberdeen University Press) 211; illus; bibliog; index. Foreword by Naomi Mitchison regards Clark 1968 as inadequate on the scientific work and especially weak with respect to subject's life in India.

Hale, George Ellery (1868–1938), American astrophysicist.

1966   Helen Wright, *Explorer of the universe a biography of George Ellery Hale* (NY: E.P. Dutton & Co., Inc.) 480; illus; bibliog; index. Introduction by Ira S. Bowen. Uses MS sources.

1993   Osterbrock see Ritchey.

Hales, Stephen (1677–1761), English chemist and plant physiologist.

1929   A.E. Clark-Kennedy, *Stephen Hales DD FRS an eighteenth century biography* (Cambridge: Cambridge University Press) 256; illus; index. Initial occasion from which this is expanded was address on two hundred and fiftieth anniversary of birth. Based on MS and published sources.

1980   D.G.C. Allan and R.E. Schofield, *Stephen Hales scientist and philanthropist* (London: Scolar Press) 220; bibliog; index. Authors inspired by Clark-Kennedy (1929) to further researches and new insights. Schofield focuses on scientific and technological aspects, and Allan on personal and philanthropic.

Hall, Charles Martin (1863–1914), American commercial chemist.

1955   Junius Edwards, *The immortal woodshed the story of the inventor who brought aluminum to America* (NY: Dodd, Mead & Company) 244; illus. Includes some invented dialogue.

Hall, James (1811–1898), American palaeontologist and geologist.

1921   John M. Clarke, *James Hall of Albany geologist and palaeontologist 1811–1898* (Albany: published by the author). Reprinted 1978 (NY: Arno Press) [History of geology] 565; illus; index. Author acquainted with subject; focus is on life.

Halley, Edmond (1656–1742), English astronomer and geophysicist.

1966   A. Armitage, *Edmond Halley* (London: Nelson) [British men of science] 220; illus; index. An "historical evaluation" not the definitive biography.

1969   Colin A. Ronan, *Edmond Halley genius in eclipse* (Garden City, NY: Doubleday; London: Macdonald) 251; illus; bibliog; index. Deals with the science "in sequence, just as it occurred, [to see] how his mind worked and his enthusiasms changed".

Halmos, Paul Richard (1916 – –), American mathematician (born Hungary).

1985   autobiography, *I want to be a mathematician an automathography* (NY: Springer-Verlag) 421; illus; index. Genre is described as "a mathematical biography written by its subject", neither a mathematics book nor the story of origins and life.

Hamilton, William (1730–1803), Scottish archaeologist and geologist.

1969   Brian Fothergill, *Sir William Hamilton envoy extraordinary* (London: Faber and Faber) 459; index; bibliog; illus. Paperback edition 1973. Argues that there is more to Hamilton than being the husband of Nelson's mistress.

Hamilton, William Rowan (1805–1865), Irish mathematician.

1882–91   R.P. Graves, *Life of Sir William Rowan Hamilton* (Dublin: Hodges Figgis) O'Donnell 1983 says that author is friend of subject, and that abundance of detail impedes perspective. XX

1980   Thomas L. Hankins, *Sir William Rowan Hamilton* (Baltimore: Johns Hopkins University Press) 474; bibliog; index. O'Donnell 1983 calls this the definitive biography. Author an historian of science. XX

1983   Seán O'Donnell, *William Rowan Hamilton portrait of a prodigy* (Dublin: Boole Press) [Profiles of genius series] 224; illus; index. Foreword by A.J. McConnell. Unlike Hankins 1980, this seeks "to come to grips with Hamilton's formidable personality rather than his achievements", so that "the psychological portrait also comes to resemble biography".

Hare, Robert (1781–1858), American chemist, inventor of the oxyhydrogen blowpipe.

1917   Edgar Fahs Smith, *The life of Robert Hare an American chemist 1781–1858* (Philadelphia: J.B. Lippincott Company) reprinted 1980 (NY: Arno Press) [Three centuries of science in America] 508; index. Addressed to students of chemistry; author at University of Pennsylvania.

Harrison, John (1693–1776), English horologist.

1966   Humphrey Quill, *John Harrison the man who found longitude* (London: John Baker) 255; illus; bibliog; index. Author an authority on horology.

Hassler, Ferdinand Rudolph (1770–1843), Swiss geodesist.

1929   Florian Cajori, *The chequered career of Ferdinand Rudolph Hassler first superintendent of the United States coast survey a chapter in the history of science in America* (Boston: The Christopher Publishing House) 245; index. Author is professor of history of mathematics; calls the book a biography and history.

Havinga, Egbert (1909–1988), Dutch organic chemist.

1991   autobiography, *Enjoying organic chemistry 1927–1987* (Washington, DC: American Chemical Society) [Profiles, pathways, and dreams: autobiographies of eminent chemists] 122; illus; index.

Hawking, Stephen William (1942 – –) English mathematician and theoretical physicist.

1992 Michael White and John Gribbin, *Stephen Hawking a life in science* (Harmondsworth: Viking; NY: Dutton Books) 304; index. Attempts to describe subject's "work as well as the life of the man behind the science".

Heaviside, Oliver (1850–1925), English physicist and electrical engineer.

1988 Paul J. Nahin, *Oliver Heaviside sage in solitude the life work and times of an electrical genius of the Victorian age* (NY: IEEE Press) 320; illus; bibliog; index. Published under the sponsorship of the Institute of Electrical and Electronics Engineers History Committee. Author's preface (he is an academic electrical and computer engineer) reflects on the problems of writing about technical careers, and the need for the biographer to have "an advanced technical background".

Heisenberg, Werner Karl (1901–1976), German physicist (founder of quantum mechanics).

1971 autobiography, *Physics and beyond encounters and conversations* (NY: Harper & Row, Publishers) [World Perspectives] 247. Translated from German by Arnold J. Pomerans. Hopes to reduce the gap between the cultures of art and science. Organized around conversations over 50 years, reconstructed to present a broad picture.

1984 Elisabeth Heisenberg, *Inner exile recollections of a life with Werner Heisenberg* (Boston: Birkhäuser) 170; illus. Author is wife of subject. Translated from German by S. Cappallari and C. Morris. Introduction by Victor Weisskopf, who says it "provides insight into some aspects of life under an oppressive regime".

1992 David C. Cassidy, *Uncertainty the life and science of Werner Heisenberg* (NY: W.H. Freeman and Company) 669; illus; index. Based on MS sources. Author observes that: "Every biography, and especially this one, brings together three lives: the subject's, the author's, and the reader's." Author "a physicist turned historian of science".

Helmholtz, Hermann Ludwig Ferdinand von (1821–1894), German physiologist and physicist.

1899 John Gray M'Kendrick, *Hermann Ludwig Ferdinand von Helmholtz* (London: T. Fisher Unwin) [Masters of medicine] 299; bibliog; index. Author is professor of physiology.

1906 Leo Koenigsberger, *Hermann von Helmholtz* (Oxford: Clarendon Press) 440. Translated by Frances A. Welby. Preface by Lord Kelvin. Author a mathematician colleague of subject.

Henry, Augustine (1857–1930), Scottish botanist.

1966 Sheila Pim, *The wood and the trees Augustine Henry a biography* (London: Macdonald & Co.). Second edition enlarged and revised with additional illustrations 1984 (Kilkenny: Boethius Press) 252; illus; bibliog; index. Preface to second edition acknowledges scholarship on subject's diaries by E. Charles Nelson, who provides an appendix.

Henry, Joseph (1797–1878), American physicist.

1950 Thomas Coulson, *Joseph Henry his life and work* (Princeton: Princeton University Press) 352; illus; bibliog; index. Based on MS research; written to rescue the subject from neglect and "restore him to a rightful place among the gallery of America's great men".

1961 Patricia Jahns, *Matthew Fontaine Maury & Joseph Henry scientists of the civil war* (NY: Hastings House Publishers) 308. Henry as the scientist of the north and Maury of the south.

1961 Sarah Riedman, *Trailblazer of American science the life of Joseph Henry* (Chicago: Rand McNally) 224; illus; index. No mention of Coulson; includes many photographs.

Henslow, John Stevens (1796–1861), English botanist.

1977 Jean Russell-Gebbett, *Henslow of Hitcham botanist educationalist and clergyman* (Lavenham, Suffolk: Terence Dalton Limited) 139; illus; index.

Herschel, Caroline Lucretia (1750–1848), English astronomer (born Germany).

1876 M.C. Herschel, *Memoir and correspondence of Caroline Herschel* (London: John Murray) second edition 1879, 355; index.

1895 Clerke, see Herschel, William.

1933 Constance A. Lubbock, ed., *The Herschel chronicle the life story of William Herschel and his sister Caroline Herschel* (Cambridge: Cambridge University Press) 388; index. Editor is William's granddaughter; aim is to present both lives in the setting of both family circle and contemporary history.

Herschel, John Frederick William (1792–1871), English mathematician, physicist and astronomer.

1895 Clerke, see Herschel, William.

1970 Günther Buttmann, *The shadow of the telescope a biography of John Herschel* (NY: Charles Scribner's Sons) 219; bibliog; index. Translated by B.E.J. Pagel; edited and introduction by David S. Evans. Preface states that no complete biography yet exists; this is a sketch to stimulate further study.

Herschel, William (1738–1822), English astronomer (born Germany).

1880 Edward S. Holden, *Sir William Herschel his life and works* (NY: Charles Scribner's Sons; London: W.H. Allen & Co., 1881) 238; bibliog; index. Author is at US Naval Observatory, Washington. Book is based on published sources, not papers preserved "at the family seat in England". Since two generations have passed since subject's death and no biography approaching completeness has appeared, the author makes no apology for "a conscientious attempt to make the best use of the scanty material which we do possess".

1895   Agnes M. Clerke, *The Herschels and modern astronomy* (London: Cassell and Company, Limited) [The Century Science Series] 224; illus; index. Combines lives of William, Caroline and John Herschel.

1900   James Sime, *William Herschel and his work* (Edinburgh: T. & T. Clark) [The world's epoch-makers] 265; index.

1933   Lubbock, see Herschel, Caroline.

1953   J.B. Sidgwick, *William Herschel explorer of the heavens* (London: Faber and Faber Limited) 228; illus; bibliog; index.

Hevesy, Georg Von (1885–1966), Hungarian physicist.

1985   Hilde Levi, *George de Hevesy life and work* (Bristol: A. Hilger) 147; illus; bibliog; index. XX

Hilbert, David (1862–1943), German mathematician.

1970   Constance Reid, *Hilbert* (NY: Springer-Verlag) 290; illus; index. Published 1986 with author's *Courant* in one volume with combined index (NY: Springer-Verlag). 1970 includes an appreciation of subject's mathematical work by Hermann Weyl, omitted in 1986. "To a large extent this book has been written from memory." Based on interviews with colleagues of subject and written recollections of others.

Hill, Robert Thomas (1858–1941), American geologist.

1976   Nancy Alexander, *Father of Texas geology Robert T. Hill* (Dallas: Southern Methodist University Press) [Bicentennial series in American studies] 317; illus; index. Based on MS sources.

Hind, Henry Youle (1823–1908), Canadian scientific explorer (born England).

1988   W.L. Morton, *Henry Youle Hind 1923–1908* (Toronto: University of Toronto Press) [Canadian Biographical Studies] 161; bibliog; index. Based on MSS and printed sources.

Hofmeister, Wilhelm Friedrich Benedict (1824–1877), German botanist.

1926   Karl Goebel, *Wilhelm Hofmeister the work and life of a nineteenth century botanist* (London: Ray Society) 202; illus. Includes a biographical supplement by Frau Professor Ganzenmüller (née Hofmeister); translated by H.M. Bower and edited botanically by F.O. Bower.

Hooke, Robert (1635–1702), English physicist.

1956   Margaret 'Espinasse, *Robert Hooke* (London: William Heinemann Ltd.) [The Contemporary Science Series] reprinted 1962 (Berkeley: University of California Press) 192; illus; bibliog; index. Author a non-scientist; hopes to convey her own image of subject's character. Uses MS sources.

Hooker, Joseph Dalton (1817–1911), English plant taxonomist and explorer.

1918   Leonard Huxley, *Life and letters of Sir Joseph Dalton Hooker OM GCSI* (London: John Murray) I:546 II:569 bibliog. Author is son of subject's close friend T.H. Huxley. Based on materials collected and arranged by Lady Hooker.

1963   W.B. Turill, *Joseph Dalton Hooker botanist explorer and administrator* (London: Nelson and Sons Ltd) [British men of science] 228; illus; bibliog; index. Uses 1918 Huxley and MS sources.

1967   Mea Allen, *The Hookers of Kew 1785–1911* (London: Michael Joseph) 273; illus; bibliog; index. Story of subject and his father, William Hooker. Uses MS sources.

Houghton, Douglass (1809–1845), American geologist.

1889   Alvah Bradish, *Memoir of Douglass Houghton first state geologist of Michigan* (Detroit: Raynor & Taylor printers) 302. First 75 pages is memoir; remainder of book is documentary appendices.

1954   Edsel K. Rintala, *Douglass Houghton Michigan's pioneer geologist* (Detroit: Wayne University Press) 119; bibliog; index.

Howard, Leland Ossian (1857–1950), American applied entomologist.

1933   autobiography, *Fighting the insects the story of an entomologist telling the life and experiences of the writer* (NY: The Macmillan Company) reprinted 1980 (NY: Arno Press) [Three centuries of science in America] 333. Claims the book was instigated by "a somewhat imaginative publisher".

Hubble, Edwin Powell (1889–1953), American astronomer and cosmologist.

1993   Alexander S. Sharov and Igor D. Novikov, *Edwin Hubble the discoverer of the big bang* (Cambridge: Cambridge University Press) 187; illus; bibliog; index. Translated by Vitaly Kisin. The "first complete account of the scientific life and work of Hubble . . . intended for a wide readership". Uses MS sources. Second half "describes the fundamental discoveries on the nature of the universe made subsequently, and thus sets his achievements in context".

Humboldt, Friedrich Wilhelm Heinrich Alexander von (1769–1859), German natural historian.

1851   Professor Klencke, *Alexander von Humboldt a biographical monument* (London: Ingram, Cooke, & Co.) 245. Bound together [spine: *Lives of the Brothers Humboldt*] with Schlesier, *Life of William von Humboldt* (London: Ingram, Cooke & Co., 1852). Both translated from German by Juliette Bauer. First biography is 1–245; second is 249–431. Separate title pages. Anon 1860 says Klencke "seemed to have no idea of writing, beyond its being a means of conveying *facts*". Bruhns 1873 says "compiled . . . with no direct reference to authorities, nor even made acquaintance with scientific subjects".

[1860]   anon., *The life and travels of Alexander von Humboldt with an account of his discoveries and notices of his scientific fellow-labourers and contemporaries* (London: James Blackwood) 316; index. Anonymous author bases this account on Klencke 1851 regarded, despite criticisms, as the only important biography. Written for both old and young readers, with emphasis on the "interesting and thrilling narrative" of the travels.

1866   F.A. Schwarzenberg, *Alexander von Humboldt or what may be accomplished in a lifetime* (London: Robert Hardwicke) 207. Author a prolific writer of popular and scientific works.

1873   Karl Bruhns, *Life of Alexander von Humboldt* (London: Longmans, Green, and Co.) I:412 II:447; index. Translated from German by Jane and Caroline Lassell. Compiled to celebrate centenary. English version omits third volume devoted to subject's scientific work; bibliography also omitted. Based on MS sources. Contributors are J. Löwenberg, Robert Avé-Lallemant and Alfred Dove.

1955   Helmut De Terra, *Humboldt the life and times of Alexander von Humboldt* (NY: Alfred A. Knopf) 386; bibliog; index. Places subject's life in a "modern perspective", which implies relegating the scientific work to a less prominent place than in a full-scale biography.

1960   M.Z. Thomas [Thomas Michael Zottmann], *Alexander von Humboldt scientist explorer adventurer* (London: Constable and Co.) 192; illus. Translated by Elizabeth Brommer.

1961   Val Gendron, *The dragon tree a life of Alexander Baron von Humboldt* (NY: Longmans, Green and Co.) 214; illus; bibliog; index.

1963   L. Kellner, *Alexander von Humboldt* (London: Oxford University Press) 247; illus; bibliog; index.

Hutton, James (1726–1797), Scottish geologist and philosopher.

1967   Edward Battersby Bailey, *James Hutton the founder of modern geology* (Amsterdam: Elsevier Publishing Co. Ltd.) 161. Foreword by J.E. Richey. Focuses on subject's work.

Huxley, Julian (1887–1975), English ethologist.

1970–73   autobiography, *Memories* (London: George Allen and Unwin Ltd.) I:296 II:269; illus; index.

1978   J.R. Baker, *Julian Huxley scientist and world citizen 1887–1975 a biographical memoir* (Paris: Unesco) 184; bibliog.

Huxley, Thomas Henry (1825–1895), English zoologist and palaeontologist.

1900   P. Chalmers Mitchell, *Thomas Henry Huxley a sketch of his life and work* (NY: G.P. Putnam's Sons/The Knickerbocker Press) [Leaders in science] 297; illus; index. New cheap edition 1913 (London: Methuen & Co. Ltd.) [Methuen's Shilling Library] 276; index; bibliog. Not "an intimate or authorized biography", but rather an account "of the external features of his life" and of his contributions to science and social policy. Anticipates the publication of Huxley 1900.

1900   Leonard Huxley, *Life and letters of Thomas Henry Huxley* (London: Macmillan and Co.; NY: D. Appleton, 1901) reprinted 1969 (Gregg International Publishers) I:503 II:504; illus; bibliog; index. Author is son of subject. Stress is on Huxley's aims, character and temperament, and circumstances, rather than technical scientific work.

1902   Edward Clodd, *Thomas Henry Huxley* (Edinburgh: William Blackwood and Sons) [Modern English Writers] 226; index. Based largely on Huxley 1900.

1907   J.R. Ainsworth Davis, *Thomas H. Huxley* (London: J.M. Dent & Co.; NY: E.P. Dutton & Co.) [English Men of Science] 288; bibliog; index. Stresses the scientific work; largely based on Huxley 1900.

1920   Leonard Huxley, *Thomas Henry Huxley a character sketch* (London: Watts) [Life stories of famous men] reprinted 1969 (Freeport, NY: Books for Libraries Press) [Select bibliographies reprint series] 120. Issued for the Rationalist Press Association, Limited.

1932   Clarence Edwin Ayres, *Huxley* (NY: Norton). XX

1932   Houston Peterson, *Huxley prophet of science* (London: Longmans, Green and Co.) reprinted 1977 (NY: AMS Press) 338; index; bibliog. Regards subject "as a symbol and symptom of fifty stirring years". Refers to friend Mr Rudler who helped edit lectures into books from the original stenographic notes (210).

1934   E.W. MacBride, *Huxley* (London: Duckworth) [Great lives] 143; bibliog.

1955   William Irvine, see Darwin, Charles.

1959   Cyril Bibby, *T.H. Huxley scientist humanist and educator* (London: Watts; NY: Horizon Press, 1960) 330; illus; bibliog; index. Forewords by Julian Huxley and Aldous Huxley. Occasion is centenary of publication of *Origin*. Stresses subject's scientific humanism.

1972   Cyril Bibby, *Scientist extraordinary the life and scientific works of Thomas Henry Huxley 1825–1895* (Oxford: Pergamon Press; NY: St Martin's Press [The Commonwealth and International Library of Science, Technology, Engineering and Liberal Studies]) 208; illus; bibliog.

1974   autobiography, see Darwin, Charles.

1991   J. Vernon Jensen, *Thomas Henry Huxley communicating for science* (Newark: University of Delaware Press; London: Associated University Presses) 253; bibliog; index. A "rhetorical biography", which seeks to get "inside his public rhetoric . . . and his interpersonal communication networks". Uses MS sources.

Huygens, Christiaan (1629–1695), Dutch physicist and mathematician.

1947   A.E. Bell, *Christian Huygens and the development of science in the seventeenth century* (London: Edward Arnold & Co.) 220; illus; bibliog; index. Author a chemist and educator.

Infeld, Leopold (1878–1968), Polish theoretical physicist.

1941   autobiography, *Quest the evolution of a scientist* (NY: Doubleday, Doran & Co., Inc.) 342. Also published London (Victor Gollancz Ltd.) 312. Second edition 1980 with title *Quest an autobiography* (NY: Chelsea Publishing Company) 361.

1978   autobiography, *Why I left Canada reflections on science and politics* (Montreal: McGill-Queen's University Press) 212; illus; index. Translated by Helen Infeld; edited with introduction and notes by Lewis Pyenson.

Ipatieff, Vladimir Nikolaievich (1867–1952), Russian chemist.

1946   autobiography, *The life of a chemist* (Stanford: Stanford University Press) [Hoover Library on War, Revolution, and Peace] 658; illus; index. Published in series "to present various aspects of Russian life and institutions before and since the Revolution of 1917". Edited by Xenia Joukoff Eudin, Helen Dwight Fisher and Harold H. Fisher; translated by Vladimir Haensel and Mrs Ralph H. Lusher.

Jeans, James Hopwood (1877–1946), English physicist and astronomer.

1952   E.A. Milne, *Sir James Jeans a biography* (Cambridge: Cambridge University Press) 175; illus; index. With a memoir by S.C. Roberts; author died before completing revisions.

Jenkin, Henry Charles Fleeming (1833–1885), English engineer.

1887   Robert Louis Stevenson, "Memoir" in *Papers Literary Scientific &c by the late Fleeming Jenkin* (London: Longmans, Green and Co.) vol. 1. Memoir is xi–clxx. American edition 1904 (NY: Charles Scribner's Sons). Another edition 1912 (London: Longmans, Green) reprinted 1969 (Geneva: Heron Books) 229. In preface to American edition author explains that the two-volume selection of papers has not been published in the United States: "the memoir appearing alone, shorn of that other matter which was at once its occasion and its justification, so large an account of a man so little known may seem to a stranger out of all proportion". 1969 reprint has preface by Rae Jeffs.

Jenner, Edward (1749–1823), English immunologist and natural historian.

1827   John Baron, *The life of Edward Jenner LLD FRS physician extraordinary to the king &c &c with illustrations of his doctrines and selections from his correspondence* (London: Henry Colburn) 624; index. Reprinted 1838 as first of a two-volume edition. Author acquainted with subject. Uses MSS.

1931   F. Dawtrey Drewitt, *The life of Edward Jenner MD FRS naturalist and discoverer of vaccination* (London: Longmans, Green and Co.) 127. Second edition, enlarged, 1933: 151; illus; index. Written "in the hope that it may interest some who are neither doctors nor naturalists".

1959   Dorothy Fisk, *Dr Jenner of Berkeley* (London: Heinemann) 288; illus; bibliog; index.

1982   Paul Sanders, *Edward Jenner the Cheltenham Years 1795–1823 being a chronicle of the vaccination campaign* (Hanover: University Press of New England) 469; illus; index. Uses MS sources.

1991   Richard B. Fisher, *Edward Jenner 1749–1823* (London: André Deutsch) 361; illus; bibliog; index. Preface by William LeFanu. Uses MS sources.

Jessop, William (1745–1814), English civil engineer.

1979   Charles Hadfield and A.W. Skempton, *William Jessop Engineer* (Newton Abbot: David & Charles) 315; illus; index. Based on MS sources.

Johansson, Carol Edvard (1864–1943), Swedish measurement engineer.

1948   Torsten K.W. Althin, *C.E. Johansson 1864–1943 the master of measurement* (Stockholm: published privately) 165; illus; bibliog. Based on MS sources. Written at the request of the subject's firm. Translated by Cyril Marshall.

Joliot, Jean Frédéric (1900–1958), French nuclear physicist.

1966   Pierre Biquard, *Frédéric Joliot-Curie the man and his theories* (NY: Paul S. Eriksson, Inc.) [A Profile in Science] 192; illus; bibliog; index. Translated by Geoffrey Strachan from the 1962 French edition.

1976   Maurice Goldsmith, *Frédéric Joliot-Curie a biography* (London: Lawrence and Wishart) 260; illus; bibliog; index.

Jones, William (1675–1749), Welsh mathematician.

1804   Lord Teignmouth [John Shore], *Memoirs of the life writings and correspondence of Sir William Jones* (London: Sold by John Hatchard) 531. Written at the request of Lady Jones. According to Cannon, "deliberately slanted to mitigate political and religious views which were quite advanced for the time".

1964   Garland Cannon, *Oriental Jones a biography of Sir William Jones (1746–1794)* (London: Asia Publishing House for the Indian Council for Cultural Relations) 215; illus; index; bibliog. The first modern life of Jones; author has also edited the letters.

Jordan, David Starr (1851–1931), American ichthyologist.

1922   autobiography, *The days of a man being memories of a naturalist teacher and minor prophet of democracy* (Yonkers-on-Hudson, NY: World Book Company) I:710 II:906; illus; index.

1953   Edward McNall Burns, *David Starr Jordan prophet of freedom* (Stanford: Stanford University Press) 243; bibliog; index. Purpose "to present the social and political ideas of Dr Jordan". Uses MSS.

Joule, James Prescott (1818–1889), English physicist.

1989   Donald S.L. Cardwell, *James Joule a biography* (Manchester: Manchester University Press) 333; illus; index.

Just, Ernest Everett (1883–1941), American biologist.

1983   Kenneth R. Manning, *Black Apollo of science the life of Ernest Everett Just* (NY: Oxford University Press) 397; bibliog; index.

Kammerer, Paul (1880–1926), Austrian biologist.

1971   Arthur Koestler, *The case of the midwife toad* (London: Hutchinson; NY: Random House) 187; bibliog; index. Based on printed and MS sources.

Kapitza, Piotr Leonidovich (1894–1984), Russian physicist and engineer.

1990   J.W. Boag, P.E. Rubinin and D. Shoenberg, comps and eds, *Kapitza in Cambridge and Moscow life and letters of a Russian physicist* (Amsterdam; North-Holland) 429; illus; bibliog; index. Contains revised biographical memoir (by Shoenberg) which originally appeared in *Biographical Memoirs of Fellows of the Royal Society* 31 (1985). Archival work by subject's former personal assistant (Rubinin). Editors have selected letters and made translations.

Karman, Theodore von (1881–1963), Hungarian aerodynamics scientist.

1967   autobiography, *The wind and beyond Theodore von Kármán pioneer in aviation and pathfinder in space* (Boston: Little, Brown, and Company) 376; illus; bibliog; index. Completed by Lee Edson after subject's death, using MS sources.

1992   Michael H. Gorn, *The universal man Theodore von Kármán's life in aeronautics* (Washington: Smithsonian Institution Press) [Smithsonian history of aviation series] 202; illus; bibliog; index. Intended for "the general reader". Uses MS sources and includes anecdotes.

Keeler, James Edward (1857–1900), American astronomer.

1984   Donald E. Osterbrock, *James E. Keeler pioneer American astrophysicist and the early development of American astrophysics* (Cambridge: Cambridge University Press)

411; illus; bibliog; index. A "record of his life in science". Includes information on the careers of subject's associates. Uses MS sources.

Keir, James (1735–1820), Scottish industrial chemist.

[1859]   Amelia Moilliet, *Sketch of the life of James Keir esq FRS with a selection from his correspondence* (London: printed for private circulation) 164. Introductory letter by Alexander Blair to grandson of author (who was daughter of subject) calls this a "little domestic memorial".

Kelly, William (1811–1888), American engineer.

1924   John Newton Boucher, *William Kelly a true history of the called Bessemer process* (Greensburg, PA: published privately) 258; illus; index. Written at the request of subject's widow.

Kelvin. See Thomson, William.

Kettering, Charles Franklin (1876–1958), American engineer.

1957   T.A. Boyd, *Professional amateur the biography of Charles Franklin Kettering* (NY: E.P. Dutton & Co., Inc.) reprinted 1972 (NY: Arno Press) [Technology and society] 242; illus; index. Foreword by Alfred P. Sloan, Jr (an associate of subject), who says this is an attempt at "a simple and sympathetic story of the man and his accomplishments".

1960   Sigmund A. Lavine, *Kettering master inventor* (NY: Dodd, Mead & Company) 173; illus. Author a teacher and writer; meant for young people, according to the acknowledgements, but more detailed and substantial than most scientific biographies for children.

1961   Rosamond McPherson Young, *Boss Ket a life of Charles F. Kettering* (NY: Longmans, Green and Co.) 210; bibliog.

1983   Stuart W. Leslie, *Boss Kettering* (NY: Columbia University Press) 382; illus; index. First biography to use subject's files.

King, Clarence Rivers (1842–1901), American geologist.

1958   Thurman Wilkins, *Clarence King a biography* (NY: The Macmillan Company) 441; illus; bibliog; index. Revised and enlarged edition 1988 (Albuquerque: University of New Mexico Press). Based on subject's papers and other materials. 1988 edition, written with the help of Caroline Lawson Hinkley, adds about 35,000 words and takes advantage of intervening scholarship and MS materials missed earlier. The preface implies that the first edition was well received.

Kinnersley, Ebenezer (1711–1778), English physicist (electricity).

1964   J.A. Leo Lemay, *Ebenezer Kinnersley Franklin's friend* (Philadelphia: University of Pennsylvania Press) 143; illus; bibliog; index. Calls subject "the greatest scientific popularizer of colonial America"; quotes sources extensively.

Kircher, Athanasius (1602–1680), German polymath.

1974 P. Conor Reilly, *Athanasius Kircher S.J. master of a hundred arts 1602–1680* (Wiesbaden-Rom: Edizione del Mondo) [Studia Kircheriana] 207; bibliog; index. Focus on subject's life and personality – no detailed explanations of his work.

Kopal, Zdeněk (1914 – –), Czech astronomer.

1986 autobiography, *Of stars and men reminiscences of an astronomer* (Bristol: Adam Hilger) 486; illus; index. Written at the invitation of the Institute of Physics. Meant to be "a basis for a broader historical survey of the past" of astronomy.

Kovalevsky, Sonya (1850–1891), Russian mathematician.

1895 A.C. Leffler (Edgren), *Sonia Kovalevsky biography and autobiography* (London: Walter Scott, Ltd.) 317; illus. Translated by L. von Cossell. First part is author's "memoir", (1–166); second part is subject's "Reminiscences of childhood", which is published elsewhere as *Life in Russia*. Author (who prefers a poetic "analysis of the soul" to "objective truth") is Duchess of Cajanello and friend of subject.

1978 autobiography, *A Russian childhood* (NY: Springer-Verlag) 250; bibliog. Translated, edited and introduced by Beatrice Stillman. Includes an analysis of subject's mathematics by P.Y. Kochina. First published 1889; this based on 1974 Russian edition.

1983 Don H. Kennedy, *Little Sparrow a portrait of Sophia Kovalevsky* (Athens: Ohio University Press) 341; illus; bibliog; index. "Not about a mathematician as such, but about an unusual woman who happens to have a secure place in the history of science as she does in Russian literature." Koblitz 1983 says author is hampered by lack of Russian language; he depended on translations made by his wife, Nina Kennedy, a descendant of the subject.

1983 Ann Hibner Koblitz, *A convergence of lives Sofia Kovalevskaia scientist writer revolutionary* (Boston: Birkhäuser) 305; bibliog; index. Places subject in the contemporary nihilist milieu, in order to explore her science, feminism and social activism. Uses MS sources.

Kramers, Hendrik Anthony (1894–1952), Dutch theoretical physicist.

1987 M. Dresden, *H.A. Kramers between tradition and revolution* (NY: Springer-Verlag) 563; illus; index. Empasizes subject's work. Author was acquainted with subject; does not claim to be exhaustive. Uses MS sources and interviews.

Krebs, Hans Adolf (1900–1981), German biochemist.

1981 autobiography, *Hans Krebs reminiscences and reflections* (Oxford: Clarendon

Press) 298; illus; bibliog; index. Written in collaboration with Anne Martin. Addressed to a general audience.

1991 Frederic Lawrence Holmes, *Hans Krebs the formation of a scientific life 1900–1933* (NY: Oxford University Press) [Monographs on the history and philosophy of biology] 298; illus; bibliog; index. Preface by Joseph S. Fruton. First of two volumes; focus is on the scientific life; written with co-operation of subject.

Kropotkin, Petr Alekeevich (1842–1921), Russian geographer.

1930 autobiography, *Memoirs of a revolutionist* (NY: Houghton Mifflin Company) [The Riverside Library] 502. Published 1968 (NY: Horizon Press) reprinted 1970 (NY: Grove) [An Evergreen Book] 519. Published 1989 (Montreal: Black Rose Books) 468. First appeared 1899 in the *Atlantic Monthly*. 1930 has introduction by George Brandes. 1968 has new foreword by Barnett Newman. 1989 has introduction by George Woodcock. Miller 1976 says text is not always accurate and Woodcock is outdated.

1950 George Woodcock and Ivan Avakumović, *The anarchist prince a biographical study of Peter Kropotkin* (London: T.V. Boardman) reprinted 1971 (NY: Schocken Books) [Studies in the libertarian and utopian tradition] 463; illus; bibliog; index. Also published 1988 (NY: Dover Publications) 557; illus. 1988 edition has new introduction and notes by Nicolas Walter.

1976 Martin A. Miller, *Kropotkin* (Chicago: The University of Chicago Press) 342; bibliog; index. Started as a dissertation. Uses MS sources.

Lamarck, Jean Baptiste Pierre Antoine de Monet (1744–1829), French biologist.

1901 Alpheus S. Packard, *Lamarck the founder of evolution; his life and work* (London: Longmans, Green, and Co.) 451; illus; bibliog; index. Includes translations of subject's writings on organic evolution.

Lanchester, Frederick William (1868–1946), English automotive engineer.

1960 P.W. Kingsford, *F.W. Lanchester the life of an engineer* (London: Edward Arnold (Publishers) Ltd.) 246; illus; bibliog. Written to help students and others "to understand 'the tiger of technology' ".

Langley, Samuel Pierpont (1834–1906), American astrophysicist.

1966 J. Gordon Vaeth, *Langley man of science and flight* (NY: The Ronald Press Company) 117; illus; bibliog; index. A "story of the man and his work" for the general reader, not scientific specialists.

Langmuir, Irving (1881–1957), American physical chemist.

1962 Albert Rosenfeld et al., *Langmuir the man and the scientist* (Oxford: Pergamon Press) 460; bibliog. Biography is part 1 (1–229), followed by subject's philosophy of science introduced by Joel H. Hildebrand and by contributions *in memoriam* by Eric Rideal and P.W. Bridgman.

Lavoisier, Antoine Laurent (1743–1794), French chemist.

1931   J.A. Cochrane, *Lavoisier* (London: Constable & Company Ltd.) 264; illus; index. Indebted to out-of-print Grimaux biography (Paris 1888, in French).

1935   Douglas McKie, *Antoine Lavoisier the father of modern chemistry* (London: Victor Gollancz) 303; illus; index. Introduction by F.G. Donnan. Author lectures in history of science. Stress is on the contribution to chemistry.

1941   Sidney J. French, *Torch and crucible the life and death of Antoine Lavoisier* (Princeton: Princeton University Press) 285; bibliog; index. Uses invented dialogue. Relies on Grimaux, though critical for passing over science.

1952   Douglas McKie, *Antoine Lavoisier scientist economist social reformer* (NY: Henry Schuman) [The Life of science library] reprinted 1980 (NY: Da Capo Press) [Da Capo Series in Science] 440; illus; bibliog; index. Also published 1952 (London: Constable) 335; illus; bibliog; index. Relies on Grimaux biography.

1970   Andrew Susac, *The clock the balance and the guillotine the life of Antoine Lavoisier* (Garden City, NY: Doubleday) 206. XX

1975   Henry Guerlac, *Antoine-Laurent Lavoisier chemist and revolutionary* (NY: Scribner) [DSB editions] 174; illus; bibliog; index. A revised and expanded version of the article which originally appeared in the *Dictionary of Scientific Biography*. XX

1985   Frederic Lawrence Holmes, *Lavoisier and the chemistry of life an exploration of scientific creativity* (Madison: University of Wisconsin Press) [Wisconsin Publications in the history of science and medicine] 565; illus; index. "Account assumes a familiarity with the broad outlines of Lavoisier's career"; recommends Guerlac 1975 as background. Objective is to portray in detail the subject's investigations, "which incorporate ideas, rather than on the ideas themselves".

1993   Arthur Donovan, *Antoine Lavoisier science administration and revolution* (Oxford: Blackwell) [Blackwell science biographies] 351; illus; bibliog; index. Aims to "render the public career . . . more intelligible, his scientific achievement more accessible, and the meaning of his life and death more comprehensible".

Lawrence, Ernest Orlando (1901–1958), American physicist.

1968   Herbert Childs, *An American genius the life of Ernest Orlando Lawrence* (NY: E.P. Dutton & Co. Inc.) 576; illus; index. Biography "for the general public", rather than "strictly scientific".

Lawson, Andrew Cowper (1861–1952), Scottish geologist.

1970   Francis E. Vaughan, *Andrew C. Lawson scientist teacher philosopher* (Glendale, CA: The Arthur H. Clark Company) 474; illus; index. Author was subject's student; book is a tribute by former students.

Leakey, Louis Seymour Bazett (1903–1972), Kenyan anthropologist and palaeontologist.

1937   autobiography, *White African* (London: Hodder and Stoughton) 320; illus. Published 1966 (Cambridge, MA: Schenkman Publishing Company, Inc.) reprinted 1973 (NY: Ballantine Books) 274; illus. 1966 has foreword by Kirtley F. Mather and a new preface by the author. Account of "the lighter side" of his "scientific expeditions in East Africa".

1974   autobiography, *By the evidence memoirs 1932–1951* (NY: Harcourt Brace Jovanovich) 276; illus; index.

1975   Sonia Cole, *Leakey's luck the life of Louis Seymour Bazett Leakey 1903–1972* (London: Collins) 448; illus; index. Commissioned by subject's wife; uses MS sources.

LeConte, Joseph (1823–1901), American biologist.

1982   Lester D. Stephens, *Joseph Leconte gentle prophet of evolution* (Baton Rouge: Louisiana State University Press) [Southern biography series] 340; illus; bibliog; index. Portrays subject as "a product of his age". Uses MS sources.

Leeuwenhoek, Antony van (1632–1723), Dutch microscopist.

1932   Clifford Dobell, *Antony von Leeuwenhoek and his "little animals" being some account of the father of protozoology and bacteriology and his multifarious discoveries in these disciplines* (London: John Bale, Sons & Danielsson, Ltd.) Reissued 1958 (NY: Russell & Russell, Inc.) and 1960 (NY: Dover Publications, Inc.) 435; illus; bibliog; index. "Collected, translated, and edited from his printed works, unpublished manuscripts, and contemporary records." Quotes extensively from MS sources. Introduction by Cornelius B. van Niel.

1959   A. Schierbeek, *Measuring the invisible world the life and works of Antoni van Leeuwenhoek FRS* (London: Abelard-Schuman) [The Life of science library] 223; illus; bibliog; index. Focuses on subject's work, with a biographical chapter by Maria Rooseboom.

1982   L.C. Palm and H.A.M. Snelders, eds, *Antoni van Leeuwenhoek 1632–1723 studies on the life and work of the Delft scientist commemorating the 350th anniversary of his birthday* (Amsterdam: Rodopi) [Nieuwe Nederlandse bijdragen tot de geschiedenis der geneeskunde en der natuurwetenschappen] 209; illus; index. "By its nature this volume is heterogenous." Uses MS sources.

Leibniz, Gottfried Wilhelm (1646–1716), German mathematician and polymath.

1929   Herbert Wildon Carr, *Leibniz* (London: Ernest Benn Limited) [Leaders of philosophy] reprinted 1960 (NY: Dover Publications, Inc.) 222; bibliog; index. Uses MS sources and focuses on subject as philosopher.

1985   E.J. Aiton, *Leibniz a biography* (Bristol: Adam Hilger Ltd.) 370; illus; bibliog; index. Uses some MS sources. Seeks broader audience than just specialists.

Leith, Charles Kenneth (1875–1956), American geologist.

1971   Sylvia Wallace McGrath, *Charles Kenneth Leith scientific adviser* (Madison: University of Wisconsin Press) 255; illus; bibliog; index. Based on MS sources.

Lemieux, Raymond U. (1920 – –), Canadian chemist.

1990   autobiography, *Explorations with sugars how sweet it was* (Washington, DC: American Chemical Society) [Profiles, pathways, and dreams: autobiographies of eminent chemists] 185; illus; index. Focuses on subject's science; contains mostly chemical formulae and equations.

Lesley, Peter J. (1819–1903), American geologist.

1909   Mary Lesley Ames, *Life and Letters of Peter and Susan Lesley* (NY: G.P. Putnam's Sons/The Knickerbocker Press) I:526 II:562; illus; index. Author is daughter of subject. Based on MS sources (family letters). "Not so much . . . a full record of the external events of their lives as . . . a faithful picture of their personalities."

Liebig, Justus von (1803–1873), German chemist.

1876   A.W. Hofmann, *The life-work of Liebig* (London: Macmillan) 145. Text is a "discourse", the Faraday lecture for 1875. Author is professor of chemistry.

1895   W.A. Shenstone, *Justus von Liebig his life and work 1803–1873* (London: Cassell and Company, Limited) [The Century Science Series] 219; index. Stresses career and achievements over private life.

Lindemann, Frederick Alexander [Viscount Cherwell] (1886–1957), English physicist (born Germany).

1961   The Earl of Birkenhead, *The Prof in Two Worlds the Official Life of Professor F.A. Lindemann Viscount Cherwell* (London: Collins) 383; illus; bibliog; index. Written at the request of subject's brother. Author a friend.

Linnaeus, Carl [from 1762 Carl von Linné] (1707–1778), Swedish botanist and zoologist.

1794   D.H. Stoever, *The life of Sir Charles Linnæus* (London: B. and J. White) 435; bibliog. Translated from German by Joseph Trapp. Based on documents and interviews with contemporaries of subject.

1837   D.C. Carr, *The life of Linnæus the celebrated Swedish naturalist* (Holt: [self-published]) 111. Author is a Norfolk schoolmaster; dedicated to his 11-year-old son, about to begin studying botany.

1844   anon., *Linnæus and Jussieu on the rise and progress of systematic botany* (London: John W. Parker) 112. Described on the title page as a popular biography with an historical introduction and sequel.

1858   Miss [Cecelia Lucy] Brightwell, *A life of Linnæus* (London: John van Voorst) 191. "Designed for the instruction and entertainment, more especially, of the young, and of those who feel that they owe a debt of gratitude" for the Linnaean system of classification.

1923   Bejamin Daydon Jackson, ed., *Linnæus afterwards Carl von Linné the story of his life adapted from the Swedish of Theodor Magnus Fries Emeritus Professor of Botany in the University of Uppsala and and brought down to the present time in the light of recent research* (London: H.F. & G. Witherby) 416; illus; bibliog; index. First published in Swedish 1903; translator/adapter is general secretary of the Linnean Society; omits part of the original including references.

1952   Knut Hagberg, *Carl Linnaeus* (London: Jonathan Cape) 264; illus. Translated from Swedish by Alan Blair. Based on subject's autobiographies and on Fries biography (Jackson 1923).

1953   Norah Gourlie, *The prince of botanists Carl Linnaeus* (London: H.F. & G. Witherby) 292; bibliog; index.

1967   Alice Dickinson, *Carl Linnaeus pioneer of modern botany* (London: Franklin Watts) 209; illus; bibliog; index.

1971   Wilfrid Blunt, *The compleat naturalist a life of Linnaeus* (London: Collins; issued in paperback 1984) 256; illus; bibliog; index. Includes an appendix by William Stearn, on Linnaean classification. Primarily for the general reader; coffee-table format.

Liouville, Joseph (1809–1882), French mathematician.

1990   Jesper Lützen, *Joseph Liouville 1809–1882 master of pure and applied mathematics* (NY: Springer-Verlag) [Studies in the history of mathematics and physical sciences] 884; illus; bibliog; index. Uses MS sources.

Lloyd, John Uri (1849–1936), American chemist and pharmacist.

1972   Corinne Miller Simons, *John Uri Lloyd his life and works 1849–1936 with a history of the Lloyd Library* (Cincinnati: privately printed by the author) 337; illus. "This chronicle intends merely to preserve and enumerate the authentic facts of his life while they are still fresh in the memories of those who knew him." Uses MS sources.

Lockyer, Joseph Norman (1836–1920), English astrophysicist.

1928   T. Mary Lockyer and Winifred L. Lockyer, *Life and work of Sir Norman Lockyer* (London: Macmillan and Co., Limited) 474; illus; index. Written by subject's second wife and his daughter, with the assistance of Prof. H. Dingle (but 1972 Meadows suggests Dingle was author and Lockyers edited). Biography followed by contributions of several of subject's colleagues, analysing his scientific discoveries.

1972   A.J. Meadows, *Science and controversy a biography of Sir Norman Lockyer* (London: Macmillan; Cambridge: MIT Press) 331; illus; index. Does not address subject's childhood. Uses MS sources.

Lodge, Oliver Joseph (1851–1940), English physicist.

1931   autobiography, *Past Years* (London: Hodder and Stoughton) 364; illus; index. Written at age eighty.

1974   W.P. Jolly, *Sir Oliver Lodge* (London: Constable) 256; illus; index. Uses MS sources.

Loeb, Jacques (1859–1924), American biologist.

1987   Philip J. Pauly, *Controlling life Jacques Loeb and the engineering ideal in biology* (NY: Oxford University Press) 252; index. Written from the perspective of "scientific work as cultural activity". Uses subject's life to examine the field in which he worked, as well as to critique the writing of the history of biology.

Logan, William (1798–1875), Canadian geologist.

1883   Bernard J. Harrington, *Life of Sir William E. Logan . . . first director of the geological survey of Canada* (Montreal: Dawson Brothers, Publishers) 432; illus; bibliog; index. Preface explains that "the work was entrusted" to author. Aims to use subject's letters, journals and reports to write a memoir; concerned with subject as a Canadian.

Lomonosov, Mikhail Vasilievich (1711–1765), Russian chemist and physicist.

1952   Boris N. Menshutkin, *Russia's Lomonosov chemist courtier physicist poet* (Princeton: Princeton University Press) 208; illus; index. Translated from the 1937 Russian edition by Jeannette Eyre Thal and Edward J. Webster under the direction of W. Chapin Huntington. Published for the Russian Translation Project of the American Council of Learned Societies.

1954   B.B. Kudryavstev, *The life and work of Mikhail Vasilyevich Lomonosov* (Moscow: Foreign Languages Publishing House) 118; illus. Patriotic point of view; popular style.

1984   G.E. Pavlova and A.S. Fedorov, *Mikhail Vasilievich Lomonosov his life and work* (Moscow: Mir Publishers) 312; illus; bibliog. Translated from the Russian edition of 1980 by Arthur Aksenov; translation edited by Richard Hainsworth. Identifies subject as the founder of Russian science.

Lovell, Bernard (1913 – –), English astronomer.

1984   Dudley Saward, *Bernard Lovell a biography* (London: Robert Hale) 320; illus; index. Based on interviews and MS sources. Author is friend of subject.

1990   autobiography, *Astronomer by chance* (London: Macmillan) 380; illus; index.

Lowell, Percival (1855–1916), American astronomer.

1935   A. Lawrence Lowell, *Biography of Percival Lowell* (NY: The Macmillan Company) 212; illus.

Lubbock, John (1834–1913), English entomologist and anthropologist.

1914   Horatio G. Hutchinson, *Life of Sir John Lubbock Lord Avebury* (London: Macmillan and Co., Limited) I:338 II:334; index. Author acquainted with subject; "the record of his achievements and of the value in which they were held by those associated in them". Uses MS sources.

Lyell, Charles (1797–1875), Scottish geologist.

1962   Edward Bailey, *Charles Lyell* (London: Thomas Nelson and Sons Ltd.) [British men of science] 214; illus; index. Focuses on subject's work and career; also discusses some of his contemporaries.

1965   F.J. North, *Sir Charles Lyell interpreter of the principles of geology* (London: Arthur Barker Limited) [Creators of the modern world] 128; illus; index. For the general reader – not an in-depth analysis of subject's work.

1972   Leonard G. Wilson, *Charles Lyell the years to 1841 the revolution in geology* (New Haven: Yale University Press) 553; illus; bibliog; index. Uses MS sources.

Lyman, Benjamin Smith (1835–1920), American geologist.

1937   Gonpei Kuwada, *Biography of Benjamin Smith Lyman* (Tokyo: published privately) 104; illus. XX

Mach, Ernst (1838–1916), Moravian physicist.

1972   John T. Blackmore, *Ernst Mach his life work and influence* (Berkeley: University of California Press) 414; illus; bibliog; index. Author calls book first full-scale biography on subject. Uses MS sources. Second half focuses on friends and opponents of subject. Aims to make him "better known to the educated public" and to "emphasize the central and controversial influence of Mach's philosophical ideas on the development of twentieth-century physics and philosophy of science".

Macintosh, Charles (1766–1843), Scottish technologist (inventor of waterproof fabrics).

1847   George Macintosh, *Biographical memoir of the late Charles Macintosh* (Glasgow: published privately) 188. Author is son of subject. Based on "authentic documents". XX

Macintosh, Charles (1839–1922), Scottish naturalist.

1923   Henry Coates, *A Perthshire Naturalist Charles Macintosh of Inver* (London: T. Fisher Unwin Ltd.) 244; illus; bibliog; index. With introduction by J. Arthur Thomson and Patrick Geddes, and a chapter on Scottish folk-music by Herbert Wiseman. Occasion was death of subject, whom the author met at the 1875 Perth Fungus Show. Includes material on social life in the Highlands. Abridged edition 1924 under title *Charlie Macintosh post-runner naturalist & musician* 142; illus.

Mairan, Jean Jacques d'Ortous de (1678–1771), French physicist.

1970   Abby R. Kleinbaum, "Jean Jacques Dortous de Mairan (1678–1771) a study of an enlightenment scientist" (Columbia University PhD dissertation). XX

Malesherbes, Chrétien Guillaume de Lamoignon de (1721–1794), French agronomist and botanist.

1938   John M.S. Allison, *Lamoignon de Malesherbes defender and reformer of the French monarchy 1721–1794* (New Haven: Yale University Press) 177; illus; index. Uses MS sources, but author was unable to obtain access to all of subject's papers; contains bibliographical note. Not concerned with subject's work in science.

Mantell, Gideon Algernon (1790–1852), English geologist.

1927   Sidney Spokes, *Gideon Algernon Mantell LlD FRCS FRS Surgeon and geologist* (London: John Bale, Sons & Danielsson, Ltd) 263; illus; index. Based on printed records and some MS letters; does not claim to be considered a "whole-truth" biography.

Marconi, Guglielmo (1874–1937), Italian engineer and physicist.

1935   B.L. Jacot [de Boinod] and D.M.B. Collier, *Marconi Master of Space* (London: Hutchinson & Co.) 287; illus. XX

1937   Orrin E. Dunlap, *Marconi the man and his wireless* (NY: The Macmillan Company) 306; illus; index. Endorsed by subject; enthusiastic tribute.

1943   Douglas Coe [Samuel Epstein and Beryl (Williams) Epstein], *Marconi pioneer of radio* (NY: J. Messner, Inc.) 272; illus; bibliog. Illustrated by Kreigh Collins. XX

1962   Degna Marconi, *My father Marconi* (London: Frederick Muller, Limited) 306; illus; index. Second edition, with minor revisions, 1982 (Ottawa: Balmuir Book Publishing Ltd.) 258; illus. Based on interviews, MS sources and family memories.

1972   W.P. Jolly, *Marconi* (London: Constable) 292; illus; index. No introduction. Uses MS sources.

1992   Mary K. MacLeod, *Whisper in the air Marconi the Canada years 1902–1946* (Hantsport, Nova Scotia: Lancelot Press) 135; illus; bibliog. Uses MS sources.

Marey, Etienne-Jules (1830–1904), French pioneer of photography.

1992   Marta Braun, *Picturing time the work of Etienne-Jules Marey (1830–1904)* (Chicago: University of Chicago Press) 450; illus; bibliog; index. Author a scholar of film and photography. Based on newly discovered photographic archives, interviews with associates of subject and MS sources. Text is divided to discuss subject's "work" and "legacy" and is followed by three catalogue appendices.

Mark, Herman Francis (1895–1992), Austrian organic chemist.

1993   autobiography, *From small organic molecules to large a century of progress* (Washington, DC: American Chemical Society) [Profiles, pathways, and dreams: autobiographies of eminent chemists] 148; illus; index.

Markham, Clements Robert (1830–1916), English geographer.

1917   Albert H. Markham, *The life of Sir Clements R Markham KCB FRS LLD* (London: John Murray) 384. Uses MS sources.

Marsh, Othniel Charles (1831–1899), American palaeontologist.

1940   Charles Schuchert and Clara Mae LeVene, *O.C. Marsh pioneer in palaeontology* (New Haven: Yale University Press) reprinted 1978 (NY: Arno Press) [Biologists and their world] 541; illus; index. "No attempt to minimize the unfortunate aspects of his career, but with strong emphasis on his far-reaching achievements in Vertebrate Paleontology." Uses MSS.

Martin, Benjamin (1704(?)–1782), English scientific instrument-maker.

1976   John R. Millburn, *Benjamin Martin author instrument-maker and country showman* (Leyden: Noordhoff International Publishing) 244; illus; index. Lack of archival sources on subject's early life results in abbreviated treatment.

Marum, Martinus van (1750?–1830), Dutch botanist and naturalist.

1969–76   Robert James Forbes, E. Lefebvre and J.G. de Bruijn, eds, *Martinus van Marum life and work* (Haarlem: H.D. Tjeenk Willink & Zoon) I:415 II:401 III:386 IV:401 V:445 VI:435; illus; bibliog; index. Each chapter is by a different author. Uses MS sources and includes translations of some of subject's works and correspondence.

Maskelyne, Nevil (1732–1811), English astronomer.

1989   Derek Howse, *Nevil Maskelyne the seaman's astronomer* (Cambridge: Cambridge University Press) 280; illus; bibliog; index. Foreword by Sir Francis Graham Smith. First biography; written for the general reader as well as for the scientific historian.

Maury, Matthew Fontaine (1806–1873), American oceanographer.

1888   Diana Fontaine Maury Corbin, *A life of Matthew Fontaine Maury U.S.N. and C.S.N.* (London: Sampson Low, Marston, Searle & Rivington) 326. Author is subject's daughter. Purpose is "to establish the claim of its subject to a place among the greatest benefactors of his race". Williams blames publisher for the errors.

1927   Charles Lee Lewis, *Matthew Fontaine Maury the pathfinder of the seas* (Annapolis: The United States Naval Institute) reprinted 1969 (NY: AMS Press) and 1980 (NY: Arno Press) [Navies and men] 264; illus; bibliog; index. Author is on faculty of US Naval Academy; foreword by Richard E. Byrd, Commander USN (Retired). Based chiefly on subject's papers; refers to Corbin's *Life*; Williams says it is basically sound but some areas are covered inadequately.

1928   Jacquelin Ambler Caskie, *Life and letters of Matthew Fontaine Maury* (Richmond, VA: Richmond Press, Inc.) 191; illus.

1930   John Wayland, *The pathfinder of the seas the life of Matthew Fontaine Maury* (Richmond: Garrett & Massie, Inc.) 191; illus; index. Introduction by William J. Showalter; acknowledges debt to earlier writers, and claims many new facts.

1943   Hildegarde Hawthorne, *Matthew Fontaine Maury trail maker of the seas* (NY: Longmans, Green and Co.) 226. No introduction or notes.

1963   Frances Leigh Williams. *Matthew Fontaine Maury scientist of the sea* (New Brunswick, NJ: Rutgers University Press) 720; illus; bibliog; index. For both specialist and general reader; corrects many errors in early biographies.

1966   Frances Leigh Williams, *Ocean Pathfinder a biography of Matthew Fontaine Maury* (NY: Harcourt, Brace & World, Inc.) 192; illus; index. Foreword refers only to four years of research, not to her earlier book. Dialogue is based on things subject and contemporaries said or wrote, but sometimes changed for the sake of brevity.

Mawson, Douglas (1882–1958), English geologist.

1964   Paquita Mawson, *Mawson of the Antarctic the life of Sir Douglas Mawson FRS OBE* (London: Longmans) 240; illus; index. Foreword by HRH the Duke of Edinburgh. Author is subject's widow.

Maxwell, James Clerk (1831–1879), Scottish physicist.

1882   Lewis Campbell and William Garnett, *The life of James Clerk Maxwell with a selection from his correspondence and occasional writings and a sketch of his contributions to science* (London: Macmillan) 662. New edition abridged and revised 1884, 421. Based on MS materials and memories of contemporaries. Appends poems and stresses early life. New edition corrects errors, adds material and suppresses "some doubtful statements". Selection of poems is smaller than first edition, and Cambridge essays are relegated to an Appendix.

1896   R.T. Glazebrook, *James Clerk Maxwell and modern physics* (London: Cassell and Company) [The Century Science Series] 224; index. Based on 1882 Campbell and Garnett.

1975   C.W.F. Everitt, *James Clerk Maxwell physicist and natural philosopher* (NY:

Charles Scribner's Sons) [*DSB* Editions] 205; illus; bibliog; index. Author a professor of physics. Series consists of books developed and expanded from articles in the *Dictionary of Scientific Biography* (which is published by Scribner's).

1981 Ivan Tolstoy, *James Clerk Maxwell a biography* (Edinburgh: Canongate) 184; illus; bibliog; index. "A book for the lay reader", not a definitive biography. Emphasis is on subject's "wholeness".

1983 Martin Goldman, *The demon in the aether the story of James Clerk Maxwell* (Edinburgh: Paul Harris Publishing) 224; index.

Mayer, Julius Robert von (1814–1878), German physicist.

1993 Kenneth L. Caneva, *Robert Mayer and the conservation of energy* (Princeton: Princeton University Press) 439; illus; bibliog; index. Author an historian of science. Based on MS sources. Not a biography in the conventional sense, but "attempts a meaningful integration of Mayer's life and work", and to situate him in the contemporary intellectual context.

McAdam, John Loudon (1756–1836), Scottish engineer.

1936 Roy Devereux [Margaret Rose Roy (McAdam) Pember-Devereux], *John Loudon McAdam chapters in the history of highways* (London: Oxford University Press/Humphrey Milford) 184; illus; bibliog. Based on MS sources and government documents. Author is great-great-granddaughter of subject. Copyright held by author and Tarmac Limited.

1980 W.J. Reader, *Macadam the McAdam family and the turnpike roads 1798–1861* (London: Heinemann) 242; illus; bibliog; index.

McCollum, Elmer Verner (1879–1967), American organic chemist.

1964 autobiography, *From Kansas farm boy to scientist the autobiography of Elmer Verner McCollum* (Lawrence: University of Kansas Press) 253; illus; index.

McCormick, Cyrus Hall (1809–1884), American agricultural engineer.

1909 Herbert N. Casson, *Cyprus Hall McCormick his life and work* (Chicago: A.C. McClurg & Co.) 264; illus; index.

1930–35 William T. Hutchinson, *Cyrus Hall McCormick* (NY: The Century Co.) I: 493 II:793; illus; index. Based on MS sources. Foreword by William E. Dodd. Volume 1 subtitled *Seed-time 1809–1856*; volume 2 subtitled *Harvest 1856–1884*.

McLennan, John Cunningham (1867–1935) Canadian physicist.

1939 H.H. Langton, *Sir John Cunningham McLennan a memoir* (Toronto: University of Toronto Press) 123; illus; bibliog. Includes a chapter on subject's scientific work by E.F. Burton.

Mendel, Johann Gregor (1822–1884), Czech geneticist.

1932   Hugo Iltis, *Life of Mendel* (London: George Allen & Unwin Ltd.) 336; illus; bibliog; index. Reprinted 1966. Translation of 1924 German edition by Eden and Cedar Paul. Preface stresses the paucity of sources.

Mendeléeff, Dmitry Ivanovich (1834–1907), Russian chemist.

1954   O.N. Pisarzhevsky, *Dmitry Ivanovich Mendeleyev his life and work* (Moscow: Foreign Languages Publishing House) [Men of Russian Science] 101; illus.

Mercer, John (1791–1866), English textile chemist.

1886   Edward A. Parnell, *The life and labours of John Mercer FRS FCS etc the self-taught chemical philosopher* (London: Longmans, Green, and Co.) 342; index. Attempts to "do justice to Mr Mercer as a man, a technical inventor, and a chemist".

Merriam, Clinton Hart (1855–1942), American biologist.

1977   Keir B. Sterling, *Last of the naturalists the career of C. Hart Merriam* (NY: Arno Press) [Natural sciences in America] 472; illus; bibliog; index. Revised from author's dissertation. Uses MS sources.

Merrifield, Robert Bruce (1921 – –), American peptide chemist.

1993   autobiography, *Life during a golden age of peptide chemistry The concept and development of solid-phase peptide synthesis* (Washington: American Chemical Society) [Profiles, pathways, and dreams: autobiographies of eminent chemists] 297; illus; bibliog; index.

Me(t)chnikov, Ilya (Elie) (1845–1916), Ukrainian zoologist.

1921   Olga Metchnikoff, *Life of Elie Metchnikoff 1845–1916* (London: Constable and Company Ltd.) 297; bibliog; index. Preface by Ray Lankester. Author is wife of subject.

Michelson, Albert Abraham (1852–1931), American physicist and optician (born Poland).

1958   John Henry Wilson, *Albert A. Michelson America's first Nobel prize physicist* (NY: J. Messner) 190. XX

1960   Bernard Jaffe, *Michelson and the speed of light* (Garden City, NY: Anchor Books) reprinted 1979 (Westport, CT: Greenwood Press) 197; illus; bibliog; index. XX

1973   Dorothy Michelson Livingstone, *The master of light a biography of Albert A. Michelson* (NY: Charles Scribner's Sons; Chicago: University of Chicago Press) 376; illus; index. Author is daughter of subject.

Michurin, Ivan Vladimirovich (1855–1935), naturalist.

1954   A.N. Bakharev, *I.V. Michurin the great remaker of nature* (Moscow: Foreign Languages Publishing House) 151; illus. Translated from Russian; Soviet perspective.

Miller, Hugh (1802–1856), Scottish geologist.

1854   autobiography, *My schools and schoolmasters or the story of my education* (Boston, Lincs.: Gould and Lincoln) 537; another edition 1857 (Edinburgh: T. Constable and Co.) 562; another edition 1870 (London: William P. Nimmo) 562. Michael Shortland, in an edition of an earlier brief memoir of Miller's edited by him and published 1995 says that this was a reworking of that document, and became a classic of working-class autobiography.

1858   Thomas N. Brown, *The life and times of Hugh Miller* (NY: Rudd & Carleton; Glasgow: Richard Griffin & Co.) 346. Second edition 1858, *Labour & Triumph the life and times of Hugh Miller* (Glasgow: Richard Griffin and Company) 315. Characterizes subject as "Scotland's representative man". Based on public documents; no personal material used.

1871   Peter Bayne, The life and letters of Hugh Miller (London: Strahan & Co.; NY: Hurst & Company) I:431 II:497; 2 vols. Author is subject's successor as editor of the *Witness*. American edition has publishers' prefatory note.

1896   W. Keith Leask, *Hugh Miller* (Edinburgh: Oliphant Anderson & Ferrier [Famous Scots Series]; NY: Charles Scribner's Sons) 157; bibliog. Notes that complete life is impossible because MS material was lost.

1981   George Rosie, *Hugh Miller outrage and order a biography and selected writings* (Edinburgh: Mainstream Publishing) 236; bibliog. Introduction by Neal Ascherson. Written to redress the "shameful neglect" of subject's work in the twentieth century. Calls for "a full-scale modern biography".

Millikan, Robert Andrews (1868–1953), American physicist.

1950   autobiography, *The autobiography of Robert A. Millikan* (NY: Prentice-Hall, Inc.) 311; illus; index. "This book represents an effort to record and appraise some of the changes which have come under the eyes of one particular observer of the rapidly changing scene."

1982   Robert H. Kargon, *The rise of Robert Millikan portrait of a life in American science* (Ithaca: Cornell University Press) 204; illus; bibliog; index. Uses MS sources. Not a full biography; "an essay . . . on themes that are illustrated and illuminated by Millikan's life in American science".

Milne, John (1850–1913), English seismologist.

1980   A.L. Herbert-Gustar and P.A. Nott, *John Milne father of modern seismology* (Tenterden, Kent: Paul Norbury Publications Limited) 196; illus; bibliog. "No experience in the field of seismology is required by the reader." Includes anecdotes.

Mitchell, John (1711–1768), American botanist.

1974   Edmund Berkeley and Dorothy Smith Berkeley, *Dr John Mitchell the man who made the map of North America* (Chapel Hill: University of North Carolina Press) 283; illus; bibliog; index.

Mitchell, Maria (1818–1889), American astronomer.

1896   Phebe Mitchell Kendall, *Maria Mitchell life letters and journals* (Boston: Lee and Shepard Publishers) reprinted 1971 (Freeport, NY: Books for Libraries Press) 293; illus. Wright says Kendall destroyed much personal and undignified material.

1949   Helen Wright, *Sweeper in the sky the life of Maria Mitchell first woman astronomer in America* (NY: The Macmillan Company) 253; illus; bibliog; index. Based on MS material.

Mivart, St George Jackson (1827–1900), English biologist and naturalist.

1960   Jacob W. Gruber, *A conscience in conflict the life of St George Jackson Mivart* (NY: Columbia University Press for Temple University Publications) 266; index. "Concern with Mivart is not so much with the man as with the mind"; discusses subject's conflicts with the Catholic Church. Uses MS sources.

Molyneux, William (1656–1698), Irish astronomer and physicist.

1982   J.G. Simms, *William Molyneux of Dublin 1656–1698* (Blackrock: Irish Academic Press) 176; illus; bibliog; index. Author died before revisions complete; edited by P.H. Kelly.

Mond, Ludwig (1839–1909), German industrial chemist.

1956   J.M. Cohen, *The life of Ludwig Mond* (London: Methuen & Co. Ltd.) 295; illus; index. Includes a note by Robert Mathias, nephew of subject and foreword by Sir Alexander Fleck, chairman of Imperial Chemical Industries.

Montgomery, Edmund (1835–1911), Scottish cell biologist and philosopher.

1951   I.K. Stevens, *The hermit philosopher of Liendo* (Dallas: Southern Methodist University Press) 402; illus; bibliog; index. "A thorough study of his writings in light of their setting in contemporary thought and in comparison with currently accepted notions."

Moore, Jonas (1617–1679), English mathematician.

1993   Frances Willmoth, *Sir Jonas Moore practical mathematics and restoration science* (Woodbridge, Suffolk: Boydell Press) 244; illus; bibliog; index. Seeks to correct John Aubrey's and earlier biographical sketches; began as a PhD dissertation.

Morgan, Thomas Hunt (1866–1945), American geneticist.

1976 Ian Shine and Sylvia Wrobel, *Thomas Hunt Morgan pioneer of genetics* (Lexington: The University Press of Kentucky) [The Kentucky Bicentennial Bookshelf] 159; illus; bibliog; index. Presents subject as a neglected scientist and Kentuckian. Foreword by George W. Beadle.

1978 Garland E. Allen, *Thomas Hunt Morgan the man and his science* (Princeton: Princeton University Press) 447; illus; bibliog; index. Focuses on "the personal and scientific work" of subject; form is a "scientific biography", in that it uses the life to explore the science in contemporary context.

Morland, Samuel (1625–1695), English mathematician and technologist.

1970 H.W. Dickinson, *Sir Samuel Morland diplomat and inventor 1625–1695* (Cambridge: W. Heffer and Sons Limited for the Newcomen Society) [Newcomen Society for the Study of the History of Engineering and Technology, Extra Publication] 133; illus; bibliog; index. Occasion is fiftieth anniversary of Newcomen Society and centenary of author, who was keeper of Mechanical Engineering at the Science Museum, London.

Morley, Edward Williams (1838–1923), American chemist and physicist.

1957 Howard Williams, *Edward Williams Morley his influence on science in America* (Easton, PA: Chemical Education Publishing Company) 282; illus; bibliog. Author is teacher of chemistry. Uses MS sources.

Morse, Jedidiah (1761–1826), American geographer.

1874 William Sprague, *The life of Jedidiah Morse, D.D.* (NY: Anson D.F. Randolph & Company) 333; index. First "continuous history of his life"; chronology followed by chapters on diverse aspects, including chapter 3 on subject's "labours as a geographer".

1983 Joseph W. Phillips, *Jedidiah Morse and New England Congregationalism* (New Brunswick, NJ: Rutgers University Press) 290; index; bibliog. Attempts to explain subject's career "in the context of the development of evangelical Protestantism". Uses MS sources.

Morse, Philip McCord, 1903 – – , American physicist.

1977 autobiography, *In at the beginnings: a physicist's life* (Cambridge MA: The MIT Press) 375; illus; index. Seeks to provide the story of an average scientist, "at the second, rather than at the top, level".

Morse, Samuel Finley Breese (1791–1872), American artist and telegraph technologist.

1875 Samuel Irenæus Prime, *The life of Samuel F.B. Morse LlD inventor of the electromagnetic recording telegraph* (NY: D. Appleton and Company) reprinted 1974 (NY: Arno Press) [Telecommunications] 776; illus. Prepared at request of subject's executors.

1943   Carleton Mabee, *The American Leonardo a life of Samuel F.B. Morse* (NY: Alfred A. Knopf) 420; illus; index. Introduction by Allan Nevins.

1989   Paul J. Staiti, *Samuel F.B. Morse* (Cambridge: Cambridge University Press) [Cambridge monographs on American artists] 298; illus; bibliog; index. Juxtaposes narrative and interpretation to "advance a novel view of a familiar figure in American art".

Moseley, Henry Gwyn Jeffreys (1887–1915), English physicist.

1974   J.L. Heilbron, *H.G.J. Mosely the life and letters of an English physicist 1887–1915* (Berkeley: University of California Press) 312; illus; bibliog; index. Stresses subject's self-conscious utilization of the "gradually increasing opportunities for scientific careers". Life is 1–139; remainder is full text of most letters.

Mott, Nevill Francis (1905 – –), English physicist.

1986   autobiography, *A life in science* (London: Taylor & Francis) 198; illus; index. Written "because I have lived through a heroic period in the development of science", during which less has been written about solid state physics than other fields.

Müller, Ferdinand von (1825–1896), Australian naturalist (born Germany).

1981   Edward Kynaston, *A man on edge a life of Baron Sir Ferdinand von Mueller* (London: Allen Lane) 389; bibliog; index.

Muller, Fleimann Joseph (1890–1967), American geneticist.

1981   Elof Axel Carlson, *Genes radiation and society the life and work of H.J. Muller* (Ithaca: Cornell University Press) 457; illus; index. "Guided by the belief that Muller's life was symbolic of the human plight in the twentieth century." Uses MS sources.

Murchison, Roderick Impey (1792–1871), Scottish geologist.

1875   Archibald Geikie, *Life of Sir Roderick I. Murchison based on his journals and letters with notices of his scientific contemporaries and a sketch of the rise and growth of palaeozoic geology in Britain* (London: John Murray) I:378 II:375; illus; bibliog; index.

1989   Robert A. Stafford, *Scientist of empire Sir Robert Murchison scientific exploration and Victorian imperialism* (Cambridge: Cambridge University Press) 293; illus; bibliog; index. Focuses on subject's work. Uses MS sources.

Muybridge, Eadweard James (1830–1904), American technologist (investigator of animal locomotion by photography) (born England).

1975   Gordon Hendricks, *Eadweard Muybridge the father of the motion picture* (NY: Grossman Publishers) 271; illus; bibliog; index. Author a student of film history.

1976   Robert Bartlett Haas, *Muybridge man in motion* (Berkeley: University of California Press) 207; illus; index. Based on MS and printed sources and subject's photographs, with which the book is illustrated.

Nakanishi, Koji (1925 – –), Japanese organic chemist (born Hong Kong).

1991   autobiography, *A wandering natural products chemist* (Washington, DC: American Chemical Society) [Profiles, pathways, and dreams: autobiographies of eminent chemists] 230; illus; index. Contains mostly science.

Nansen, Fridtjof (1861–1930), Norwegian zoologist and explorer.

1896   W.C. Brögger and Nordahl Rolfsen, *Fridtiof Nansen 1861–1893* (London: Longmans, Green, and Co.) 402; illus; index. Translated by William Archer from a Copenhagen edition of 1893 written while the fate of subject's expedition was unknown; translator's preface states successful outcome.

[1897]   J. Arthur Bain, *Life of Fridtjof Nansen Scientist and Explorer* (London: Simpkin Marshall, Hamilton, Kent & Co. Ltd; Sheffield: J. Arthur Bain) 290; illus. New edition [1897] revised and enlarged under title *Life and Explorations of Fridtjof Nansen* and later as *Life and adventures of Nansen the great Arctic explorer* (London: The Walter Scott Publishing Co., Ltd.) [Evergreen Library] 449; illus. Abridged edition 1897 under title *Fridtjof Nansen his life and explorations* (London: Partridge) 160; illus. Author a bookseller and traveller, friend of subject. Includes an account of the 1893–96 expedition. Preface dated January 1897; revised edition preface December 1897.

1930   S. Stuart Starritt, *The Life of Nansen* (London: The Religious Tract Society) 143; illus. Popular style.

1932   E.E. Reynolds, *Nansen* (London: Geoffrey Bles) 274; illus; bibliog; index. Offers "a straightforward account of the chief incidents in his public life".

1933   Charles Turley, *Nansen of Norway* (London: Methuen & Co.) 210; index. Based on earlier biographies.

1959   Edward Shackleton, *Nansen the explorer* (London: H.F. & G. Witherby Ltd.) 209; illus; index. Relies "almost wholly on published sources".

Nasmyth, James (1808–1890), Scottish engineer.

1883   autobiography, *James Nasmyth engineer an autobiography* (London: John Murray) 450; illus; index. New edition revised and corrected (NY: Harper) 461. Edited by Samuel Smiles.

Nef, John Ulrie (1862–1915), Swiss chemist.

1973   autobiography, *Search for meaning the autobiography of a nonconformist* (Washington: Public Affairs Press) 349; bibliog. "The story told in this book suggests that the most stable foundation for happiness rests with a new humanism for a united humanity."

Nelson, Aven (1859–1952), American botanist.

1984   Roger L. Williams, *Aven Nelson of Wyoming* (Boulder: Colorado Associated University Press) 407; illus; bibliog; index. Based on MS sources.

Nernst, Hermann Walther (1864–1941), German chemist.

1973   Kurt Mendelssohn, *The world of Walther Nernst the rise and fall of German science* (London: Macmillan; Pittsburgh: University of Pittsburgh Press) 191; illus; index.

Newcomb, Simon (1835–1909), American astronomer.

1903   autobiography *The reminiscences of an astronomer* (Boston and NY: Houghton, Mifflin and Company; Cambridge: The Riverside Press) 424; index.

Newcomen, Thomas, (1663–1729), English engineer.

1963   L.T.C. Rolt, *Thomas Newcomen the prehistory of the steam engine* (Dawlish: David and Charles; London: Macdonald) 158; illus; bibliog; index. Life of subject is embedded in a narrative of the development of the technology and the people involved with it.

Newsom, Carroll V. (1904 – –), American mathematician.

1983   autobiography, *Problems are for solving an autobiography* (Bryn Mawr: Dorrance & Company) 353.

Newton, Isaac (1642–1727), English natural philosopher and mathematician.

1831   David Brewster, *The life of Sir Isaac Newton* (London: John Murray) 366; illus. New edition 1875 (London: William Tegg & Co.) 346. Based on MS materials. Occasion is centenary. 1875 is revised and edited by W.T. Lynn, who notes author's death in 1868; follows the text of 1831 but collates it with the 1855 biography and adds notes to bring it up to date.

1855   David Brewster, *Memoirs of the life writings, and discoveries of Sir Isaac Newton* (Edinburgh: Thomas Constable and Co.) reprinted 1965 (NY: Johnson Reprint Cor.) [The Sources of Science] I:478 II:564; illus; index. Second edition 1860 (Edinburgh: Edmonston and Douglas). Based on MS sources, including some not available for author's 1831 biography. 1965 reprint has new introduction by Richard S. Westfall.

1858   E.F. King, *A biographical sketch of Sir Isaac Newton* (Grantham: S. Ridge & Son; London: Simpkin, Marshall, & Co.) 118. Includes reports of orations at the inauguration of the statue at Grantham. Compiled from Brewster 1831 and other works.

1927   S. Brodetsky, *Sir Isaac Newton a brief account of his life and work* (London: Methuen & Co.; Boston: J.W. Luce, 1928) 161; illus; index. For the general reader, including children, who seek insight into the heroes of science.

1931   R. De Villamil, *Newton the man* (London: Gordon D. Knox) reprinted 1972 (NY: Johnson Reprint Corporation) [The Sources of Science] 111. Foreword by Albert Einstein. Introduction to the reprint, by I. Bernard Cohen, notes that this is a "kind of 'mystery book' for historians of science" – little is known of the author and there are "curious" bibliographical problems, since Knox was not a regular imprint. Book includes catalogue of subject's library.

1934   Louis Trenchard More, *Isaac Newton a biography* (NY: Charles Scribner's Sons) reprinted 1962 (NY: Dover Publications) 675; bibliog; index. Uses MS sources. Westfall (1980) says it failed to supersede Brewster (1855).

1938   J.W.N. Sullivan, *Isaac Newton 1642–1727* (London: Macmillan and Co.) 275. Includes memoir of the author (a science writer) by Charles Singer.

1939   John Dougall, *Sir Isaac Newton* (London: Blackie & Son) 208; illus. XX

1950   E.N. da C. Andrade, *Sir Isaac Newton his life and work* (London: Max Parrish) [Personal portraits] 111; illus. Also published 1954 (London: Collins; Garden City, NY: Doubleday) [Brief Lives] reprinted 1958 (Garden City, NY: Doubleday/Anchor Books [Science Study Series] 144; illus. Author's personal admiration for subject is stressed. Westfall (1980) calls this the best of the popular biographies.

1960   H.D. Anthony, *Sir Isaac Newton* (London: Abelard-Schuman) [Life of Science Library] 224; illus; bibliog; index. Also published 1961 (NY: Collier Books) 188; index; bibliog. Occasion is tercentenary of the Royal Society. Includes newly discovered MS sources.

1968   Frank E. Manuel, *A portrait of Isaac Newton* (Cambridge: The Belknap Press of Harvard University Press) 478; illus; index. A psychoanalytic interpretation; according to Westfall (1980) does not attempt to deal with the scientific career.

1980   Richard S. Westfall, *Never at rest a biography of Isaac Newton* (Cambridge: Cambridge University Press; paperback edition 1993) 908; illus; bibliog; index. Focus is on Newton the scientist, and on the science as "a developing endeavour". Preface to paperback comments on reviews and says typographical and factual errors corrected.

1984   Gale E. Christianson, *In the presence of the Creator Isaac Newton and his times* (NY: Free Press; London: Collier Macmillan) 623; illus; bibliog; index.

1992   A. Rupert Hall, *Isaac Newton adventurer in thought* (Oxford: Blackwell) [Blackwell science biographies] 468; illus; bibliog; index. "Chiefly directed to Newton the mathematician and philosopher."

1993   Richard S. Westfall, *The life of Isaac Newton* (Cambridge: Cambridge University Press; Canto paperback edition 1994) 328; illus; bibliog; index. A condensation of Westfall 1980, with reduced technical content, aimed at a general audience; no footnotes.

Neyman, Jerzy (1894–1981), American mathematician (born Russia).

1982   Constance Reid, *Neyman from life* (NY: Springer-Verlag) 298; illus; index. Based on interviews with subject, his papers, and recollections of others.

Niépce, Joseph Nicéphore (1765–1833), French photography technologist.

1935   Victor Fouque, *The truth concerning the invention of photography Nicéphore Niépce his life letters and works* (NY: Tennant and Ward) reprinted 1973 (NY: Arno Press) [The Literature of Photography] 163. Translated from the 1867 Paris edition by by Edward Epstein, who notes: "This translation is offered not to the casual reader or as a literary work, but to the student of the History of Photography." Uses MS sources.

Nobel, Alfred Bernhard (1833–1896), Swedish inventor and philanthropist.

1929   Ragnar Sohlman and Henrik Schück, *Nobel dynamite and peace* (NY: Cosmopolitan Book Corporation) 353; illus. British edition called *The life of Alfred Nobel* 353; illus. Translated by Brian and Beatrix Lunn. Quotes extensively from subject's correspondence.

1942   Herta E. Pauli, *Alfred Nobel dynamite king architect of peace* (NY: L.B. Fischer) 325.

1960   Nicholas Halasz, *Nobel a biography* (London: Robert Hale Limited) 189; illus; index. No introduction, table of contents, chapter titles or documentation. Contains invented dialogue; contains little on subject's childhood and emphasizes political issues. Uses MS sources.

1962   Erik Bergengren, *Alred Nobel the man and his work* (London: Thomas Nelson and Sons Ltd.) 222; illus; bibliog; index. Translated from 1960 Swedish edition by Alan Blair, with a supplement on the Nobel institutions and the Nobel prizes by Nils. K. Staåhle. Tells of "the man behind the work", criticizes previous biographies as "romanticized". Uses MSS.

1993   Kenne Fant, *Alfred Nobel a biography* (NY: Arcade Publishing) 342; illus; index. Translated from 1991 Swedish edition by Marianne Ruth. Uses MS sources.

Noether, Amalie Emmy (1882–1935), German mathematician.

1981   James W. Brewer and Martha K. Smith, eds, *Emmy Noether a tribute to her life and work* (NY: Mariel Dekkek, Inc.) [Monographs and textbooks in pure and applied mathematics] 180; index. "This book progresses from the primarily biographical to the primarily mathematical."

1981   Auguste Dick, *Emmy Noether 1882–1935* (Boston: Birkhäuser) 193; illus; index. Translated by H.I. Blocher. Uses MS sources.

Nordenskiöld, Nils Adolf Erik (1832–1901), Finnish geographer and explorer.

1973   George Kish, *North-east passage Adolf Nordenskiöld his life and times* (Amsterdam: Nico Israel) 283; illus; index. "The story of a man, of a land reborn, Sweden, and of a time of change, the nineteenth century." Uses MSS.

Nozoe, Tetsuo (1902 – –), Japanese organic chemist.

1991 autobiography, *Seventy years in organic chemistry* (Washington: American Chemical Society) [Profiles, pathways, and dreams: autobiographies of eminent chemists] 267; illus; bibliog; index. XX

Nuttall, Thomas (1786–1859), English botanist and ornithologist.

1967 Jeanette E. Graustein, *Thomas Nuttall explorations in America* (Cambridge: Harvard University Press) 481; illus; index. Critical of previous writings on subject as inaccurate. Uses MS sources.

Oken (or Okenfuss), Lorenz (1779–1851), German natural philosopher.

1883 Alexander Ecker, *Lorenz Oken a biographical sketch* (London: Kegan Paul, Trench & Co.) 183; bibliog. Translated by Alfred Tulk from 1880 Stuttgart edition; occasion is centenary; includes selections from subject's correspondence. Aim was to collect, correct and amplify scattered materials for a biography.

Oliphant, Marcus Laurence Elwin (1901 – –), Australian nuclear physicist.

1981 Stewart Cockburn and David Ellyard, *Oliphant the life and times of Sir Mark Oliphant* (Adelaide: Axiom Books) 369; illus; bibliog; index. Foreword by Paul Hasluck notes that the text analyses the subject's place in Australian history, political as well as scientific.

Oppenheimer, J. Robert (1904–1967), American theoretical physicist.

1969 Peter Michelmore, *The Swift years the Robert Oppenheimer story* (NY: Dodd, Mead) 273; illus; bibliog; index. Uses MS sources.

[1969] Denise Royal, *The story of J. Robert Oppenheimer* (NY: St Martin's Press) 196; illus; bibliog; index. "The influence of the times on the man, and the impact of the man on his times."

1980 Peter Goodchild, *J. Robert Oppenheimer "Shatterer of worlds"* (London: British Broadcasting Corporation) 301; illus; bibliog. Published in conjunction with the BBC/WGBH television series.

Oughtred, William (1575–1660), English mathematician.

1916 Florian Cajori, *William Oughtred a great seventeenth-century teacher of mathematics* (Chicago: The Chicago Open Court Publishing Company) 100; index. Organized thematically; focuses on subject's work and influence.

Owen, David Dale (1807–1860), American geologist (born Scotland).

1943   W.B. Hendrickson, *David Dale Owen Pioneer geologist of the middle west* (Indianapolis: The Indiana Historical Bureau) [Indiana Historical Collections] 180; illus; bibliog. XX

Owen, Richard (1804–1892), English anatomist.

1894–95   Richard Owen, *The life of Richard Owen* (London: John Murray) I:409 II:393; illus; index. Author is subject's grandson. "With the scientific portions revised by C. Davies Sherborn and an essay by the Right. Hon. T.H. Huxley, F.R.S." Uses MS sources.

1992   Jacob W. Gruber and John C. Thackeray, *Richard Owen commemoration three studies* (London: Natural History Museum Publications) 181; illus; bibliog; index. Uses MS sources.

Palmer, Edward (1831–1911), American naturalist (born England).

1956   Rogers McVaugh, *Edward Palmer plant explorer of the American West* (Norman: University of Oklahoma Press) 430; illus. XX

Parkes, Alan S. (1900 – –), English biologist.

1985   autobiography, *Alan S. Parkes off-beat biologist* (Cambridge: The Galton Foundation) 485; illus; index. Primarily "a work of reminiscence". Publisher is a registered charity.

1988   autobiography, *Biologist at large the background to off-beat biologist* (Cambridge: published by the author) 465; illus; index. "In writing *off-beat*, it had become obvious that one volume... would not accommodate all I had to say." Written for relatives, friends and colleagues, and for biographers and archivists.

Parsons, Charles Algernon (1854–1931), Irish engineer.

1933   Rollo Appleyard, *Charles Parsons his life and work* (London: Constable & Co. Ltd.) 334; illus; bibliog; index.

Pascal, Blaise (1623–1662), French mathematician and physicist.

1844   Gilberte Perier, *The life of Mr Paschal with his letters relating to the Jesuits* (London: printed for the author) I:228 II:320. Translated into English by "W.A.".

1902   Emile Boutroux, *Pascal* (Manchester: Sherratt and Hughes) 211; illus; index. Translated by Ellen Margaret Creak. Text is followed by 71 separately paginated pages of notes. Emphasis is religious.

1909   Viscount St Cyres, *Pascal* (London: Smith, Elder & Co.) 441; bibliog; index. Stresses "the more dramatic sides of his scientific career".

1927   Mary Duclaux [A. Mary F. Robinson], *Portrait of Pascal* (London: T. Fisher Unwin Ltd./Ernest Benn Limited) 232; bibliog; index.

1927   Roger H. Soltau, *Pascal the man and the message* (London: Blackie & Son Limited) 216; bibliog; index. Originated as lectures to students of French. Stress is on the religious experience.

1936   Morris Bishop, *Pascal the life of genius* (NY: Reynal & Hitchcock; London: G. Bell & Sons, 1937) 398; illus; index.

1952   Jean Mesnard, *Pascal his life and works* (London: Harvill Press; NY: Philosophical Library) 211; illus; bibliog. Translated from 1951 Paris edition by G.S. Fraser. Aims to portray Pascal the Christian, the scientist and the man of the world. Preface by Ronald Knox.

1959   Ernest Mortimer, *Blaise Pascal the life and work of a realist* (London: Methuen & Co. Ltd) 240; illus; bibliog; index. Starts with "the wish that modern thought might be more ready to admit quality as belonging to the realm of fact".

1966   Morris Bishop, *Blaise Pascal* (NY: Dell) [The Laurel great lives and thought] 256. Life is 96 pages; remainder is selected works.

1986   Francis X.J. Coleman, *Neither angel nor beast the life and work of Blaise Pascal* (NY: Routledge & Kegan Paul) 227; illus; bibliog; index. Author a professor of philosophy. Part one is "scenes from the life"; part two is "views on the works".

Pasteur, Louis (1822–1895), French chemist.

1886   René Vallery-Radot, *Louis Pasteur his life and labours* (NY: D. Appleton and Company) 300. A new translation under title *The Life of Pasteur* published 1901 (London: Constable) I:222 II:202; index. Issued in one volume [1906] by Constable and in NY by Doubleday, Page and Company: 484; index. Written by subject's son-in-law (whose name is given in 1886 edition as Renie Valery Radot). "A filial tribute . . . written under the immediate supervision of M. Pasteur" and translated at his request. 1886 edition translated from the French by Lady Claud Hamilton, with an introduction by John Tyndall. 1901 edition translated by Mrs R.L. Devonshire with an introduction by William Osler (who says "this is a biography for young men of science, and for others who wish to learn what science has done, and may do, for humanity").

1898   Percy Frankland and Grace Coleridge Frankland, *Pasteur* (London: Cassell and Company, Limited) [The Century Science Series] 224; illus; index. Hopes to "raise the veil" on the subject and his work.

1920   Emile Duclaux, *Pasteur the history of a mind* (Philadelphia: W.B. Saunders Company) reprinted 1973 (Metuchen, NJ: Scarecrow Reprint Corporation, under the auspices of The Library of the NY Academy of Medicine) [The history of medicine series] 363; illus; index. Translated by Erwin F. Smith and Florence Hedges, with a foreword by René Dubos. Author was subject's student and associate and succeeded him as director of the Pasteur Institute. Calls the book an "intellectual biography" that "takes the reader into the 'mind behind the man' and traces the origin and development of his scientific discoveries". Dubos says it "tells little about Pasteur the man".

[1924]   S.J. Holmes, *Louis Pasteur* (London: Chapman & Hall, Ltd.) 246; illus; index. Another edition 1961 (NY: Dover Publications, Inc.) 149; illus; index. Written for students and general readers; based on Vallery-Radot and other published sources; author a professor of zoology. His preface to 1960 edition notes that impetus for the book was a struggle, in California during the early 1920s, over proposed legislation to restrict animal experimentation.

[1932] Piers Compton, *The Genius of Louis Pasteur* (London: Alexander Ouseley, Ltd.; NY: The Macmillan Company) 361; illus; index. Presents subject as "scientist of the heart".

1950 René J. Dubos, *Louis Pasteur free lance of science* (Boston: Little, Brown and Company) 418; illus; bibliog; index.

1960 René Dubos, *Pasteur and modern science* (Garden City, NY: Anchor Books/ Doubleday & Company, Inc.) [The Science Study Series] 159; index. New edition 1988 (Madison, WI: Science Tech Publishers; NY: Springer-Verlag) 168; illus; index. "Distilled" from Dubos 1950; 1988 text edited by Thomas D. Brock; foreword by Gerald L. Geison, who says there is "no proper scholarly biography" on subject. Series offers students and the general public "the writing of distinguished authors on . . . physics".

1960 Madeleine P. Grant, *Louis Pasteur fighting hero of science* (London: Ernest Benn Limited) 220; illus; index. Author is professor of biology and bacteriology. Popular style.

1963 Hilaire Cuny, *Louis Pasteur the man and his theories* (London: Souvenir Press; NY: P.S. Eriksson, 1966) [Profiles in Science] 190; illus; bibliog; index. Translated by Patrick Evans. Biography is followed by "selected writings".

Peano, Giuseppe (1858–1932), Italian mathematician.

1980 Hubert C. Kennedy, *Peano life and works of Giuseppe Peano* (Dordrecht: D. Reidel Publishing Company) [Studies in the history of modern science] 230; bibliog; index.

Pearson, Karl (1857–1936), English statistician.

1938 E.S. Pearson, *Karl Pearson an appreciation of some aspects of his life and work* (Cambridge: The University Press) 170; illus. Author is subject's son. Based on two journal articles in *Biometrika*. Uses MS sources.

Peierls, Rudolf Ernst (1907 – –), English atomic physicist (born Germany).

1985 autobiography, *Bird of passage recollections of a physicist* (Princeton: Princeton University Press) 350; illus; index. Described as written from a memory that "functions . . . like a leaking pot; some of the contents disappear, but what stays is genuine" and "should be more or less correct".

Peirce, Charles Sanders (1839–1914), American mathematician and philosopher of science.

1990 Girard Deledalle, *Charles S. Peirce an intellectual biography*. Translated from French and introduced by Susan Petrilli (Philadelphia: John Benjamins Publishing

Company) 91; bibliog; index. Introduction says it "offers a specific and personal reading" of the subject.

1993   Joseph Brent, *Charles Sanders Peirce a life* (Bloomington: Indiana University Press) 388; illus; bibliog; index. Foreword by Thomas A. Sebeok (semiotician and Peirce scholar at Indiana University) says this book was a 1960 PhD dissertation at the University of California at Los Angeles; Sebeok discovered it, sought out the author and encouraged him to revise and expand the original work. The Department of Philosophy at Harvard University, which had then refused permission to quote from the subject's papers, now granted such permission.

Perkin, William Henry (1860–1929), English organic chemist.

1932   A.J. Greenaway et al., *The life and work of Professor William Henry Perkin MA ScD LlD PhD FRS* (London: The Chemical Society) 138; illus; bibliog. Occasion is death of subject; a special number of Society's journal.

Pettijohn, Francis John (1904 – –), American geologist.

1984   autobiography, *Memoirs of an unrepentant field geologist a candid profile of some geologists and their science 1921–1981* (Chicago: University of Chicago Press) 260; illus; bibliog; index.

Petty, William (1623–1687), English geographer.

1895   Edmond Fitzmaurice, *The life of Sir William Petty 1623–1687 . . . chiefly derived from private documents hitherto unpublished* (London: John Murray) 335; illus; index. Based on MS sources.

1954   E. Strauss, *Sir William Petty portrait of a genius* (London: The Bodley Head) 260; illus; bibliog; index. Based entirely on printed sources, "its purpose is the systematic use of this information for the reconstruction of Petty's mind and character".

Pfeffer, Wilhelm (1845–1920), German botanist.

1975   Erwin Bünning, *Ahead of his time Wilhelm Pfeffer early advances in plant biology* (Ottawa: Carleton University Press) [Carleton science series] 199; illus; bibliog; index. Translated from 1975 German edition by Helmut William Pfeffer, grandson of subject.

Planck, Max Carl Ernst Ludwig (1858–1947), German physicist.

1986   J.L. Heilbron, *The dilemmas of an upright man Max Planck as spokesman for German science* (Berkeley: University of California Press) 238; illus; bibliog; index. Focus is on the post-war "reconstruction of [the subject's] world picture and his politics". Based on MS sources. Text originated as an introduction to the subject's essays.

Playfair, Lyon (1818–1898), Scottish chemist (born India).

1899   Wemyss Reid, *Memoirs and correspondence of Lyon Playfair first Lord Playfair of St Andrews PC GCB LlD FRS &c* (London: Cassell and Company, Limited) 487; index. Cites subject's correspondence.

Porter, Russell Williams (1871–1949), American astronomer.

1976   Berton C. Willard, *Russell W. Porter arctic explorer artist telescope maker* (Freeport, ME: The Bond Wheelwright Company Publishers) 274; illus; bibliog. Based on MS sources including subject's diaries. Preface by David O. Woodbury.

Prelog, Vladimir (– –), Yugoslav organic chemist.

1991   autobiography, *My 123 semesters of chemistry studies* (Washington: American Chemical Society) [Profiles, pathways, and dreams: autobiographies of eminent chemists] 120; illus; bibliog; index. Translated from German by Otto Theodor Benfey and David Ginsburg.

Priestley, Joseph (1733–1804), English chemist and theologian.

1906   T.E. Thorpe, *Joseph Priestley* (London: J.M. Dent & Co.; NY: E.P. Dutton & Co.) 228; index; illus. [English men of science] Based on subject's autobiography and other sources.

1931   Anne Holt, *A life of Joseph Priestly* (London: Oxford University Press) 221; bibliog; index. Introduction by Francis W. Hirst. Calls previous studies "inadequate" but praises 1906 for concentrating primarily on subject's work. Focuses on character and philosophy of subject. Uses MS sources.

1965   F.W. Gibbs, *Joseph Priestley adventurer in science and champion of truth* (London: Nelson) [British men of science] 258; illus; index. Includes bibliographical note. Uses MS sources. Author is "sketching the broad outline" of subject's life and work.

1966   autobiography, *A scientific autobiography of Joseph Priestley 1733–1804 selected scientific correspondence* (Cambridge, MA: M.I.T Press) 415; bibliog; index. Edited with commentary by Robert E. Schofield, who "attempts to relate the letters to Priestley's work as a whole". and says autobiography contains little on his scientific career.

1970   autobiography, *Autobiography of Joseph Priestley memoirs written by himself* (Bath: Adams & Dart) 159; index. Introduction by Jack Lindsay; also includes text of Priestley's *An Account of Further discoveries in Air.*

Pritchard, Charles (1808–1893), English astronomer.

1897   Ada Pritchard, *Charles Pritchard DD FRS FRAS FRGS late Savilian professor of astronomy in the University of Oxford memoirs of his life* (London: Seeley and Co. Limited) index. Compiled by subject's daughter, with an account of subject's astronomical work by his successor Prof. H.H. Turner; also an account of his theological work by the Bishop of Worcester.

Przheval'skii, Nikolai Mikhailovich (1839–1888), Russian geographer.

1976   Donald Rayfield, *The dream of Lhasa the life of Nikolay Przhevalsky (1839–88) explorer of Central Asia* (London: Paul Elek) 221; illus; bibliog; index.

Rabi, Isidor Isaac (1898 – –), American physicist (born Poland).

1987   John S. Rigden, *Rabi scientist and citizen* (NY: Basic Books) [Alfred P. Sloan Foundation Series] 302; illus; index. Based on interviews with subject and associates. Author an historian of science.

Raman, Chandrasekhara Venkata (1888–1970), Indian physicist.

1988   G. Venkataraman, *Journey into light life and science of C.V. Raman* (Bangalore: Indian Academy of Sciences in co-operation with Indian National Science Academy) 570; illus; bibliog; index. "A scientific biography with appeal to the entire community of scientists . . . somewhat at the level of *Scientific American*." Contains equations.

Ramanujan Iyengar, Srinivasa (1887–1920), Indian mathematician.

1967   S.R. Ranganathan, *Ramanujan the man and the mathematician* (London: Asia Publishing House) [Great thinkers of India] 138; illus; index. "This biography concerns itself largely with the human aspect." Divided into very short sections; contains anecdotes.

1980   Ashis Nandy. See Bose, Jagadis Chunder.

1991   Robert Kanigel, *The man who knew infinity a life of the genius Ramanujan* (NY: Charles Scribner's Sons) 438; illus; bibliog; index. For the general reader; intended to provide a "flavour" of subject's thinking and his work.

Ramsay, Andrew Crombie (1814–1891), Scottish geologist.

1895   Archibald Geikie, *Memoir of Sir Andrew Crombie Ramsay* (London: Macmillan and Co.) 397; illus; bibliog; index. Author a colleague of subject; a "labour of love", as much as possible in subject's own words.

Ramsay, William (1852–1916), Scottish chemist.

1918   William A. Tilden, *Sir William Ramsay KCB FRS Memorials of his life and work* (London: Macmillan and Co., Limited) 311; illus; index. Author acquainted with subject; contains anecdotes. Uses MS sources and quotes extensively from correspondence. Travers 1956 says treatment of subject's later work is "completely lacking in atmosphere".

1956   Morris W. Travers, *A life of Sir William Ramsay KCB FRS* (London: Edward

Arnold Publishers Ltd.) 308; illus; index. Seeks to "analyse the thought of a man committed both to science and to politics". Uses Tilden 1918 and MS sources.

Raspail, François Vincent (1794–1878), French biologist.

1968   Dora B. Weiner, *Raspail scientist and reformer* (NY: Columbia University Press) 336; illus; bibliog; index. Author an historian of science; aims to "shed . . . light on that frontier between the sciences and the humanities". Includes a chapter by Simone Raspail, great-granddaughter of subject and a biologist-pharmacist, who replicated subject's experiments.

Raspe, Rudolf Erich (1737–1794), German geologist.

1950   John Carswell, *The prospector being the life and times of Rudolf Erich Raspe 1737–1794* (London: The Cresset Press; NY: Dutton) 277; illus; bibliography; index. NY edition has title *The romantic rogue being the singular life and adventures of Rudolph Eric Raspe creator of Baron Munchausen*. Author observes that, on the basis of his experience with subject, he cannot agree with Samuel Smiles' belief that a failure does not deserve a biography.

Ravenel, Henry William (1814–1887), American botanist.

1987   Tamara Miner Haygood, *Henry William Ravenel 1814–1887 South Carolina scientist in the civil war era* (Tuscaloosa: University of Alabama Press) 204; illus; index; bibliog. Context is historiographical debate about Clement Eaton's thesis that southern intellectual life was stifled. Argues that Eaton overlooked naturalists like subject.

Ray John (1627–1705), English systemizer of botanical and zoological description.

1846   Edwin Lankester, ed., *Memorials of John Ray* (London: printed for the Ray Society) 220; index. Includes life of Ray by Dr Derham, plus biographical and critical notes by Sir J.E. Smith, Cuvier, and Dupetit Thouars and "A catalogue of the published works of John Ray, arranged chronologically".

1942   Charles E. Raven, *John Ray naturalist his life and work* (Cambridge: University Press) 502; index. Second edition 1950 with new notes; bibliographical information in the introduction.

Ray, Prafulla [or Praphulla] Chandra (1861–1944), Indian chemist.

1932   autobiography, *Life and experiences of a Bengali chemist* (Calcutta: Chuckervertty, Chatterjee & Co. Ltd.; London: Kegan Paul, Trench, Trübner & Co. Ltd) I:557; II:469; index. Second volume includes excerpts from reviews of the first.

1972   J. Sen Gupta, *P.C. Ray* (New Delhi: National Book Trust) [National biography series] 126.

Rayleigh. See Strutt, John William.

Reclus, Elisée, (1830–1905), French geographer.

1978   Gary S. Dunbar, *Elisée Reclus historian of nature* (Hamden, CT: Archon Books) 193; illus; bibliog; index. "Presented as a simple narrative of the efforts of one man ... to come to grips with the overarching issues of his day" which are also the problems of the modern era. Referring to earlier works on subject, author says "a new book is necessary to introduce Reclus to a new generation", particularly in the English-speaking world.

1988   Marie Fleming, *The geography of freedom the odyssey of Elisée Reclus* (Montreal: Black Rose Books) 246; bibliog; index. Introduction by George Woodcock. Attempts to explain and redress neglect of subject.

Remsen, Ira (1846–1927), American chemist and educator.

1940   Frederick H. Getman, *The Life of Ira Remsen* (Easton, PA: Journal of Chemical Education) reprinted 1980 (NY: Arno Press) [Three centuries of science in America] 172; illus. "Investigations carried out by Ira Remsen or under his direction." Uses MS sources.

Rennell, James (1742–1830), English geographer.

1895   Clements R. Markham, *Major James Rennell and the rise of modern English geography* (London: Cassell [The century science series]; NY: Macmillan & Co.) 232; bibliog; index. XX

Rennie, John (1761–1821), Scottish civil engineer.

1861   Samuel Smiles, "Life of John Rennie," *Lives of the Engineers* (London: John Murray) II:7 91–284; index. 1874 edition in five volumes. New edition 1968 based on the 1862 two-volume printing (Newton Abbot: David & Charles Reprints) with introduction by L.T.C. Rolt. The classic "account of some of the principal men by whom the material development of England has been promoted".

1963   Cyril T.G. Boucher, *John Rennie 1761–1821 the life and work of a great engineer* (Manchester: Manchester University Press) 149; illus; bibliog; index. Seeks to correct the technological and other deficiencies of Smiles 1861. Includes use of MS eight-volume life by subject's son.

Ricardo, Harry Ralph (1885–1974), English mechanical engineer.

1968   autobiography, *Memories and machines the pattern of my life* (London: Constable) reprinted 1990 ([London]: Ricardo Consulting Engineers Ltd.) 264; illus; index. Second edition 1992 (Warrendale, PA: Society of Automotive Engineers) [Society of Automotive Engineers historical series] 282; illus; index. Second edition includes a postscript by Cecil French, a preface and biographical notes by Don Goodsell, and additional illustrations.

Ritchey, George Willis (1864–1945), American astronomer.

1993 Donald E. Osterbrock, *Pauper & prince Ritchey Hale & big American telescopes* (Tucson: University of Arizona Press) 359; illus; bibliog; index. Author an academic astrophysicist-astronomer and historian of astronomy. The focus of the book is on Ritchey, but description of their relationship includes telescope-building part of Hale's life.

Rittenhouse, David (1732–1796), American technologist and astronomer.

1813 William Barton, *Memoirs of the life of David Rittenhouse LLD FRS late president of the American philosophical society &c interspersed with various notices of many distinguished men with an appendix, containing sundry philosophical and other papers, most of which have not hitherto been published* (Philadelphia: Edward Parker) 614; illus. Author is counsellor at law. Ford says this biography "omits many enlightening incidents, especially any fact that does not flatter Rittenhouse".

1946 Edward Ford, *David Rittenhouse astronomer-patriot 1732–1796.* (Philadelphia: University of Pennsylvania Press) 226; index; bibliog. [Pennsylvania Lives] Foreword by Thomas D. Cope. Hindle calls this "a surprisingly full chronicle of the external facts".

1964 Brooke Hindle, *David Rittenhouse* (Princeton: Princeton University Press) reprinted 1980 (NY: Arno Press) [Three centuries of science in America] 394; illus; index; bibliog. Author is at NY University; based on MS research.

Roberts, John D. (1918 – –), American chemist.

1990 autobiography, *The right place at the right time* (Washington: American Chemical Society) [Profiles, pathways, and dreams: autobiographies of American chemists] 299; illus; index. Contains mostly science.

Robinson, Robert (1886–1975), English organic chemist.

1976 autobiography, *Memoirs of a minor prophet 70 years of organic chemistry* (Amsterdam: Elsevier) 252; bibliog. The present volume covers the period before 1932, when subject was appointed to a Chair at Oxford. Acknowledges the consultative assistance of Renée H. Jaeger, who helped overcome the problems associated with writing from memory. Unfinished; intended second volume interrupted by author's death.

1990 Trevor I. Williams, *Robert Robinson chemist extraordinary* (Oxford: Clarendon Press) 201; illus; bibliog; index. Written at request of subject's daughter; author was acquainted with subject. Based on limited MS sources and on interviews.

Rogers, William Barton (1804–1882), Scottish geologist.

1896 Mrs W.B. Rogers, *Life and letters of William Barton Rogers* (Boston: Houghton Mifflin and Company) 2 vols. Author-editor was assisted by William T. Sedgwick. XX

Romanes, George John (1848–1894), English biologist (born Canada).

1896 [Ethel Duncan Romanes], *The life and letters of George John Romanes* (London: Longmans, Green) 360; index. Book is "written and edited" by widow of subject; she tries "to let him, especially in matters scientific, speak for himself". Based on MS sources.

Röntgen, Wilhelm Conrad (1845–1923), German physicist.

1970 K.T. Claxton, *Wilhelm Roentgen* (London: Heron Books) [The Great Nobel prizes] 311; illus; index.

1971 W. Robert Nitske, *The life of Wilhelm Conrad Röntgen, discoverer of the X ray* (Tucson: The University of Arizona Press) 355; illus; bibliog; index.

Roscoe, Henry Enfield (1833–1915), English chemist.

1906 autobiography, *The life and experiences of Sir Henry Enfield Roscoe DCL LlD FRS* (London: Macmillan and Co., Limited) 420; illus; index.

1916 Edward Thorpe, *The Right Honourable Sir Henry Enfield Roscoe PC DCL FRS a biographical sketch* (London: Longmans, Green and Co.) 207; index. Author a co-worker and friend of subject. Expansion of Royal Society and Chemical Society obituary notices.

Ross, James Clark (1800–1862), English polar navigator.

1973 Ernest S. Dodge, *The polar Rosses John and James Clark Ross and their explorations* (London: Faber and Faber) [Great Travellers] 260; illus; bibliog; index. Uses MS sources.

Rossi, Bruno Bendetto (1905 – –), Italian physicist.

1990 autobiography, *Moments in the life of a scientist* (Cambridge: Cambridge University Press) 181; illus; index. Includes a postscript by Nora Rossi, wife of subject and a foreword by Philip Morrison.

Rumford. See Thompson, Benjamin.

Rush, Benjamin (1745–1813), American chemist.

1934 Nathan G. Goodman, *Benjamin Rush physician and citizen 1746–1813* (Philadelphia: University of Pennsylvania Press; London: Humphrey Milford/Oxford University Press) 421; illus; bibliog; index. Written to redress neglect.

1948 autobiography, *The autobiography of Benjamin Rush his travels through life together with his commonplace book for 1789–1813* (Westwood, CT: Greenwood Press) 399; illus; bibliog. Reprinted 1970. XX

1960   Carl Binger, *Revolutionary doctor Benjamin Rush 1746–1813* (NY: W.W. Norton & Company Inc.) 326; index. Author is a medical doctor with similar interests to subject.

1971   David Freeman Hawke, *Benjamin Rush revolutionary gadfly* (Indianapolis: The Bobbs-Merrill Company, Inc.) 490; bibliog; index. Covers 43 years of subject's 68-year life, and thus does not emphasize the medical side of his career.

Russell, Bertrand Arthur William (1872–1970), English mathematician.

1965   Herbert Gottschalk, *Bertrand Russell a life* (London: John Baker) 128. Translated from the 1962 German edition by Edward Fitzgerald. Chronological account of subject's life; work is not emphasized.

1967–69   autobiography, *The autobiography of Bertrand Russell* (London: George Allen and Unwin) I:230 II:268 III:232; illus; index. (NY: Simon and Schuster) I:230 II:268 III:339. Issued 1975 in one volume (London: Unwin Books) 751; illus; bibliog; index.

1969   William Ready, *Necessary Russell an introduction to the life and times of Bertrand Russell* (Toronto: The Copp Clark Publishing Company) 118. Project described as a "child of the Russell Archives" [at McMaster University]. Author praises Wood and autobiography.

1975   Ronald W. Clark, *The Life of Bertrand Russell* (London: Jonathan Cape and Weidenfeld & Nicolson; NY: Alfred A. Knopf, 1976) 766; illus; bibliog; index. Uses MS sources.

1981   Ronald Clark, *Bertrand Russell and his world* (London: Thames and Hudson) 127; illus; bibliog; index. No introduction or chapter divisions; numerous photographs.

1988   Alan Ryan, *Bertrand Russell a political life* (London: Allen Lane, the Penguin Press; NY: Hill and Wang) 226; bibliog; index. An analysis of subject's theories and ideas. Author has mixed opinion of Clark 1975 and calls autobiography "sentimental".

1989   Andrew Brink, *Bertrand Russell a psychobiography of a moralist* (Atlantic Highlands, NJ: Humanities Press International, Inc.) 174; bibliog; index. Uses MS sources. Focuses on subject's politics and beliefs rather than on his scientific work.

1992   Caroline Moorehead, *Bertrand Russell a life* (London: Sinclair-Stevenson) 596; bibliog; index. Uses MS sources.

Russell, Edward John (1872–1965), English agricultural scientist.

1956   autobiography, *The land called me* (London: George Allen & Unwin Ltd.) 286; illus; index.

Rutherford, Ernest (1871–1937), New Zealand nuclear physicist.

1939   Ivor B.N. Evans, *Man of Power the life story of Baron Rutherford of Nelson OM FRS* (London: Stanley Paul & Co. Ltd.) 288; illus; index. Published 1943 as *Rutherford of Nelson* (Harmondsworth and NY: Penguin Books) 232; index. Outline of subject's scientific achievements, "together with the story of the vast work he did in the interests of British industry and in the safeguarding of the freedom of knowledge against intolerance". 1943 edition (wartime Pelican paperback) notes that the whole text has been completely revised, but there are no main structural alterations; the index is new.

1939   A.S. Eve, *Rutherford being the life and letters of the Rt. Hon. Lord Rutherford OM* (Cambridge: Cambridge University Press; NY: The Macmillan Company) 451; illus; index. Author is professor of physics; foreword by Earl Baldwin of Bewdley, Chancellor of the University of Cambridge.

1940   Norman Feather, *Lord Rutherford* (London: Blackie & Son Limited) reprinted 1973 (London: Priory Press Ltd.) 195; illus; index. 1940 edition has foreword by W.H. Bragg; 1973 reprint has foreword by H.S.W. Massey. Author a former colleague in the subject's laboratory. Emphasis is on career in science.

1955   John Rowland, *Ernest Rutherford atom pioneer* (London: Werner Laurie) 160; illus; index. Foreword acknowledges debt to Eve and Evans.

1964   John Rowland, *Ernest Rutherford master of the atom* (London: Arthur Barker Limited) [Creators of the modern world]; (London: Weidenfeld & Nicolson (Educational) Ltd.) [Pathfinder biographies] 123; illus; bibliog; index. Not specifically for children.

1970   C.L. Boltz, *Ernest Rutherford* (London: Distributed by Heron Books) [The Great Nobel prizes] 375; illus; index. Copyright by Edito-Service S.A. Geneva. Series editor's foreword by Courtland Canby.

1983   David Wilson, *Rutherford simple genius* (London: Hodder and Stoughton; Cambridge: The MIT Press) 638; illus; index; bibliog. Tries to show subject "outside the laboratory as well". Introduction does not allude directly to earlier biographies, but to the problem of those who did and did not know where the subject's discoveries would lead.

Sabine, Wallace Clement Ware (1868–1919), American physicist.

1933   William Dana Orcutt, *Wallace Clement Sabine a study in achievement* (Norwood, MA: Privately printed by the Plimpton Press) 376; index; bibliog; illus. Author stresses subject's reserve, and describes this as "a deferential attempt to pierce that 'protective crust of reserve' ".

Sakharov, Andrei Dmitrievich (1921–1989), Russian theoretical physicist.

1989   George Bailey, *The making of Andrei Sakharov* (London: Allen Lane/The Penguin Press) 453; bibliog; index. Places the subject in the context of the history of science, particularly physics.

1990–91   autobiography, (NY: Alfred A. Knopf Inc.; London: Hutchinson) reprinted 1992 (NY: Vintage Books) I:771 II:168; illus; bibliog; index. Volume 1, entitled *Memoirs*, is translated by Richard Lourie; volume 2, entitled *Moscow and beyond 1986 to 1989* is translated by Antonina Bouis. Both have a foreword by Edward Kline.

1991   anon., *Andrei Sakharov facets of a life* (Gif-sur-Yvette, France: Edition Frontieres) [Legends of our time] 730; illus; bibliog. Authorship attributed to the Academy of Sciences of the USSR, P.N. Lebedev Physics Institute, I.E. Tamm Theory Department.

Salam, Abdus (1926 – –), Pakistani theoretical physicist.

1982   Abdul Ghani, *Abdus Salam a Nobel laureate from a Muslim country a biographical sketch* (Karachi: Màaref Printers) 234; illus; bibliog. XX

1992   Jagjit Singh, *Abdus Salam a biography* (New Delhi: Penguin Books) 213; illus; bibliog; index. XX

Saussure, Horace Bénédict de (1740–1799), Swiss geologist and meteorologist.

1920   Douglas W. Freshfield, *The life of Horace Benedict de Saussure* (London: Edward Arnold) 479; illus; index. Written with the collaboration of Henry F. Montagnier. Uses MS sources to portray subject as politican, patriot, educational reformer, geologist, explorer, philosopher and citizen: "de Saussure's life as a whole".

Say, Thomas (1787–1834), American entomologist and conchologist.

1931   Harry B. Weiss and Grace M. Ziegler, *Thomas Say early American naturalist* (Springfield, IL: Charles C. Thomas) 260; illus; index. With a foreword by L.O. Howard. "More concerned with Say's life than with his scientific achievements, although to a certain extent the two are inseparable." Written as a factual account, in the hope that subject's character will "emerge of itself".

1992   Patricia Tyson Stroud, *Thomas Say new world naturalist* (Philadelphia: The Barara Foundation, University of Pennsylvania Press) 340; illus; bibliog; index. Uses new correspondence which has surfaced since Weiss's 1931 account to correct previous image of subject.

Schrödinger, Erwin (1887–1961), Austrian theoretical physicist.

1989   Walter Moore, *Schrödinger life and thought* (Cambridge: Cambridge University Press) 513; illus; index. For the general reader.

Scott, William Berryman (1858–1947), American palaeontologist and geologist.

1939   autobiography, *Some memories of a palaeontologist* (Princeton: Princeton University Press) reprinted 1980 (NY: Arno Press) 336. Preface says this is an abridgement of an autobiography written as a family memoir.

Sedgwick, Adam (1785–1873), English geologist.

1890   John Willis Clark and Thomas McKenny Hughes, *The life and letters of the Reverend Adam Sedgwick* (Cambridge: Cambridge University Press) I:539, II:640; illus; index. Authors acquainted with subject.

1982   Colin Speakman, *Adam Sedgwick geologist and dalesman 1785–1873 a biography in twelve themes* (Broad Oak: Broad Oak Press Limited, The Geological Society of London and Trinity College, Cambridge) 145; illus; bibliog; index. Uses Clark's 1890 account with new material to discuss subject's philosophy and influence, including locating the subject in his community.

See, Thomas Jefferson Jackson (1866–1962), American astronomer.

1913 W. Webb, *Brief biography and popular account of the unparalleled discoveries of T.J.J. See AM LtM ScM (Missou) AM PhD (Berol) Famous astronomer natural philo-sopher and founder of the new sciences of cosmogony and geogony* (Lynn, MA: Thos. P. Nichols & Son Co., Publishers; London: Wm. Wesley & Son) 298; illus; index. Flowery prose style.

Shapley, Harlow (1885–1972), American astronomer.

1969 autobiography, *Ad astra per aspera through rugged ways to the stars* (NY: Charles Scribner's Sons) [Scribners scientific memoirs] 180; illus; bibliog; index.

Shelford, Victor Ernest (1877–1968), American ecologist.

1991 Robert A. Croker, *Pioneer ecologist the life and work of Victor Ernest Shelford 1877–1968* (Washington: Smithsonian Institution) 222; illus; bibliog; index. Foreword by François Vuilleumien. Context is "the emergence and development of animal ecology as a self-conscious scientific discipline".

Shklovskiĭ, Iosif Samuilovich (1916 – –), Russian astronomer.

1991 autobiography, *Five billion vodka bottles to the moon tales of a soviet scientist* (NY: W.W. Norton & Company) 268; index. Translated and adapted by Mary Fleming Zirin and Harold Zirin, whose foreword notes that "these tales from life circulated in typescript throughout the Soviet scientific community". Introduction by Herbert Friedman.

Shreve, Forrest (1878–1950), American plant ecologist.

1988 Janice Emily Bowers, *A sense of place the life and work of Forrest Shreve* (Tucson: University of Arizona Press) 195; illus; bibliog; index. Based on interviews and MS sources.

Siemens, Charles William (1823–1883), English engineer (born Germany).

1888 William Pole, *The life of Sir William Siemens* (London: John Murray) 412; illus; index. Published uniformly with the subject's works. Author a friend. Based on MS sources.

Sikorsky, Igor Ivanovich (1889–1972), American aeronautical engineer (born Ukraine).

1987   K.N. Finne, *Igor Sikorsky the Russian years* (Washington: Smithsonian Institution Press; Shrewsbury: Airlife) 223; illus; bibliog; index. Edited by Carl J. Boborow and Von Hardesty; translated and adapted by Hardesty. An "aviation classic" written in 1930, abbreviated and amplified for an English-reading audience.

Silliman, Benjamin (1779–1864), American chemist.

1866   George P. Fisher, *Life of Benjamin Silliman MD LLD late professor of chemistry, mineralogy, and geology in Yale college chiefly from his MS reminiscences diaries and correspondence.* (NY: Charles Scribner and Company) I:407 II:408; index. Author is a Yale professor, who used the subject's nine-volume MS autobiography; Fulton says he "included a large assemblage of material essentially without critical evaluation".

1947   John F. Fulton, *Benjamin Silliman 1779–1864 pathfinder in American science* (NY: Henry Schuman) [Yale University School of Medicine Historical Library publication no. 16] [The life of science library] reprinted 1968 (NY: Greenwood Press) 294; illus; bibliog; index. Co-author Elizabeth H. Thomson. The occasion is the centenary of Sheffield School.

1989   Chandos Michael Brown, *Benjamin Silliman a life in the young republic* (Princeton: Princeton University Press) 377; illus; bibliog; index. A cultural, not a scientific biography; the stress is "not his *exceptionality* but his *representativeness*". This work is identified with the new history of science.

Simon, Franz Eugen (1893–1956), German physicist.

1966   Nancy Arms, *A prophet in two countries the life of F.E. Simon* (Oxford: Pergamon Press) [The Commonwealth and International Library of Science, Technology, Engineering and Liberal Studies. History Division. Biography Section] 171; bibliog; index. Focuses on subject's life; contains complete list of his scientific publications. Uses MS sources.

Simpson, Thomas (1710–1761), English mathematician.

1929   Frances Marguerite Clarke, *Thomas Simpson and his times.* PhD thesis, Columbia University, 1929. XX

Simson, Robert (1687–1768), Scottish mathematician.

1812   William Trail, *Account of the life and writings of Robert Simson MD* (London: G. and W. Nicol) 191.

Sinclair, Clive Marles (1940 – –), English computer engineer.

1985   Rodney Dale, *The Sinclair Story* (London: Duckworth) 184; illus. Occasion is crisis in subject's business; based on interviews with subject and others.

1986   Ian Adamson and Richard Kennedy, *Sinclair and the "Sunrise" Technology the deconstruction of a myth* (Harmondsworth: Penguin Books) 263. An "exercise in demystification, . . . the presentation of a detailed case history that reveals the inherent fallibility of the 'entrepreneurial solution' to economic crisis and the durability of media-generated mythology".

Slaught, Herbert Ellsworth (1861–1937), American mathematician.

1948   Harris Jeremiah Dark, *The life and works of Herbert Ellsworth Slaught* (Nashville, TN: George Peabody College for Teachers) 152; bibliog. Purpose is "to make a systematic and permanent record of the essential facts in the life and career" of subject. Based on printed and MS sources, and interviews.

Slichter, Charles Sumner (1864–1946), American mathematician.

1972   Mark H. Ingraham, *Charles Sumner Slichter the golden vector* (Madison: The University of Wisconsin Press) 316; illus; index. Based on MS sources. Purpose is to portray both personality and accomplishments of subject.

Smeaton, John (1724–1792), English engineer and instrument-maker.

1793   John Holmes, *A short narrative of the genius life and works of the late Mr J. Smeaton civil engineer* (London: published privately). XX

1844   anon, *Smeaton and lighthouses A popular biography with an historical introduction and sequel* (London: John W. Parker) 120. Stress is more on context than on life of subject.

1861   Samuel Smiles, "Life of John Smeaton", *Lives of the Engineers* (London: John Murray) II:6 1–90; index. 1874 edition in five volumes. New edition 1968 based on the 1862 two-volume printing (Newton Abbot: David & Charles Reprints) with introduction by L.T.C. Rolt. The classic "account of some of the principal men by whom the material development of England has been promoted".

Smith, Alec (1927 – –), English entomologist.

1993   autobiography, *Insect man a fight against malaria in Africa* (London: The Radcliffe Press) 212; illus; index.

Smith, Erwin Frink (1854–1927), American plant pathologist and bacteriologist.

1952   Andrew Denny Rodgers, *Erwin Frink Smith a story of North American plant pathology* (Philadelphia: American Philosophical Society) [Memoirs of the American Philosophical Society] 675; illus; index. Focuses on subject's work. Uses MS sources.

Smith, James Edward (1759–1828), English botanist.

1832   Pleasance Smith, *Memoir and correspondence of the late Sir James Edward Smith MD* (London: Longman, Rees, Orme, Brown, Green, and Longman) I:610 II:610; index. Author ("editor") is wife of subject. Includes text of subject's lecture to the London Institution, 2 May 1825.

Smith, William (1769–1839), English geologist.

1844   John Phillips, *Memoirs of William Smith LlD* (London: John Murray) reprinted 1978 (NY: Arno Press) [History of geology] 150; illus. Based on MS sources; author was literary executor, and student of subject. Regards the biography as a contribution to the history of English geology.

Smithson, James (1765–1829), English chemist (born France).

1965   Leonard Carmichael and J.C. Long, *James Smithson and the Smithsonian story* (NY: G.W. Putnam's Sons) 316; illus; bibliog; index. Biography, written by Long, is part two (41–143) of three-part volume on the Smithsonian Institution.

Smyth, Charles Piazzi (1819–1900), Italian astronomer and meteorologist.

1988   H.A. Brück and M.T. Brück, *The peripatetic astronomer the life of Charles Piazzi Smyth* (Bristol: Adam Hilger) 274; illus; bibliog; index. The "main source of material for this book are Piazzi Smyth's own publications . . . and the archives of the Royal Society of Edinburgh and the Royal Observatory Edinburgh".

Soddy, Frederick (1877–1956), English radiochemist.

1958   Muriel Howorth, *Pioneer research on the atom Rutherford and Soddy in a glorious chapter of science the life story of Frederick Soddy MA LLD FRS Nobel laureate* (London: New World Publications) 352; illus. XX

Somerville, Mary (1780–1872), Scottish mathematician and physicist.

1874   autobiography, *Personal recollections, from early life to old age, of Mary Somerville; with selections from her correspondence* (Boston: Roberts Bros.) 377. Edited by Martha Somerville, daughter of subject.

1983   Elizabeth Chambers Patterson, *Mary Somerville and the cultivation of science 1815–1840* (The Hague: Martinus Nijhoff) [International archives of the history of ideas] 264; bibliog; index. Considers only scientific aspects of subject's life; focuses on her participation in London science.

Sonnerat, Pierre (1748–1814), French natural historian.

1976   Madeleine Ly-Tio-Fane, *Pierre Sonnerat 1748–1814 an account of his life and work* (Cassis, Mauritius: published by the author) 157; illus; bibliog; index. Based on MS sources; originated as a University of London PhD dissertation.

Sorby, Henry Clifton (1826–1908), English geologist and metallurgist.

1963   Norman Higham, *A very scientific gentleman; the major achievements of Henry Clifton Sorby.* (Oxford: Pergamon Press) [The Commonwealth and International Library of Science, Technology, Engineering and Liberal Studies. History of science and technology division] 160; illus; bibliog; index. Uses MS sources. Foreword by Cyril Stanley Smith.

Sperry, Elmer Ambrose (1860–1930), American engineer and technologist.

1971   Tomas Parke Hughes, *Elmer Sperry inventor and engineer* (Baltimore: The Johns Hopkins Press) 348; illus; bibliog; index. Uses MS materials; research was sponsored by the Centre for the Study of Recent American History by a grant from the subject's descendants.

Spinks, John William Tranter (1908 – –), Canadian chemist (born England).

1980   autobiography, *Two blades of grass an autobiography* (Saskatoon: Western Producer Prairie Books) 224; illus; bibliog; index. Author regards his insight as being "that of a scientist in an academic setting".

Steacie, Edgar William Richard (1900–1962), Canadian physical chemist.

1989   M. Christine King, *E.W.R. Steacie and science in Canada* (Toronto: University of Toronto Press) 243; illus; bibliog; index. Author died before revisions complete; edited by Diane Mew.

Steinmetz, Charles Proteus (1865–1923), German engineer.

1924   John Winthrop Hammond, *Charles Proteus Steinmetz a biography* (NY: The Century Co.) 489; illus; index. Portrays subject as a "world-builder" and an "idealist". Text approved by subject.

1929   Jonathan Norton Leonard, *Loki the life of Charles Proteus Steinmetz* (Garden City, NY: Doubleday, Doran & Company) 291; illus. Includes invented dialogue; written with the co-operation of General Electric.

1959   Henry Thomas, *Charles Steinmetz* (NY: G.P. Putnam's Sons) [Lives to remember] 126.

1992   Ronald R. Kline, *Steinmetz engineer and socialist* (Baltimore: The Johns Hopkins University Press) [Johns Hopkins studies in the history of technology new series] 401; illus; bibliog; index. An "intellectual biography set in the economic, political and social contexts of the Progressive Era, as well as a cultural history of the Steinmetz myth". Comments on scarcity of archival records concerning subject's private life.

Steklov, Vladimir Andreevich (1864–1926), Russian mathematician.

1983   V.S. Vladimirov and I.I. Markush, *Academician Steklov mathematician extraordinary* (Moscow: Mir Publishers) [Outstanding Soviet scientists] 125. Revised from the 1981 Russian edition; translated by C.A. Hainsworth and R.A. Hainsworth. Uses MS sources.

Steller, Georg Wilhelm (1709–1746), Russian geographer and biologist.

1936   Leonhard Stejneger, *George Wilhelm Steller the pioneer of Alaskan natural history* (Cambridge: Harvard University Press) 623; illus; bibliog; index. "The plain tale of the life of a great naturalist." Uses MS sources.

Steno, Nicolaus [or Stensen, Niels] (1638–1686), Danish anatomist and geologist.

1961   Raffaello Cioni, *Niels Stensen scientist-bishop* (NY: P.J. Kenedy & Sons) 192; index. Translated by Genevieve M. Camera; preface by John LaFarge.

Stephenson, George (1781–1848), English railway engineer.

1857   Samuel Smiles, *The life of George Stephenson railway engineer* (London: John Murray; NY: Harper, 1858) 517. Third edition, revised with additions 1857 (London: John Murray; Boston: Ticknor and Fields) 546. Fourth edition 1862 ([London: John Murray]; Boston: Ticknor and Fields) 463. Fifth edition revised, with additions 1858 (London: John Murray) reprinted 1971 (Ann Arbor: Plutarch Press) 557; index. Abridged edition 1859 under title *The story of the life of George Stephenson railway engineer*: 356; illus; index. Appeared 1862 as "Lives of George and Robert Stephenson", volume 3 of *Lives of the Engineers* (London: John Murray) 512; illus; index. New edition of abridgement, thoroughly revised 1864, under title *The story of the life of George Stephenson including a memoir of his son Robert Stephenson*: 338; illus; index. Text of 1857 first edition published 1975 (London: The Folio Society) 304; illus. 1857 revision adds material on subject's life in Liverpool, Alton Grange and Tapton House. 1862 revision is expanded to include Robert Stephenson. 1864 revision of abridgement reflects the death of Robert Stephenson. 1975 edition has introduction by Eric de Maré; text is taken from 1874, author's last revision.

1948   Ada Louise Barrett, *George Stephenson father of railways* (NY: The Paebar Company) 287; bibliog. Based on published sources; addressed to general reader.

1960   L.T.C. Rolt, *George and Robert Stephenson the railway revolution* (London: Longmans; NY: St Martin's Press, 1962) 356; illus; bibliog; index. Argues that a "fresh assessment" of the two subjects must deal with both "on a perfectly equal footing". Includes drawings and maps by Kenneth Lindley. NY edition has title *The railway revolution George and Robert Stephenson*.

1971   John Rowland, *Railway pioneer the story of George Stephenson* (NY: Roy Publishers) 121. XX

1975   Hunter Davies, *A biographical study of the father of railways George Stephenson* (London: Weidenfeld and Nicolson) 337; illus; bibliog; index. Subtitle is: On the occasion of the one hundred and fiftieth anniversary of the opening of the world's first public railway, the Stockton and Darlington, 1825–1975, including an account of railway mania and a consideration of Stephensonia today. A biography by a generalist, not a railway writer.

Stone, Francis Gordon Albert (1925 – –), British chemist.

1993   autobiography, *Leaving no stone unturned pathways in organometallic chemistry* (Washington: American Chemical Society) [Profiles, pathways, and dreams: autobiographies of eminent chemists] 240; illus; bibliog; index. XX.

Strutt, John William [Third Baron Rayleigh] (1842–1919), English mathematical physicist.

1924   Lord Rayleigh, *John William Strutt Third Baron Rayleigh OM FRS sometime President of the Royal Society and Chancellor of the University of Cambridge* (London: Edward Arnold & Co.; (NY: Longmans, Green & Co. under title *Life of John William Strutt, third Baron Rayleigh OM*) 403; illus; index. New augmented edition 1968 (Madison: University of Wisconsin Press) 439; illus; index. Written by subject's son, whose "aim [is] not so much to give an account of . . . Father's scientific work as to depict him as a man". 1968 has annotations by the author and foreword by John N. Howard

1970   Robert Bruce Lindsay, *Lord Rayleigh the man and his work* (Oxford: Pergamon Press) [Men of Physics] 251; bibliog. XX

Struve, Otto Wilhelm (Otton Vasilievich) (1819–1905) **and Otto** (1897–1963), Russian astronomers.

1988   Alan H. Batten, *Resolute and undertaking characters: the lives of Wilhelm and Otto Struve* (Dordrecht: D. Reidel Publishing. Co.) [Astrophysics and space science library] 259; illus; bibliog; index.

Sutherland, William (1859–1911), Scottish theoretical physical chemist.

1920   William Alexander Osborne, *William Sutherland a biography* (Melbourne: Lothian Book Pub. Co.) 101; illus; bibliog. XX

Swallow, Ellen Henrietta (1842–1911), American ecologist.

1973   Robert Clarke, *Ellen Swallow the woman who founded ecology* (Chicago: Follett Publishing Company) 276; illus; bibliog; index.

Swammerdam, Jan (1637–1680), Dutch anatomist, biologist.

1967   A. Schierbeek, *Jan Swammerdam his life and works* (Amsterdam: Swets & Zeitlinger) 202; illus; bibliog. Translation of Dutch edition. XX

Swan, Joseph Wilson (1828–1917), English chemist (inventor of the Swan incandescent filament lamp).

1929   M.E.S. and K.R.S. [Mary Edmonds Swan and Kenneth Raydon Swan], *Sir Joseph Wilson Swan FRS a memoir* (London: Ernest Benn Limited) 183; illus; index. Authors are daughter and son of subject.

Swedenborg, Emanuel (1688–1772), Swedish geologist and theologian.

1866   William White, *Life of Emanuel Swedenborg together with a brief synopsis of his writings both philosophical and theological* (Philadelphia: J.B. Lippincott Company) 266. "Pretends to nothing but simplicity, and would be ranked as a handbook, a guide, a directory." Author calls subject "the most gifted and extraordinary man that has ever lived". Described by Trobridge (1907) as "able" but biased and unreliable in terms of facts.

1907   George Trobridge, *Swedenborg life and teaching* (London: Frederick Warne & Company; London: Swedenborg Society under title *Life of Emanuel Swedenborg*, and in subsequent reissues as *Swedenborg life and teaching*) 140. Second edition 1929 enlarged with illustrations. Third edition 1930 abridged. Revised edition 1935 (London: Swedenborg Society, (Incorporated)) 343; index. Fourth edition 1969 (NY: Swedenborg Foundation, Incorporated) 298. Calls book "a portrait of the whole man".

1948   Signe Toksvig, *Emanuel Swedenborg scientist and mystic* (London: Faber and Faber; New Haven: Yale University Press) reprinted 1972 (Freeport, NY: Books for Libraries Press) reprinted 1983 (NY: Swedenborg Foundation) 389; illus; bibliog; index. Uses MS sources.

1971   Cyriel Odhner Sigstedt, *The Swedenborg epic the life and works of Emanuel Swedenborg* (NY: AMS Press) [Communal Societies in America Series] 517; illus; bibliog; index. First published 1952 (NY: Bookman Associates). "Strictly chronological"; attempts exhaustive use of documents.

Szent-Györgyi, Albert Von (1893–1986), American biochemist (born Hungary).

1988   Ralph W. Moss, *Free radical Albert Szent-Gyorgyi and the battle over Vitamin C* (NY: Paragon House Publishers) 316; illus; index.

Szilard, Leo (1898–1964), American physicist (born Hungary).

1972   Arnulf E. Esterer and Louise A. Esterer, *Prophet of the atomic age Leo Szilard* (NY: Julian Messner) 189; bibliog; index. Authors are a chemist and an educator.

1992   William Lanouette with Bela Silard, *Genius in the shadows a biography of Leo*

Szilard (NY: Charles Scribner's Sons) 587; illus; bibliog; index. Author is a journalist; Silard is brother of subject. Foreword by Jonas Salk, who says the biography "reveals a multifaceted singularity".

Talbot, William Henry Fox (1800–1877), English photochemist and mathematician.

1965   Arthur H. Booth, *William Henry Fox Talbot father of photography* (London: Arthur Barker Limited) [Creators of the Modern World] 119; illus; index. The first biography, based on MS sources, some received from H. White whose work is in progress.

1977   H.J.P. Arnold, *William Henry Fox Talbot pioneer of photography and man of science* (London: Hutchinson Benham) 383; illus; bibliog; index. Project sponsored by Kodak Ltd; occasion is centenary of death.

1980   Gail Buckland, *Fox Talbot and the invention of photography* (Boston: D.R. Godine; London: Scolar Press) 216; illus; bibliog; index. Biography and reproductions of photographs.

Teilhard de Chardin, Pierre (1881–1955), French palaeontologist and geologist.

1960   Nicolas Corte [Lion Christiani], *Pierre Teilhard de Chardin his life and spirit* (London: Barrie and Rockliff) 120; bibliog; index. Translated from 1957 French edition by Martin Jarett-Kerr, whose preface "fill[s] in some of the gaps in this necessarily brief study" with new material.

1962   Charles E. Raven, *Teilhard de Chardin scientist and seer* (London: Collins) 221; index. An "account of his life and thought and of his special significance for English readers".

1965   Claude Cuénot, *Teilhard de Chardin a biographical study* (Baltimore: Helicon) 494; illus; index. No introduction.

1965   Paul Grenet, *Teilhard de Chardin the man and his theories* (London: Souvenir Press; NY: Paul S. Eriksson, Inc., 1966) [Profiles in Science] 176; illus; bibliog; index. Translated from 1961 French edition by R.A. Rudorff. Portrays subject as a Catholic and as a scientist. Uses some of subject's correspondence.

1967   Robert Speaight, *The life of Teilhard de Chardin* (NY: Harper & Row, Publishers; London: Collins under title *Teilhard de Chardin a biography*) 360; illus; bibliog; index. Uses MS sources to focus on subject's "dual vocation" in theology and science.

1977   Mary Lukas and Ellen Lukas, *Teilhard* (Garden City, NY: Doubleday and Company, Inc.) 360; illus; index. Aim is that subject's work be "re-examined and reinstated into its place as a part of the common human heritage".

Telford, Thomas (1757–1834), Scottish civil engineer.

1861   Samuel Smiles, "Life of Thomas Telford", *Lives of the Engineers* (London: John Murray) II:8 285–493; index. 1874 edition in five volumes; New edition 1968 based on the 1862 two-volume printing (Newton Abbot: David & Charles Reprints) with introduction by L.T.C. Rolt. The classic "account of some of the principal men by whom the material development of England has been promoted".

1867   Samuel Smiles, *The Life of Thomas Telford civil engineer with an introductory history of roads and travelling in Great Britain* (London: John Murray) 331; illus; index. A revised and enlarged edition of Smiles 1861.

1935   Alexander Gibb, *The story of Telford the rise of civil engineering* (London: Alexander Maclehose) 357; illus; bibliog; index. Foreword by Lord Macmillan of Aberfeldy. "Neither a formal biography . . . nor a technical description of his works. It is, indeed, no more than an attempt to present some sort of picture of the man."

1958   L.T.C. Rolt, *Thomas Telford* (London: Longmans, Green) 211; illus; bibliog. XX

1973   Brian Bracegirdle and Patricia H. Miles, *Thomas Telford* (Newton Abbot: David and Charles) [Great engineers and their works] 112; illus; bibliog; index. XX

Teller, Edward (1908 – –), American physicist (born Hungary).

1976   Stanley A. Blumberg and Gwinn Owens, *Energy and conflict the life and times of Edward Teller* (NY: G.P. Putnam's Sons) 492; illus; index. Authors are journalists. Based on interviews with subject and associates. Introduction discusses difficulties of objectivity when author disagrees politically with subject.

1990   Stanley A. Blumberg and Louis G. Panos, *Edward Teller giant of the golden age of physics* (NY: Charles Scribner's Sons) 306; illus; bibliog; index. Includes subject's involvement in defence issues of the 1980s.

Tesla, Nikola (1856–1943), American electrical engineer (born Croatia).

1944   John J. O'Neill, *Prodigal genius the life of Nikola Tesla* (NY: Ives Washburn, Inc.) reprinted 1968 (London: Neville Spearman) paperback issue 1980 (London: Granada) 326; index. Author is friend of subject and science writer: Uses MS sources.

1959   Arthur J. Beckhard, *Nikola Tesla electrical genius* (NY: Messner; London: Dennis Dobson, 1961) 192; bibliog; index. Popular style with invented dialogue; acknowledges O'Neill 1944.

1981   Margaret Cheney, *Tesla man out of time* (Englewood Cliffs, NJ: Prentice-Hall) 320; illus; bibliog. Author says O'Neil 1944 passed over subject's relations with others.

Thomas, Sidney Gilchrist (1850–1885), English metallurgist.

1891   R.W. Burnie, ed., *Memoir and letters of Sidney Gilchrist Thomas* (London: John Murray) 314.

1940   Lilian Gilchrist Thompson, *Sidney Gilchrist Thomas an invention and its consequences* (London: Faber and Faber Limited) 328; index. Author is sister of subject; based on Burnie 1891.

Thompson, Benjamin [Count Rumford], (1753–1814), American physicist.

[1871]   George E. Ellis, *Memoir of Sir Benjamin Thompson Count Rumford with notices of his daughter* (Philadelphia: American Academy of Arts and Sciences) reprinted 1972

(Farnborough, Hants.: Gregg Press) [The Loyalist Library]) 680; illus; bibliog; index. Published in connection with an edition of Rumford's complete works. Uses MS sources. Emphasis is on subject's life as opposed to his work. Sparrow says it is scholarly but lacks objectivity; Thompson calls it a soporific tome, which has difficulty coming to terms with the subject's loyalism. 1972 reprint has new introduction and preface by George Athan Billias.

1935   James Alden Thompson, *Count Rumford of Massachusetts* (NY: Farrar & Rinehart Incorporated) 275; illus; bibliog. Author a remote descendant; focus is on subject's "color" not his scientific achievement.

1953   Egon Larsen [Egon Lehrburger], *An American in Europe the life of Benjamin Thompson Count Rumford* (London: Rider and Company) 224; illus; bibliog. According to foreword of Rideal, this is an admiring portrait.

1962   Sanborn C. Brown, *Count Rumford physicist extraordinary* (Garden City, NY: Anchor Books (Doubleday & Company, Inc.) [Science study series] reprinted 1979 (Westport, CT: Greenwood Press) 178; illus; bibliog. Series for students and the general public. This paperback by a professor of physics at MIT is the "overture" to author's 1979 biography.

1964   W.J. Sparrow, *Knight of the White Eagle a biography of Sir Benjamin Thompson Count Rumford (1753–1814)* (London: Hutchinson; NY: Thomas Y. Crowell Company), 1965 under title *Knight of the White Eagle Sir Benjamin Thompson Count Rumford of Woburn Mass)* 302; illus; index; bibliog. First substantial biography to be written and published in Britain; focus on the scientific work.

1967   Duane Bradley, *Count Rumford* (Princeton: D. Van Nostrand Company, Inc.) 176; illus; index. A chatty narrative biography stressing subject's expatriation, animosity and dishonest dealings.

1979   Sanborn C. Brown, *Benjamin Thompson Count Rumford* (Cambridge: The MIT Press) 361; illus; bibliog; index. Presents "a picture of a scientist as he really lives".

Thompson, D'Arcy Wentworth (1860–1948), Scottish naturalist.

1958   Ruth D'Arcy Thompson, *D'Arcy Wentworth Thompson the scholar-naturalist 1860–1948* (London: Oxford University Press) 244; illus; index. Postscript by P.B. Medawar. Author is subject's daughter.

Thompson, Silvanus Phillips (1851–1916), English applied physicist and electrical engineer.

1920   Jane Smeal Henderson, and Helen G. Thompson *Silvanus Philips Thompson DSc LlD. FRS his life and letters* (NY: E.P. Dutton and Company) 372; illus; index. Written by subject's wife and daughter. Uses MSS.

Thomson, Elihu (1853–1937), American electrical engineer (born England).

1944   David O. Woodbury, *Beloved scientist Elihu Thompson a guiding spirit of the electrical age* (NY: Whittlesey House) reprinted 1960 (Boston: The Museum of Science)

358; illus; index. Foreword by Owen D. Young. Anecdotal style. 1960 reprint has title *Elihu Thompson beloved scientist 1853–1937 inventive genius engineer educator pioneer of the electrical age).*

1991   W. Bernard Carlson, *Innovation as a social process Elihu Thompson and the rise of General Electric 1870–1900* (Cambridge: Cambridge University Press) 377; illus; index. Focus is on subject as inventor, from point of view of business and technology. Intended as a "prehistory" of Hughes's story of the evolution of electrical systems; says Passer had access to fewer MS sources and took a macroeconomic perspective.

Thomson, Joseph John (1856–1940), English physicist.

1936   autobiography, *Recollections and reflections* (London: G. Bell and Sons) 451. XX

1942   Lord Rayleigh, *The life of Sir J.J. Thomson, OM* (Cambridge: Cambridge University Press) 299; illus. XX

1964   George Paget Thomson, *J.J. Thomson and the Cavendish Laboratory in his day* (London: Nelson) 186; illus; index. Aimed at readers with a slight, "perhaps somewhat rusty" knowledge of physics. Stresses both technical and intellectual impediments to scientific discovery.

Thomson, William [Baron Kelvin] (1824–1907), Irish physicist.

1908   Andrew Gray, *Lord Kelvin an account of his scientific life and work* (London: J.M. Dent & Co; NY: E.P. Dutton & Co.) reprinted 1973 (NY: Chelsea Publishing company) [English Men of Science] 319; illus; index. Author is professor of natural philosophy at University of Glasgow; aims to give an account of the scientific activity, with less emphasis on the life. This text an extension of an article in the *Glasgow Herald* (19 December 1907).

1910   Silvanus P. Thompson, *The life of William Thomson Baron Kelvin of Largs* (London: Macmillan and Co.) 2 vols, 1297; illus; index. Based on MS sources; begun before subject's death, with his co-operation. Sharlin 1979 says it is eulogistic and sometimes misleading but has not been superseded.

1925   Agnes Gardner King, *Kelvin the man a biographical sketch* (London: Hodder and Stoughton Limited) 142; illus; index. Author is niece of subject. Written to make him "a living personality . . . and to reveal the wonderful happiness of a pure life, inspired by a high ideal and filled with strenuous work".

1938   Alexander Russell, *Lord Kelvin* (London: Blackie & Son) 163; index. Author was a student of subject; "a slight sketch of his work and his influence on his contemporaries".

1979   Harold Issadore Sharlin and Tiby Sharlin, *Lord Kelvin the dynamic Victorian* (University Park: The Pennsylvania State University Press) 272; illus; index. Uses MS sources and also relies heavily on Thompson. Attempts "to integrate the subject's life and work and to place the result in a broader historical context".

1989   Crosbie Smith and M. Norton Wise, *Energy and empire a biographical study of Lord Kelvin* (Cambridge: Cambridge University Press) 866; illus; bibliog; index. Analyses the subject's political, religious and scientific ideology. Based on MS sources; authors are historians of science.

Thurston, Robert Henry (1839–1903), American steam engineer.

1929 William Frederick Durand, *Robert Henry Thurston a biography the record of a life of achievement as engineer educator and author* (NY: American Society of Mechanical Engineers) 301; illus; bibliog; index.

Tizard, Henry Thomas (1885–1959), English physical chemist.

1965 Ronald W. Clark, *Tizard* (London: Methuen & Co.; Cambridge: The MIT Press) 458; illus; bibliog; index. Author a biographer of scientists. Based on MS sources. Foreword by Solly Zuckerman. Foreword to the American edition by Vannevar Bush.

Todd, Alexander Robertus (1907 – –), Scottish bio-organic chemist.

1983 autobiography, *A time to remember the autobiography of a chemist* (Cambridge: Cambridge University Press) 257. Decision to write was based on experience of preparing biographical memoirs of Fellows of the Royal Society, and awareness of lack of information about lives and careers. Stresses rise from humble beginnings. Six appendices are texts of addresses to professional societies.

Tombaugh, Clyde William (1906 – –), American astronomer.

1991 David H. Levy, *Clyde Tombaugh discoverer of planet Pluto* (Tucson: The University of Arizona Press) 211; illus; bibliog; index. Based on interviews with subject and associates, and MS and printed sources.

Torrey, John (1796–1873), American botanist.

1942 Andrew Denny Rodgers III, *John Torrey a story of North American botany* (Princeton: Princeton University Press; London: Humphrey Milford, Oxford University Press; facsimile published 1965 (NY: Hafner Publishing Company) 352; index; bibliog. Foreword by S.W. Geiser.

Tradescant, John (1608–1662), English natural historian.

1964 Mea Allen, *The Tradescants their plants gardens and museum* (London: Michael Joseph) 345; illus; bibliog; index. Author calls book the first attempt to tell subject's story. Leith-Ross 1984 says it is incomplete and sometimes inaccurate.

1984 Prudence Leith-Ross, *The John Tradescants gardeners to the rose and lily queen* (London: Peter Owen) 320; illus; index. Uses MS sources.

Trembley, Abraham (1710–1784), Swiss zoologist.

1952 John R. Baker, *Abraham Trembley of Geneva scientist and philosopher 1710–1784* (London: Edward Arnold) 259; illus; bibliog; index. Author's "purpose has been to present the discoveries of [subject] in a convenient form, to place them in a right perspective amid the scientific ideas of the XVIIIth century, and to relate them to the biological knowledge of the present day".

Trevithick, Richard (1771–1833), English engineer.

1872   Francis Trevithick, *Life of Richard Trevithick with an account of his inventions* (London: E. & F.N. Spon) I:388 II:403; illus; index. Based on MS sources. Author is son of subject. Illustrated with wood engravings by W.J. Welch.

1934   H.W. Dickinson and Arthur Titley, *Richard Trevithick the engineer and the man* (Cambridge: Cambridge University Press) 290; illus; bibliog; index. Aims at a "fairer perspective of events" than was possible for Trevithick 1872. Occasion is centenary; publication sponsored by Babcock and Wilcox Limited as memorial contribution.

Turing, Alan Mathison (1912–1954), English mathematician.

1959   Sara Turing, *Alan M. Turing* (Cambridge: W. Heffer & Sons, Ltd.) 157; bibliog; index. Author is mother of subject; Hodges 1983 says she was unaware of his war work and of much else, but did understand that he was planning to build a computer.

1983   Andrew Hodges, *Alan Turing the enigma* (London: Burnett Books; NY: Simon and Schuster, Inc.) reprinted 1985 (London: Unwin Paperbacks) [Counterpoint] and 1992 (London: Vintage) 587; illus; index. 1992 has new preface, which describes the book as "claiming to cover [subject's] conception . . . of the electronic computer, his critical role in the Second World War, his description of Mind and his founding of Artificial Intelligence".

Twort, Frederick William (1877–1950), English microbiologist.

1993   Antony Twort, *In focus out of step a biography of Frederick William Twort FRS 1877–1950* (Phoenix Mill, NH: Alan Sutton) 340; illus; index. Author is subject's son.

Tyndall, John (1820–1893), English naturalist (born Ireland).

1945   A.S. Eve and C.H. Creasey, *Life and work of John Tyndall* (London: Macmillan and Co. Ltd.) 404; illus; index. Chapter on Tyndall as a mountaineer by Lord Schuster. Preface by Granville Proby, who is nephew of subject, gives history of subject's widow's long-delayed and ultimately unsuccessful attempt to write the life. This was followed by putting the MS sources into the hands of Eve, who fell ill and left it to be completed by Creasey. Uses MSS.

Tyrrell, Joseph Burr (1858–1957), Canadian geologist.

1978   Alex Inglis, *Northern vagabond the life and career of J.B. Tyrrell* (Toronto: McClelland and Stewart) 256; illus; bibliog; index. Uses MS sources. Focus on subject's career with little attention to early life.

Vauban, Sébastien Le Prestre de (1633–1707), French military and civil engineer.

1938   Reginald Blomfield, *Sebastien le Prestre de Vauban 1633–1707* (NY: Barnes & Noble, Inc.; London: Methuen & Co. Ltd.) 216; illus; bibliog; index. Reprinted 1971. Hebbert (1989) says his concern with subject's "activities as an engineer and architect tended to obscure the character and personality of the man".

1924   Daniel Halévy, *Vauban builder of fortresses* (London: Geoffrey Bles) 256. Translated from 1923 Paris edition with notes by C.J.C. Street. Blomfield says author's "eloquence and enthusiasm leave one rather breathless".

1989   F.J. Hebbert and G.A. Rothrock, *Soldier of France Sebastien le Prestre de Vauban 1633–1707* (NY: Peter Lang) [American university studies. Series IX, History] 274; illus; bibliog; index. Uses MS sources.

Vavilov, Nikolai Ivanovich (1887–1943), Russian botanist (plant geneticist).

1984   Mark Popovsky, *The Vavilov affair* (Hamden, CT: Archon Books) 216; index. Foreword by Andrei Sakharov says book is "bitter but truthful . . . reveals the true stature of [subject], undistorted by the lies, embellishments and half-truths of official publications". Uses MS sources.

Vavilov, Sergei Ivanovich (1891–1951), Russian physicist.

1989   L.V. Levshin, *My lifelong road to light* (Moscow: Mir Publishers) [Outstanding Soviet scientists] 264; illus; bibliog. Revised and translated from 1987 Russian edition by G.G. Egorov. Author acquainted with subject.

Vermuyden, Cornelius (1595–1677), Dutch drainage engineer.

1925   J. Korthals-Althes, *Sir Cornelius Vermuyden the lifework of a great anglo-dutchman in land-reclamation and drainage* (London: Williams & Norgate; The Hague: W.P. Van Stockum) 208 and 202. Author is concerned with contemporary public policy with respect to land-drainage and related issues. Harris 1953 says it "dealt almost exclusively with Vermuyden's work in Hatfield Chase, Yorkshire, and disposed of his work in the Great Level . . . in two or three pages", and therefore fails to "achieve [its] professed aim". Text is followed by 202 pages of appendices.

1953   L.E. Harris, *Vermuyden and the Fens a study of Sir Cornelius Vermuyden and the Great Level* (London: Cleaver-Hume Press Ltd.) 168; illus; bibliog; index. Hopes to destroy misconceptions and give to subject "credit too long witheld".

Vernadskii, Vladìmir Ivanovich (1863–1945), Russian mineralogist.

1982   R.K. Balandin, *Vladimir Vernadsky* (Moscow: Mir Publishers) [Outstanding Soviet scientists] 207; illus. Translated and revised from the 1979 Russian edition by Alexander Repeyev. "Our concern in this book is not esoteric scientific problems" but rather to "usher the reader into the rich spiritual world of Vernadsky".

1990   Kendall E. Bailes, *Science and Russian culture in an age of revolutions V.I. Vernadsky and his scientific school 1863–1945* (Bloomington: Indiana University Press) [Indiana-Michigan series in Russian and East European studies] 238; illus; bibliog; index. Uses MS sources.

Volta, Alessandro (1745–1827), Italian physicist.

1964   Bern Dibner, *Alessandro Volta and the electric battery* (NY: Franklin Watts, Inc.) [Immortals of science] 135; illus; index. Not exclusively on subject.

Von Braun, Wernher Magnus Maximilian (1912–1977), American space engineer (born Germany).

1967   Heather M. David, *Wernher von Braun* (NY: Putnam) [Lives to remember] 255; bibliog. XX

1976   Erik Bergaust, *Wernher von Braun* (Washington: National Space Institute) 589; illus; bibliog; index. Based on interviews with the subject. Described as authoritative and definitive. This is not a new edition of author's 1960 Doubleday & Co. *Reaching for the Stars* although portions were "obtained" from that book.

Von Neumann, Johann (1903–1957), American mathematician and computer scientist (born Hungary).

1980   Steve J. Heims, *John von Neumann and Norbert Weiner from mathematics to the technologies of life and death* (Cambridge: The MIT Press) 547; illus; index. Belongs to the genre "of the double biographical essay".

1990   William Aspray, *John von Neumann and the origins of modern computing* (Cambridge: The MIT Press) 376; bibliog; index. Stress is on computing; not the "full intellectual biography" which remains unwritten.

1992   Norman Macrae, *John von Neumann* (NY: Pantheon Books) 405; bibliog; index. Stresses controversies.

1992   William Poundstone, *Prisoner's Dilemma* (NY: Doubleday; Oxford: Oxford University Press, 1993) 290; bibliog; index. Based on MS sources. Combines subject's life with a history of the cold war and an investigation of the effect of game theory on public policy.

Waksman, Selman Abraham (1888–1973), American microbiologist (born Russia).

1958   autobiography, *My life with the microbes* (London: Robert Hale Limited) 320; index. Presented as "the story of a life of a searcher for knowledge".

Wallace, Alfred Russel (1823–1913), English naturalist.

1905   autobiography, *My life a record of events and opinions* (London: Chapman and

Hall; NY: Dodd, Mead & Company) reprinted 1974 (NY: AMS Press) I:435 II:464; illus; index. One-volume edition 1908 (London: Chapman & Hall, Ltd.) Written at the request of the publishers. 1908 edition omits "superfluous matter" including early writings.

1916   James Marchant, *Alfred Russel Wallace letters and reminiscences* (London: Cassell and Company, Ltd.) I:216, II:291; illus; bibliog; index.

1964   Wilma George, *Biologist philosopher a study of the life and writings of Alfred Russell Wallace* (London: Abelard-Schuman) [The Life of science library] 320; bibliog; index. Events of the life are background for a study of the ideas in biological thought. Uses MS sources.

1966   Amabel Williams-Ellis, *Darwin's moon a life of Alfred Russel Wallace* (London: Blackie) 261; illus; index. For the general reader.

1980   Arnold C. Brackman, *A delicate arrangement the strange case of Charles Darwin and Alfred Russel Wallace* (NY: Times Books) 370; illus; bibliog; index. Popular style. Focus is on "the conspiracy against Wallace and its cover-up".

1983   Harry Clements, *Alfred Russel Wallace biologist and social reformer* (London: Hutchinson) 215. Published two years after author's death, with a foreword by his son Richard Clements. "Not intended to be a biography in the ordinary sense of the term" but an attempt "to present the many problems which faced him as a thinking man".

Wallis, Barnes Neville (1887–1979), English engineer.

1972   J.E. Morpurgo, *Barnes Wallis a biography* (London: Longman) 400; illus; index. Penguin edition 1973. Updated reissue 1981 (London: Ian Allan Ltd.) Based on MS sources and written with co-operation of subject, who is friend of author.

Wallis, John (1616–1703), English mathematician.

1938   J.F. Scott, *The mathematical work of John Wallis DD FRS (1616–1703)* (London: Taylor and Francis) 240; index. Foreword by E.N. da C. Andrade.

Warburg, Otto Heinrich (1883–1970), German biochemist.

1981   Hans Krebs, *Otto Warburg cell physiologist biochemist and eccentric* (Oxford: Clarendon Press) 141; illus; bibliog; index. Written in collaboration with Roswitha Schmid; translated by author and Anne Martin.

Waterton, Charles (1782–1865), English naturalist.

1949   Richard Aldington, *The strange life of Charles Waterton 1782–1865* (London: Evans Brothers Limited) 200; illus; bibliog; index. Bibliography is annotated.

1976   Gilbert Phelps, *Squire Waterton* (Wakefield: E.P. Publishing Limited) 167; illus; bibliog. Uses MS sources.

1989   Julia Blackburn, *Charles Waterton 1782–1865 traveller and conservationist*

(London: The Bodley Head) 243; illus; bibliog; index. Foreword by Gerald Durell; an attempt to refocus attention on subject's science as opposed to his eccentricity.

Watson, Richard (1781–1833), English chemist.

1817   Richard Watson, *Anecdotes of the life of Richard Watson Bishop of Landaff written by himself at different intervals and revised in 1814* (London: T. Cadell and W. Davies) 551. Second edition 1817, I:440 II:476; index.

Watson-Watt, Robert Alexander (1892–1973), Scottish radio engineer.

1957   autobiography, *Three steps to victory a personal account by radar's greatest pioneer* (London: Odhams Press Limited) 480; illus; index. Published 1959 under title *The pulse of radar the autobiography of Sir Robert Watson-Watt* (NY: Dial Press) 438. Author explains that "this book began as [an] autobiography . . . [and] relentlessly forced itself toward the shape of a biography. It is now the biography of a system". American edition is heavily revised.

Watt, James (1736–1819), Scottish engineer and chemist.

1856   George Williamson, *Memorials of the lineage early life education and development of the genius of James Watt* (Edinburgh: Printed for the Watt Club) 262; illus. Edited by James Williamson.

1858   James Patrick Muirhead, *The life of James Watt with selections from his correspondence* (London: John Murray) 580; illus. Published 1859 (NY: D. Appleton & Co.) 424. Addressed to the general reader. Note in 1859: "The Publishers have omitted portions of the original English edition which appeared unimportant and uninteresting to the American reader."

1865   Samuel Smiles, *Lives of Boulton and Watt.* See Boulton, Matthew.

1901   William Jacks, *James Watt* (Glasgow: printed for private circulation) 215. XX

1905   Andrew Carnegie, *James Watt* (Edinburgh: Oliphant, Anderson and Ferrier) [Famous Scots Series] 164; index. Also published (NY: Doubleday, Page & Company) 241. Popular account by the American industrialist and philanthropist, written at the request of the Edinburgh publisher.

1925   T.H. Marshall, *James Watt 1736–1819* (London: Leonard Parsons; Boston: Small, Maynard and Company) [The Roadmaker series] 192; index.

Wedgwood, Josiah (1730–1795), English ceramic technologist and chemist.

1865   Llewellyn Jewitt, *The Wedgwoods being a life of Josiah Wedgwood with notices of his works and their productions Memoirs of the Wedgwood and other families and a history of the early potteries of Staffordshire* (London: Virtue Brothers and Co.) 435; illus; index. Author has "scrupulously avoided any reference or allusion" to subject's letters and has "never sought to see them".

1865–66   Eliza Meteyard, *The life of Josiah Wedgwood from his private correspondence and family papers* (London: Hurst and Blackett Publishers) I:504 II:643; illus; index. Based on newly discovered MS sources and includes an introductory sketch of the art of pottery in England. Reilly (1992) says author was neither historian nor ceramist and admired the subject too uncritically.

1894   A.H. Church, *Josiah Wedgwood master-potter* (London: Seeley and Co., Limited) [The portfolio: monographs on artistic subjects, edited by P.G. Hamerton] 104; bibliog. New edition 1903 revised and enlarged.

1894   Samuel Smiles, *Josiah Wedgwood FRS his personal history* (London: John Murray; NY: Harper & Brothers, Publishers, 1895). Uses newly discovered documents.

1915   Julia Wedgwood, *The personal life of Josiah Wedgwood the potter* (London: Macmillan and Co., Limited) 388; illus; index. Author is subject's great-granddaughter; text is revised, edited and introduced by C.H. Herford.

1922   William Burton, *Josiah Wedgwood and his pottery* (London: Cassell and Company, Ltd.) 195; illus; index. The "life-history" of subject and his work in pottery. Author was a chemist with Wedgwood firm.

1976   Anthony Burton, *Josiah Wedgwood a biography* (London: André Deutsch; NY: Stein and Day) 239; illus; bibliog; index. Based on MS sources. Reilley says this is not a true biography but mostly concerned with subject's "wares".

1992   Robin Reilly, *Josiah Wedgwood 1730–1795* (London: Macmillan) 412; illus; bibliog; index. Attempts an objective reassessment and a fair portrait.

Wedgwood, Thomas (1771–1805), English chemist (pioneer of photography).

1903   R.B. Litchfield, *Wedgwood, the first photographer* (London: Duckworth and Co.) reprinted 1973 (NY: Arno Press) [The Literature of Photography] 271; illus; index. Subtitle: an account of his life, his discovery and his friendship with Samuel Taylor Coleridge, including the letters of Coleridge to the Wedgwoods and an examination of accounts of alleged earlier photographic discoveries.

Wegener, Alfred Lothar (1880–1930), German meteorologist and geophysicist.

1986   Martin Schwarzbach, *Alfred Wegener the father of continental drift* (Madison, WI: Science Tech.) [Scientific revolutionaries a biographical series]. Introduction by Anthony Hallam and "an assessment of the earth science revolution" by I. Bernard Cohen. Translation of 1980 Stuttgart edition. XX

Weil, André (1906 – –), French mathematician.

1992   autobiography, *André Weil the apprenticeship of a mathematician* (Basel: Birkhäuser Verlag) 197; illus; index. Translated from 1991 French edition by Jennifer Gage. Described as an attempt "to retrace the intellectual itinerary of a mathematician".

Weizmann, Chaim (1874–1952), Israeli organic chemist and biochemist (born Russia).

1962   Meyer W. Weisgal and Joel Carmichael, eds, *Chaim Weizmann a biography by several hands* (London: Weidenfield and Nicholson) 364; illus; index. Preface by David Ben-Gurion; chronological, with each chapter by a different author: "We have aimed at producing a composite portrait that would encompass the totality of his life." Uses subject's correspondence.

1976   Barnet Litvinoff, *Weizmann last of the patriarchs* (London: Hodder and Stoughton) 288; illus; bibliog; index. "I have not seen it as my part to scatter references throughout the text; or support the narrative with bulky footnotes, a historian's practice that does not always strike this author as meritorious." Does not address subject's childhood. Uses MSS.

1986   Norman Rose, *Chaim Weizmann a biography* (NY: Viking) 520; illus; bibliog; index. Focuses on subject as Zionist leader. Uses MS sources.

1993   Jehuda Reinharz, *Chaim Weizmann the making of a statesman* (NY: Oxford University Press) [Studies in Jewish history] 536; illus; bibliog; index. Part of a multi-volume work on subject; "the present volume focuses on Weizmann as a leader and statesman of the World Zionist Organization beginning with World War One until the summer of 1922". Uses MS sources.

Werner, Alfred (1866–1919), French chemist.

1966   George B. Kauffman, *Alfred Werner founder of coordination chemistry* (Berlin: Springer-Verlag) 127; illus; index. Uses MS sources.

Westinghouse, George (1846–1914), American engineer.

1919   Francis E. Leupp, *George Westinghouse his life and achievements* (Boston: Little, Brown and Company) 304; illus; index. Based on interviews with associates, local tradition and gossip, public records and newspapers. Hopes to inspire "the young men of today".

1921   Henry G. Prout, *A life of George Westinghouse* (NY: The American Society of Mechanical Engineers) 375; illus; index. Author/editor has compiled the memories and impressions of associates of subject, with the aid of a Committee of the American Society of Mechanical Engineers.

Whately, Richard (1787–1863), English logician.

1866   E. Jane Whately, *Life and correspondence of Richard Whately late Archbishop of Dublin* (London: Longmans, Green and Co.) I:491 II:480; index. Written by subject's daughter.

1981   Donald Harman Akenson, *A Protestant in purgatory Richard Whately Archbishop of Dublin* (Hamden, CT: Archon Books) [The Conference on British Studies Biography Series] 276; bibliog; index. A non-technical portrait of subject and his interests; a "traditional biography" that eschews " 'psychobiography' ".

Wheatstone, Charles (1802–1875), English physicist.

1975   Brian Bowers, *Sir Charles Wheatstone FRS 1802–1875* (London: HMSO) 239; illus; bibliog; index. Author is on staff of the Science Museum; the book originated as a PhD thesis.

Wheeler, William Morton (1865–1937), American zoologist.

1970   Mary Alice Evans and Howard Ensign Evans, *William Morton Wheeler biologist* (Cambridge: Harvard University Press) 363; illus; bibliog; index.

Whewell, William (1794–1866), English philosopher of science and physical chemist.

1876   I. Todhunter, *William Whewell DD Master of Trinity College Cambridge an account of his writings with selections from his literary and scientific correspondence* (London: Macmillan and Co.) I:416 II:439. "I have been solicitous to guard against obtrusions of my own opinions and judgement, being desirous of making known Dr Whewell himself, his pursuits and attainments, and not of obscuring them by any interpretation of mine." Second volume consists of subject's correspondence.

1891   [Janet Mary] Stair Douglas, *The life and selections from the correspondence of William Whewell late Master of Trinity College Cambridge* (London: C. Kegan Paul & Co.) 591; index. For the general reader; author says 1876 Todhunter deals with subject's scientific correspondence, while this book is concerned with his "domestic and academic" correspondence.

1991   Menachem Fisch, *William Whewell philosopher of science* (Oxford: Clarendon Press; NY: Oxford University Press) 220; bibliog; index. "This study is concerned with the history and historiography of philosophy"; focuses on subject's work.

Whiston, William (1667–1752), English mathematician and cosmologist.

1981   Maureen Farrell, *William Whiston* (NY: Arno Press) [The Development of Science] 347; illus; bibliog; index. Originally presented as the author's thesis; discusses subject's life and work.

1985   James E. Force, *William Whiston honest Newtonian* (Cambridge: Cambridge University Press) 208; illus; index. Based on author's dissertation; foreword by Richard H. Popkin. An "attempt to focus on Whiston's uniquely Newtonian synthesis of the design argument of natural and revealed religion" and to put his work "in social and historical context".

White, Gilbert (1720–1793), English naturalist.

1901   Rashleigh Holt-White, *The life and letters of Gilbert White of Selborne* (London: John Murray) reprinted 1969 (NY: AMS Press) I:330 II:300; illus; index. "Written and edited by his great-grand-nephew." Seeks to correct misconceptions. Uses MSS.

1928   Walter Johnson, *Gilbert White pioneer poet and stylist* (London: John Murray)

340; illus; index. 1981 edition under title *Gilbert White* (London: Macdonald Futura, Publishers) [Heritage] 331; illus; index. Uses MS sources. Author calls book an opportunity of freeing subject's "memory from unjust aspersions".

1946   Walter S. Scott, *White of Selborne* (London: J. Westhouse) reprinted 1985 (Liss, Hampshire: Nimrod Book Services) [Selborne in Hampshire series] 262; illus; index. "A one-volume account of White's life, told in a continuous narrative form . . . in which the emphasis would be laid upon Gilbert White as a man, a friend, a clergyman, a University don, an agriculturalist and a gardener, rather than as a naturalist." Uses MSS.

1954   R.M. Lockley, *Gilbert White* (London: H.F. & G. Witherby, Ltd.) [Great naturalists series] 127. 1976 edition (London: White Lion Publishers) 136; illus; bibliog; index. Uses MS sources.

1986   Richard Mabey, *Gilbert White a biography of the author of The natural history of Selborne* (London: Century) 239; illus; bibliog; index. Uses MSS.

1988   Paul G.M. Foster, *Gilbert White and his records a scientific biography* (London: Christopher Helm) 240; illus; bibliog; index. Critical of previous accounts for ignoring the man and his book "within the context of a social and scientific study" in favour of the pastoral dream evoked by *Selborne*. Based on subject's records.

Whitehead, Alfred North (1861–1947), English mathematician, theoretical physicist and philosopher.

1985–90   Victor Lowe, *Alfred North Whitehead the man and his work* (Baltimore: The Johns Hopkins University Press) I:351 II:389; illus; bibliog; index. Written with the co-operation of subject. Uses MS sources including subject's correspondence. Focuses on subject as philosopher rather than as mathematician. Author died before completion; edited by J.B. Scheewind but remains incomplete.

Whitney, Eli (1765–1825), American technologist.

1952   Jeannette Mirsky and Allan Nevins, *The world of Eli Whitney* (NY: The Macmillan Company) 346; illus; bibliog; index. Another edition 1962 (NY: Collier Books) 350. Stresses that subject was "a man of ideas; his real life is the life of his mind". Uses MS sources.

Whitney, Josiah Dwight (1819–1896), American geologist.

1909   Edwin Tenney Brewster, *Life and letters of Josiah Dwight Whitney* (Boston and NY: Houghton Mifflin Company (The Riverside Press, Cambridge)) 411; illus; index; bibliog. Uses materials from subject's family and colleagues.

Whittle, Frank (1907 – –), English aeronautical engineer.

1953   autobiography, *Jet the story of a pioneer* (London: Frederick Muller Ltd.) 320; illus; index. Primarily concerns the development of the turbo-jet engine but includes a brief account of early life.

1987   John Golley, *Whittle the true story* (Shrewsbury: Airlife) 273; illus; index. Written "in association with" subject; technical editor Bill Gunston. Subject presented as "a very great Englishman . . . one of the greatest inventors of all time".

Wiener, Norbert (1894–1964), American mathematician.

1953   autobiography, *Ex-prodigy my childhood and youth* (NY: Simon and Schuster, Inc.) reprinted 1964 (Cambridge, MA: The M.I.T. Press) 309; index. Avoids temptation "to write an autobiography in the Freudian jargon".

1956   autobiography, *I am a mathematician The later life of a prodigy An autobiographical account of the mature years and career of Robert Wiener and a continuation of the account of his childhood in Ex-prodigy* (Cambridge, MA: The M.I.T. Press) 380; index. Reprinted paperback 1964. "The present book is concerned with my mature years and my scientific career."

Wigner, Eugene Paul (1902 – –), Hungarian physicist.

1992   Andrew Szanton, *The recollections of Eugene P. Wigner* (NY: Plenum Press) 335; illus; index; bibliog. Described as being an autobiography "as told to" author, who explains he organized book from tape-recorded interviews, condensing and deciding on themes. Subject's preface stresses the transitory quality of fame, and admits he is not content with a brief and "narrowly objective" profile in *American Men of Science*.

Wiley, Harvey Washington (1844–1930), American chemist.

1957   Maurice Natenberg, *The legacy of Doctor Wiley* (Chicago: Regent House) 166; illus; bibliog; index. Preface by Jonathan Forman stresses contemporary dangers of food additives and pesticides. Occasion is the fiftieth anniversary of the 1906 Pure Food and Drug Act.

1958   Oscar Edward Anderson, *The health of a nation Harvey W. Wiley and the fight for pure food* ([Chicago]: Published for the University of Cincinnati by the University of Chicago Press) 333; illus; index. Author is an historian at the University of Cincinnati.

Wilkins, John (1614–1672), English mathematician and philosopher of science.

1969   Barbara J. Shapiro, *John Wilkins 1614–1672 an intellectual biography* (Berkeley: University of California Press) 333; bibliog; index. Author says none of subject's MSS survive.

Williamson, William Crawford (1816–1895), English palaeobotanist.

1896   autobiogaphy, *Reminiscences of a Yorkshire naturalist* (London: George Redway) 228; bibliog. Edited by the subject's widow.

Williston, Samuel Wendell (1851–1918), American vertebrate palaeontologist and ento-mologist.

1971   Elizabeth Noble Shor, *Fossils and flies the life of a compleat scientist Samuel Wendell Williston 1851–1918* (Norman: University of Oklahoma Press) 285; illus; bibliog; index. Author is subject's granddaughter-in-law. Quotes extensively from subject's unpublished "Recollections" of his early years and other MS sources.

Wilson, Alexander (1766–1813), Scottish ornithologist.

1828   George Ord, *Sketch of the life of Alexander Wilson author of the American ornithology* (Philadelphia: Harrison Hall) 199. Author is FLS, an associate of subject. Hunter (1983) says author's sketch in volume 9 of *American Ornithology* was rewritten and substantially augmented with the inclusion of more letters for the three-volume octavo edition (1828–29) published by Harrison Hall; here published separately.

1856   William B.O. Peabody, "Life of Alexander Wilson," in *The Library of American Biography*, conducted by Jared Sparks (NY: Harper & Brothers Publishers) vol. 2, 1–169.

1861   C. Lucy Brightwell, *Difficulties overcome scenes in the life of Alexander Wilson the ornithologist* (London: Sampson Low, Son, and Co.) 160. Written to promote "a taste for . . . pure and elevating pursuits . . . among all classes of the community".

1906   James Southall Wilson, *Alexander Wilson poet-naturalist a study of his life with selected poems* (NY: The Neale Publishing Co.) 179. Author regards this as first real biography.

1961   Robert Cantwell, *Alexander Wilson naturalist and pioneer a biography* (Philadelphia: J.B. Lippincott Company) 319; illus; index; bibliog. Decorations by Robert Ball. "The first penetrating investigation of Wilson's life and character"; but Hunter (1983) notes and corrects "a few trifling errors".

1983   Clark Hunter, *The life and letters of Alexander Wilson* (Philadelphia: American Philosophical Society) 456; illus; bibliog; index. Full texts of letters, many of which had been suppressed.

Wilson, George (1818–1859), Scottish chemist.

1860   [Jessie Aitken Wilson], *Memoir of George Wilson* (Edinburgh: Edmonston and Douglas) 536; bibliog. New condensed edition 1866 (London: Macmillan and Co.) 384. Author, who is sister of subject, made use of his letters.

Withering, William (1741–1799), English botanist and meteorologist.

1950   T. Whitmore Peck and K. Douglas Wilkinson, *William Withering of Birmingham MD FRS FLS* (Bristol: John Wright and Sons Ltd.) 239; illus; bibliog; index. Uses MS sources.

Witt, Jan de (1625–1672), Dutch mathematician.

1978   Herbert H. Rowen, *John de Witt grand pensionary of Holland, 1625–1672* (Princeton: Princeton University Press) 949; index; bibliog. XX

1986   Herbert H. Rowen, *John de Witt statesman of the "true freedom"* (Cambridge: Cambridge University Press) 236; bibliog. Subject as statesman; a "much briefer and wholly new version" of author's 1978 biography; uses same sources.

Wood, Robert Williams (1868–1955), American experimental physicist.

1941   William Seabrook, *Doctor Wood modern wizard of the laboratory the story of an American small boy who became the most daring and original experimental physicist of our day but never grew up.* (NY: Harcourt, Brace and Company) 355; illus; bibliog.

Woodhouse, James (1770–1809), American chemist.

1918   Edgar F. Smith, *James Woodhouse a pioneer in chemistry 1770–1809* (Philadelphia: The John C. Winston Company) reprinted 1980 (NY: Arno Press) [Three centuries of science in America] 299; index. Written in "the hope that the rising generations of American chemists would seriously interest themselves in the labors of their earlier brothers".

Wright, Wilbur (1867–1912) **and Orville** (1871–1948), American aeronautical engineers.

1930   John R. McMahon, *The Wright brothers fathers of flight* (Boston: Little, Brown, and Company) 308; illus. Written to make amends for earlier false counterclaims of priority. Evidence includes "homely details". Howard 1987 says Orville Wright "detested" this book, because of "fictional conversations and many inaccuracies".

1943   Fred C. Kelly, *The Wright brothers a biography authorized by Orville Wright* (NY: Harcourt, Brace) reprinted 1989 (NY: Dover Publications) [Dover books on transportation, maritime] 340; illus; index. Aimed at non-technical readers.

1975   John Evangelist Walsh, *First flight the untold story of the Wright brothers* (NY: Crowell; London: George Allen & Unwin Ltd.) 306; illus; bibliog; index. Author a professional biographer with longstanding interest in subjects. Corrects earlier studies.

1987   Fred Howard, *Wilbur and Orville a biography of the Wright brothers* (NY: Alfred A. Knopf) 530; illus; bibliog; index. Aimed at general reader. Author is co-editor of subjects' papers.

1989   Tom D. Crouch, *The Bishop's boys a life of Wilbur and Orville Wright* (NY: W.W. Norton & Company) 606; illus; bibliog index. Author a Wright scholar.

Young, Arthur (1741–1820), English agricultural scientist.

1938   Amelia Defries, *Sheep and turnips being the life and times of Arthur Young, F.R.S., first Secretary to the Board of Agriculture* (London: Methuen & Co. Ltd.) 235. Preface by R.A. Butler; introduction by Montague Fordham, who observes that the author writes as a student of human nature, not of history and economics.

1973   John G. Gazley, *The life of Arthur Young* (Philadelphia: American Philosophical Society) [Memoirs of the American Philosophical Society] 727; illus; bibliog. XX

Young, Thomas (1773–1829), English natural philosopher.

1855   George Peacock, *Life of Thomas Young MD FRS &c* (London: John Murray) 514. Author is professor of astronomy. Based on MS sources.

1933   Frank Oldham, *Thomas Young FRS philosopher and physician* (London: Edward Arnold & Co.) 159; illus; bibliog; index.

Yukawa, Hideki (1907–1981), Japanese theoretical physicist.

1982   autobiography, *Tabibito (the traveler)* [sic] (Singapore: World Scientific) 218; illus. Translated, from an edition published 1958 by Asahi Shinburn, by L.M. Brown & R. Yoshida. Introduction by Brown, who discusses the subject's life and work to 1935.

Zacharias, Jerrold Reinach (1905–1986), American physicist.

1992   Jack S. Goldstein, *A different sort of time the life of Jerrold R. Zacharias scientist engineer educator* (Cambridge: The MIT Press) 373; illus; bibliog; index. Based on interviews with subject and his associates.

Zariski, Oscar (1899–1986), American mathematician (born Russia).

1991   Carol Parikh, *The unreal life of Oscar Zariski* (Boston: Academic Press, Inc.) 264; illus; bibliog; index. Includes a foreword for non-mathematicians by David Mumford. Based on interviews with subject and associates.

Zeppelin, Ferdinald (1838–1917), German airship technologist.

1931   Margaret Goldsmith, *Zeppelin a biography* (NY: William Morrow and Company). XX

Appendix A: Scientific Specialities

Agriculturalist
Bakewell, R.
Boussingault, J.B.J.D.
Coke, T.W.
Malesherbes, C.G.L. de
Russell, E.J.
Smith, E.F.
Young, A.
Anatomist
Clift, W.
Cuvier, G.
Owen, R.
Steno, N.
Swammerdam, J.
Astronomer
Airy, G.B.
Banneker, B.
Bok, B.J.
Bond, W.C.
Bowditch, N.
Dyson, F.W.
Eddington, A.S.
Ferguson, J.
Flamsteed, J.
Frost, E.B.
Gill, D.
Halley, E.
Herschel, C.L.
Herschel, W.
Hubble, E.P.
Keeler, J.E.
Kopal, Z.
Lovell, B.
Lowell, P.
Maskelyne, N.
Mitchell, M.
Molyneux, W.
Newcomb, S.
Porter, R.W.
Pritchard, C.
Ritchey, G.W.
See, T.J.J.
Shapley, H.
Shklovskii, I.S.
Smyth, C.P.
Struve, O.W.
Tombaugh, C.W.
Biochemist
Abel, J.J.

Chargaff, E.
Folin, O.
Funk, C.
Haldane, J.B.S.
Krebs, H.A.
Szent-Györgyi, A. Von
Warburg, O.H.
Biologist
Boveri, T.
Chambers, R.
Delbruck, M.
Garrod, A.E.
Just, E.E.
Kammerer, P.
Lamarck, J.B.P.A. de M.
LeConte, J.
Leeuwenhoek, A. van
Loeb, J.
Merriam, C.H.
Mivart, St G.J.
Montgomery, E.
Parkes, A.S.
Raspail, F.V.
Romanes, G.J.
Twort, F.W.
Waksman, S.A.
Botanist
Bailey, L.H.
Banister, J.
Banks, J.
Bartram, J.
Bentham, G.
Bessey, C.E.
Brown, R.
Colden, C.
Coulter, J.M.
Cunningham, A.
Deam, C.C.
Ehret, G.D.
Gray, A.
Henry, A.
Henslow, J.S.
Hofmeister, W.F.B.
Hooker, J.D.
Linnaeus, C.
Marum, M. van
Mitchell, J.
Nelson, A.
Nuttall, T.

Pfeffer, W.
Ravenel, H.W.
Ray, J.
Smith, J.E.
Torrey, J.
Vavilov, N.I.
Williamson, W.C.
Withering, W.
Chemist
Adams, R.
Armstrong, H.E.
Avogadro, A.
Barton, D.H.R.
Beddoes, T.
Berthelot, P.E.M.
Berzelius, J.J.
Black, J.
Boerhaave, H.
Borodin, A.P.
Calvin, M.
Collie, J.N.
Cooper, T.
Cottrell, F.G.
Cram, D.J.
Crookes, W.
Davy, H.
Dewar, M.J.S.
Djerassi, C.
Draper, J.W.
Eliel, E.L.
Faraday, M.
Foucroy, A.F. de
Frankland, E.
Gay-Lussac, J.L.
Gibbs, J.W.
Goldschmidt, V.M.
Haber, F.
Hahn, O.
Hales, S.
Hall, C.M.
Hare, R.
Havinga, E.
Ipatieff, V.N.
Keir, J.
Langmuir, I.
Lavoisier, A.L.
Lemieux, R.U.
Liebig, J. von
Lloyd, J.U.

Lomonosov, M.V.
Mark, H.F.
McCollum, E.V.
Mendeléeff, D.I.
Mercer, J.
Merrifield, R.B.
Mond, L.
Morley, E.W.
Nakanishi, K.
Nef, J.U.
Nernst, H.W.
Nozoe, T.
Pasteur, L.
Perkin, W.H.
Playfair, L.
Prelog, V.
Priestley, J.
Ramsay, W.
Ray, P.C.
Remsen, I.
Roberts, J.D.
Robinson, R.
Roscoe, H.E.
Rush, B.
Silliman, B.
Smithson, J.
Soddy, F.
Spinks, J.W.T.
Steacie, E.W.R.
Stone, F.G.A.
Sutherland, W.
Swan, J.W.
Tizard, H.T.
Todd, A.R.
Watson, R.
Wedgwood, T.
Weizmann, C.
Werner, A.
Wiley, H.W.
Wilson, G.
Woodhouse, J.

Cinematographer
Friese-Green, W.
Marey, E.J.

Ecologist
Shelford, V.
Shreve, F.
Swallow, E.H.

Engineer
Arkwright, R.
Armstrong, E.H.
Baird, J.L.

Bell, A.G.
Bessemer, H.
Bidder, G.P.
Bond, C.C.J.
Boulton, M.
Brindley, J.
Brunel, I.K.
Brunel, M.I.
Coolidge, W.D.
Cort, H.
Crompton, R.E.B.
Crompton, S.
De Forest, L.
De Havilland, G.
Diesel, R.
Doran, P.H.
Eads, J.B.
Edison, T.A.
Ericsson, J.
Evans, O.
Fairbairn, W.
Ferranti, S.Z. De
Fessenden, R.A.
Fleming, J.A.
Ford, H.
Fulton, R.
Garrett, G.W.L.
Goodyear, C.
Jenkin, H.C.F.
Jessop, W.
Johansson, C.E.
Karman, T. von
Kelly, W.
Kettering, C.F.
Lanchester, F.W.
Macintosh, C.
Marconi, G.
Martin, B.
McAdam, J.L.
McCormick, C.H.
Morse, S.F.B.
Muybridge, E.J.
Nasmyth, J.
Newcomen, T.
Niépce, J.N.
Parsons, C.A.
Rennie, J.
Ricardo, H.R.
Rittenhouse, D.
Siemens, C.W.
Sikorsky, I.I.
Sinclair, C.M.

Smeaton, J.
Sperry, E.A.
Steinmetz, C.P.
Stephenson, G.
Telford, T.
Tesla, N.
Thomson, E.
Thurston, R.H.
Trevithick, R.
Vauban, S.L.P. de
Vermuyden, C.
Von Braun, W.M.M.
Wallis, B.N.
Watson-Watt, R.A.
Watt, J.
Wedgwood, J.
Westinghouse, G.
Whitney, E.
Whittle, F.
Wright, W. and O.
Zeppelin, F.

Entomologist
Bodenheimer, F.S.
Fabre, J.H.
Howard, L.O.
Lubbock, J.
Say, T.
Smith, A.

Explorer
Amundsen, R.E.G.
David, T.W.E.
Hind, H.Y.

Geneticist
Mendel, J.G.
Morgan, T.H.
Muller, F.J.

Geographer
Bering, V.
Bougainville, L.A. De
Bowman, I.
Evans, L.
Kropotkin, P.A.
Markham, C.R.
Morse, J.
Nordenskiöld, N.A.E.
Petty, W.
Przheval'skii, N.M.
Reclus, E.
Rennell, J.
Steller, G.W.

Geologist
Agassiz, J.L.R.

Bailey, L.W.
Clarke, E.D.
Clarke, W.B.
Croll, J.
Dana, J.D.
Dawson, G.
Dawson, J.W.
Du Toit, A.L.
Eaton, A.
Edgeworth, R.L.
Ewing, W.M.
Featherstonhaugh, G.W.
Geikie, A.
Geikie, J.
Gilbert, G.K.
Haast, J.F.J. von
Hamilton, W.
Hill, R.T.
Houghton, D.
Hutton, J.
King, C.R.
Lawson, A.C.
Leith, C.K.
Lesley, P.J.
Logan, W.
Lyell, C.
Lyman, B.S.
Mantell, G.A.
Mawson, D.
Miller, H.
Murchison, R.I.
Owen, D.D.
Pettijohn, F.J.
Ramsay, A.C.
Raspe, R.E.
Rogers, W.B.
Saussure, H.B. de
Sedgwick, A.
Smith, W.
Sorby, H.C.
Swedenborg, E.
Tyrrell, J.B.
Whitney, J.D.
Horologist
Harrison, J.
Horticulturalist
Evelyn, J.
Ichthyologist
Jordan, D.S.
Inventor
Nobel, A.B.

Logician
Whately, R.
Mathematician
Abel, N.H.
Arbuthnot, J.
Babbage, C.
Barrow, I.
Bell, E.T.
Bellman, R.
Boole, G.
Byron, A.A.
Carnot, L.-N.-M.
Cartan, E.
Cauchy, A.L.
Condorcet, M.J.A.
Courant, R.
D'Alembert, J.R.
De Morgan, A.
Dodgson, C.L.
Fisher, R.A.
Fourier, J.B.J.
Friedman, A.A.
Galton, F.
Gauss, K.F.
Gödel, K.
Green, G.
Halmos, P.R.
Hamilton, W.R.
Hawking, S.W.
Herschel, J.F.W.
Hilbert, D.
Jones, W.
Kovalevsky, S.
Leibniz, G.W.
Liouville, J.
Moore, J.
Morland, S.
Newsom, C.
Neyman, J.
Noether, A.E.
Oughtred, W.
Pascal, B.
Peano, G.
Pearson, K.
Peirce, C.S.
Ramanujan Iyengar, S.
Russell, B.A.W.
Simpson, T.
Simson, R.
Slaught, H.E.
Slichter, C.S.
Somerville, M.

Steklov, V.A.
Talbot, W.H.F.
Turing, A.M.
Von Neumann, J.
Wallis, J.
Weil, A.
Whiston, W.
Whitehead, A.N.
Wiener, N.
Wilkins, J.
Witt, J. de
Zariski, O.
Metallurgist
Thomas, S.G.
Meteorologist
Abbe, C.
Bjerknes, V.F.K.
Ellis, W.
Fitzroy, R.
Wegener, A.L.
Mineralogist
Vernadskii, V. I.
Natural historian
Browne, T.
Catesby, M.
Collinson, P.
Commerson, P.
Humboldt, F.W.H.A. von
Sonnerat, P.
Tradescant, J.
Natural philosopher
Ashmole, E.
Berkeley, G.
Boyle, R.
Newton, I.
Oken, L.
Whewell, W.
Young, T.
Naturalist
Audubon, J.J.
Baird, S.F.
Bates, H.W.
Coghill, G.E.
Darwin, C.R.
Darwin, E.
Dick, R.
Doubleday, H.
Douglas, D.
Edward, T.
Frohawk, F.W.
Garden, A.
Gosse, P.H.

Jenner, E.
Macintosh, C.
Michurin, I.V.
Müller, F. von
Palmer, E.
Thompson, D.W.
Tyndall, J.
Wallace, A.R.
Waterton, C.
White, G.
Navigator
Cayley, G.
Ross, J.C.
Oceanographer
Maury, M.F.
Ornithologist
Coues, E.
Gould, J.
Wilson, A.
Palaeontologist
Broom, R.
Cope, E.D.
Hall, J.
Leakey, L.S.B.
Marsh, O.C.
Scott, W.B.
Teilhard de Chardin, P.
Williston, S.W.
Philosopher of science
Bernal, J.D.
Physicist
Abragam, A.
Alvarez, L.W.
Ambartsumyan, V.A.
Appleton, E.V.
Bache, A.D.
Bethe, H.A.
Bohr, N.H.D.
Boltzmann, L.E.
Born, M.
Bose, J.C.
Bose, S.N.
Bragg, W.H.
Brashear, J.A.
Braun, K.F.
Brewster, D.
Bridgman, P.W.
Callan, N.

Casimir, H.B.G.
Cavendish, H.
Chandrasekhar, S.
Cockcroft, J.D.
Coulomb, C.A.
Curie, M.
Curie, P.
Dalton, J.
Dirac, P.A.M.
Duhem, P.M.M.
Ehrenfest, P.
Einstein, A.
Fermi, E.
Feynman, R.P.
Forbes, J.D.
Frisch, O.R.
Goddard, R.H.
Hale, G.E.
Hassler, F.R.
Heaviside, O.
Heisenberg, W.K.
Helmholtz, H.L.F. von
Henry, J.
Hevesy, G. Von
Hooke, R.
Huygens, C.
Infeld, L.
Jeans, J.H.
Joliot, J.F.
Joule, J.P.
Kapitza, P.L.
Kinnersley, E.
Kramers, H.A.
Langley, S.P.
Lawrence, E.O.
Lindemann, F.A.
Lockyer, J.N.
Lodge, O.J.
Mach, E.
Mairan, J.J.O. de
Maxwell, J.C.
Mayer, J.R. von
McLennan, J.C.
Michelson, A.A.
Millikan, R.A.
Morse, P.
Moseley, H.G.J.
Mott, N.F.

Oliphant, M.L.E.
Oppenheimer, J.R.
Peierls, R.E.
Planck, M.C.E.L.
Rabi, I.I.
Raman, C.V.
Röntgen, W.C.
Rossi, B.B.
Rutherford, E.
Sabine, W.C.W.
Sakharov, A.D.
Salan, A.
Schrödinger, E.
Simon, F.E.
Strutt, J.W.
Szilard, L.
Teller, E.
Thompson, B.
Thompson, S.P.
Thomson, J.J.
Thomson, W.
Vavilov, S.I.
Volta, A.
Wheatstone, C.
Wigner, E.P.
Wood, R.W.
Yukawa, H.
Zacharias, J.R.
Polymath
Kircher, A.
Seismologist
Milne, J.
Writer
Châtelet, G.E. le T. de B.
Diderot, D.
Zoologist
Agassiz, A.
Aspinall, J.
Flower, W.H.
Frisch, K.R. Von
Goldschmidt, R.B.
Haeckel, E.H.P.A.
Huxley, J.
Huxley, T.H.
Metchnikov, I.
Nansen, F.
Trembley, A.
Wheeler, W.M.

Appendix B: Major Publishers (three or more biographies)

Only publishers of first editions are indexed.

Abelard-Schuman
Leeuwenhoek, A. van
Newton, I.
Wallace, A.R.
Allen & Unwin
Mendel, J.G.
Russell, B.A.W.
Russell, E.J.
American Chemical Society
Adams, R.
Barton, D.H.R.
Calvin, M.
Cram, D.J.
Dewar, M.J.S.
Djerassi, C.
Edison, T.A.
Eliel, E.L.
Havinga, E.
Lemieux, R.U.
Mark, H.F.
Merrifield, R.B.
Nakanishi, K.
Nozoe, T.
Prelog, V.
Roberts, J.D.
Stone, F.G.A.
American Philosophical Society
Dawson, J.W.
Smith, E.F.
Wilson, A.
Young, A.
Anchor Books
Michelson, A.A.
Pasteur, L.
Thompson, B.
Appleton, D.
Audubon, J.J.
Dodgson, C.L.
Morse, S.F.B.
Pasteur, L.
Archon Books
Bowman, I.
Byron, A.A.
Reclus, E.
Vavilov, N.I.

Whately, R.
Arnold, Edward
David, T.W.E.
Huygens, C.
Lanchester, F.W.
Ramsay, W.
Saussure, H.B. de
Strutt, J.W.
Trembley, A.
Young, T.
Barker, A.
Curie, M.
Lyell, C.
Rutherford, E.
Talbot, W.H.F.
Basic Books
Alvarez, L.W.
Bethe, H.A.
Djerassi, C.
Einstein, A.
Rabi, I.I.
Birkhäuser
Heisenberg, W.K.
Kovalevsky, S.
Noether, A.E.
Weil, A.
Blackie
Newton, I.
Pascal, B.
Rutherford, E.
Thomson, W.
Wallace, A.R.
Blackwell
Darwin, C.R.
Davy, H.
Lavoisier, A.L.
Newton, I.
Blackwood
Berkeley, G.
Humboldt, F.W.H.A. von
Huxley, T.H.
Bobbs-Merrill
Darwin, C.R.
Edison, T.A.
Ford, H.
Rush, B.

Bodley Head
Carnot, L.-N.-M.
Petty, W.
Waterton, C.
Cambridge University Press
Airy, G.B.
Boulton, M.
Bragg, W.H.
Browne, T.
Dirac, P.A.M.
Friedman, A.A.
Frisch, O.R.
Galton, F.
Gay-Lussac, J.L.
Hales, S.
Herschel, C.L.
Herschel, W.
Hubble, E.P.
Jeans, J.H.
Keeler, J.E.
Maskelyne, N.
Morse, S.F.B.
Murchison, R.I.
Newton, I.
Pearson, K.
Ray, J.
Rossi, B.B.
Rutherford, E.
Schrödinger, E.
Sedgwick, A.
Thomson, E.
Thomson, J.J.
Thomson, W.
Todd, A.R.
Trevithick, R.
Whiston, W.
Witt, J. de
Cape
Aspinall, J.
Linnaeus, C.
Russell, B.A.W.
Cassell
Châtelet, G.E. le T. de B.
Dalton, J.
Davy, H.

141

Faraday, M.
Herschel, C.L.
Herschel, J.F.W.
Herschel, W.
Liebig, J. von
Maxwell, J.C.
Pasteur, L.
Playfair, L.
Rennell, J.
Wallace, A.R.
Wedgwood, J.
Century
McCormick, C.H.
Steinmetz, C.P.
White, G.
Chapman & Hall
Diderot, D.
Faraday, M.
Pasteur, L.
Wallace, A.R.
Collins
Curie, M.
Darwin, C.R.
Leakey, L.S.B.
Lindemann, F.A.
Linnaeus, C.
Teilhard de Chardin, P.
Columbia University Press
Colden, C.
Kettering, C.F.
Mivart, St G.J.
Raspail, F.V.
Constable
Agassiz, A.
Black, J.
Boyle, R.
Crompton, R.E.B.
Dodgson, C.L.
Humboldt, F.W.H.A. von
Lavoisier, A.L.
Lodge, O.J.
Marconi, G.
Metchnikov, I.
Newton, I.
Parsons, C.A.
Ricardo, H.R.
Cornell University Press
Bjerknes, V.F.K.
Millikan, R.A.
Muller, F.J.
David & Charles
Banks, J.

Jessop, W.
Newcomen, T.
Telford, T.
Dent
Bentham, G.
Dalton, J.
Darwin, E.
Dodgson, C.L.
Flower, W.H.
Huxley, T.H.
Priestley, J.
Thomson, W.
Dodd, Mead
Einstein, A.
Fulton, R.
Funk, C.
Hall, C.M.
Kettering, C.F.
Oppenheimer, J.R.
Doubleday
Amundsen, R.E.G.
Bowditch, N.
Cottrell, F.G.
Curie, M.
Dalton, J.
Darwin, C.R.
Einstein, A.
Ford, H.
Gibbs, J.W.
Halley, E.
Infeld, L.
Lavoisier, A.L.
Steinmetz, C.P.
Teilhard de Chardin, P.
Von Neumann, J.
Duckworth
Huxley, T.H.
Sinclair, C.M.
Wedgwood, T.
Dutton
Hale, G.E.
Kettering, C.F.
Lawrence, E.O.
Thompson, S.P.
Faber & Faber
Bates, H.W.
Berkeley, G.
Darwin, E.
Davy, H.
Faraday, M.
Hamilton, W.
Herschel, W.

Ross, J.C.
Swedenborg, E.
Thomas, S.G.
Foreign Languages
Lomonosov, M.V.
Mendeléeff, D.I.
Michurin, I.V.
Hale, R.
Lovell, B.
Nobel, A.B.
Waksman, S.A.
Harcourt, Brace
Audubon, J.J.
Leakey, L.S.B.
Maury, M.F.
Wood, R.W.
Wright, W. and O.
Harper & Row
Casimir, H.B.G.
Heisenberg, W.K.
Teilhard de Chardin, P.
Harper Brothers
Dana, J.D.
Edison, T.A.
Wilson, A.
Harvard University Press
Arbuthnot, J.
Berkeley, G.
Cuvier, G.
Dalton, J.
Nuttall, T.
Steller, G.W.
Wheeler, W.M
Heffer, W.
Dyson, F.W.
Foucroy, A.F.
Morland, S.
Turing, A.M.
Heinemann
Clift, W.
Dalton, J.
Darwin, C.R.
Hooke, R.
Jenner, E.
McAdam, J.L.
Hilger, A.
Cockcroft, J.D.
Einstein, A.
Hevesy, G.V.
Kopal, Z.
Leibniz, G.W.
Smyth, C.P.

Hodder & Stoughton
Cayley, G.
Edison, T.A.
Fabre, J.H.
Haldane, J.B.S.
Leakey, L.S.B.
Lodge, O.J.
Rutherford, E.
Thomson, W.
Weizmann, C.
Houghton Mifflin
Brashear, J.A.
Eads, J.B.
Frost, E.B.
Kropotkin, P.A.
Newcomb, S.
Rogers, W.B.
Whitney, J.D.
Hutchinson
Babbage, C.
Baird, J.L.
Bernal, J.D.
Cavendish, H.
Darwin, C.R.
Kammerer, P.
Marconi, G.
Thompson, B.
Wallace, A.R.
Johns Hopkins University Press
Abel, J.J.
Edison, T.A.
Hamilton, W.R.
Sperry, E.A.
Steinmetz, C.P.
Whitehead, A.N.
Joseph, Michael
Darwin, C.R.
Hooker, J.D.
Tradescant, J.
Kegan Paul
Ellis, W.
Gosse, P.H.
Oken, L.
Whewell, W.
Knopf
Bohr, N.H.D.
Darwin, C.R.
Edison, T.A.
Einstein, A.
Ford, H.
Humboldt, F.W.H.A. von

Morse, S.F.B.
Sakharov, A.D.
Wright, W. and O.
Lane, J.
Banks, J.
Coke, T.W.
Fulton, R.
Lippincott
Armstrong, E.H.
Baird, S.F.
Hare, R.
Swedenborg, E.
Wilson, A.
Little Brown
Bell, A.G.
Bowditch, N.
Ewing, W.M.
Karman, T. von
Pasteur, L.
Westinghouse, G.
Wright, W. and O.
Longman
Audubon, J.J.
Babbage, C.
Bose, J.C.
Brunel, I.K.
Brunel, M.I.
Darwin, C.R.
Davy, H.
De Morgan, A.
Fairbairn, W.
Faraday, M.
Humboldt, F.W.H.A. von
Huxley, T.H.
Jenkin, H.C.F.
Jenner, E.
Kettering, C.F.
Lamarck, J.B.P.A. de M.
Maury, M.F.
Mawson, D.
Mercer, J.
Nansen, F.
Romanes, G.
Roscoe, H.E.
Smith, J.E.
Stephenson, G.
Telford, T.
Wallis, B.N.
Whately, R.
Macdonald
Edison, T.A.
Hahn, O.

Henry, A.
Macmillan
Agassiz, J.L.R.
Babbage, C.
Browne, T.
Curie, P.
Edison, T.A.
Faraday, M.
Flower, W.H.
Forbes, J.D.
Geikie, A.
Howard, L.O.
Huxley, T.H.
King, C.R.
Liebig, J. von
Lockyer, J.N.
Lovell, B.
Lowell, P.
Lubbock, J.
Marconi, G.
Maxwell, J.C.
Mitchell, M.
Nernst, H.W.
Newton, I.
Ramsay, A.C.
Ramsay, W.
Roscoe, H.E.
Thomson, W.
Tyndall, J.
Wedgwood, J.
Wedgwood, J.
Whewell, W.
Manchester University Press
Arkwright, R.
Cuvier, G.
Darwin, E.
Ferranti, S.Z. De
Joule, J.P.
Rennie, J.
McGraw-Hill
Bowditch, N.
Darwin, C.R.
Edison, T.A.
Messner
De Forest, L.
Goodyear, C.
Marconi, G.
Michelson, A.A.
Szilard, L
Tesla, N.

Methuen
Amundsen, R.E.G.
Boerhaave, H.
Davy, H.
Dodgson, C.L.
Galton, F.
Mond, L.
Nansen, F.
Newton, I.
Pascal, B.
Tizard, H.T.
Young, A.
Mir
Lomonosov, M.V.
Steklov, V.A.
Vavilov, S.I.
Vernadskii, V.I.
MIT Press
Babbage, C.
Braun, K.F.
Byron, A.A.
Edison, T.A.
Ford, H.
Gauss, K.F.
Gödel, K.
Morse, P.
Priestley, J.
Thompson, B.
Von Neumann, J.
Wiener, N.
Zacharias, J.R.
Murray, J.
Boulton, M.
Boyle, R.
Brindley, J.
Brunel, I.K.
Byron, A.A.
Commerson, P.
Darwin, C.R.
Darwin, E.
Dick, R.
Edward, T.
Gill, D.
Herschel, C.L.
Hooker, J.D.
Markham, C.R.
Murchison, R.I.
Nasmyth, J.
Newton, I.
Owen, R.
Petty, W.
Rennie, J.

Siemens, C.W.
Smeaton, J.
Smith W.
Stephenson, G.
Telford, T.
Thomas, S.G.
Watt, J.
Wedgwood, J.
White, G.
Young, T.
Nelson
Berkeley, G.
Darwin, C.R.
Davy, H.
Eddington, A.S.
Halley, E.
Hooker, J.D.
Lyell, C.
Nobel, A.B.
Priestley, J.
Thomson, J.J.
Norton
Huxley, T.H.
Rush, B.
Wright, W. and O.
Oxford University Press
Abragam, A.
Arbuthnot, J.
Ashmole, E.
Babbage, C.
Bohr, N.H.D.
Borodin, A.P.
Boyle, R.
Clarke, W.B.
D'Alembert, J.R.
Darwin, C.R.
Diderot, D.
Einstein, A.
Fourier, J.B.J.
Garrod, A.E.
Helmholtz, H.L.F. von
Humboldt, F.W.H.A. von
Just, E.E.
Krebs, H.A.
Loeb, J.
McAdam, J.L.
Priestley, J.
Robinson, R.
Thompson, D.W.
Warburg, O.H.
Weizmann, C.
Whewell, W.

Pantheon
Dodgson, C.L.
Feynman, R.P.
Von Neumann, J.
Penguin
Russell, B.A.W.
Sakharov, A.D.
Salam, A.
Sinclair, C.M.
Pergamon
Appleton, E.V.
Evelyn, J.
Frisch, K.R.V.
Huxley, T.H.
Langmuir, I.
Simon, F.E.
Sorby, H.C.
Strutt, J.W.
Princeton University Press
Bailey, L.H.
Cope, E.D.
Coulomb, C.A.
Coulter, J.M.
Henry, J.
Lavoisier, A.L.
Lomonosov, M.V.
Mayer, J.R. von
Morgan, T.H.
Peierls, R.E.
Rittenhouse, D.
Scott, W.B.
Silliman, B.
Torrey, J.
Witt, J. de
Private publication
Clarke, E.D.
Dawson, G.M.
Ferranti, S.Z. De
Goodyear, C.
Haast, J.F.J. Von
Hall, J.
Johansson, C.E.
Keir, J.
Kelly, W.
Linnaeus, C.
Lloyd, J.U.
Lyman, B.S.
Macintosh, C.
Parkes, A.S.
Pascal, B.
Smeaton, J.
Sonnerat, P.

Ford, H.
Putnam
Agassiz, J.L.R.
Audubon, J.J.
Curie, M.
Darwin, C.R.
Edison, T.A.
Einstein, A.
Huxley, T.H.
Lesley, P.J.
Smithson, J.
Steinmetz, C.P.
Teller, E.
Von Braun, W.M.M.
Reidel, D.
Avogadro, A.
Beddoes, T.
Boussingault, J.B.J.D.
Peano, G.
Struve, O.W.
Sampson Low
Audubon, J.J.
Maury, M.F.
Wilson, A.
Schuman, H.
Browne, T.
Lavoisier, A.L.
Silliman, B.
Scribners
Banneker, B.
Ericsson, J.
Ford, H.
Hahn, O.
Herschel, J.F.W.
Herschel, W.
Lavoisier, A.L.
Maxwell, J.C.
Michelson, A.A.
Newton, I.
Ramanujan Iyengar, S.
Shapley, H.
Silliman, B.
Szilard, L
Teller, E.
Simon & Schuster
Dodgson, C.L.
Einstein, A.
Wiener, N.
Smithsonian
Baird, S.F.
Karman, T. von
Shelford, V.E.

Sikorsky, I.I.
Souvenir
Fermi, E.
Pasteur, L.
Teilhard de Chardin, P.
Springer-Verlag
Borodin, A.P.
Cauchy, A.L.
Courant, R.
Gauss, K.F.
Halmos, P.R.
Hilbert, D.
Kovalevsky, S.
Kramers, H.A.
Liouville, J.
Neyman, J.
Werner, A.
Stanford University Press
Bridgman, P.W.
Ipatieff, V.N.
Jordan, D.S.
Taylor & Francis
Born, M.
Boyle, R.
Mott, N.F.
Wallis, J.
Thames & Hudson
Brunel, I.K.
Darwin, C.R.
Dodgson, C.L.
Russell, B.A.W.
University of Alabama Press
Diesel, R.
Featherstonhaugh, G.W.
Ravenel, H.W.
University of Arizona Press
Bok, B.J.
Ritchey, G.W.
Röntgen, W.C.
Shreve, F.
Tombaugh, C.W.
University of California Press
Boveri, T.
Mach, E.
Moseley, H.G.J.
Muybridge, E.J.
Planck, M.C.E.L.
Wilkins, J.

University of Chicago Press
Agassiz, J.L.R.
Chandrasekhar, S.
Coghill, G.E.
Fermi, E.
Kropotkin, P.A.
Marey, E.-J.
Pettijohn, F.J.
Wiley, H.W.
University of Illinois Press
Banister, J.
Catesby, M.
Coues, E.
University of Oklahoma Press
Audubon, J.J.
Diesel, R.
Haber, F.
Palmer, E.
Williston, S.W.
University of Pennsylvania Press
Bache, A.D.
Bartram, J.
Brashear, J.A.
Draper, J.W.
Eaton, A.
Kinnersley, E.
Rittenhouse, D.
Rush, B.
Say, T.
University of Toronto Press
Hind, H.Y.
McLennan, J.C.
Steacie, E.W.R.
University of Wisconsin Press
Lavoisier, A.L.
Leith, C.K.
Slichter, C.S.
Unwin, T. Fisher
Crookes, W.
Dodgson, C.L.
Fabre, J.H.
Haeckel, E.H.P.A.
Helmholtz, H.L.F. von
Macintosh, C.
Pascal, B.
Viking
Diderot, D.
Hawking, S.W.
Weizmann, C.

145

Watts
Darwin, C.R.
Huxley, T.H.
Watts, F.
Darwin, C.R.
Fulton, R.
Gibbs, J.W.
Linnaeus, C.
Volta, A.

Weidenfeld & Nicolson
Audubon, J.J.
Darwin, C.R.
Einstein, A.
Faraday, M.
Stephenson, G.
Weizmann, C.
Witherby, H.F.
Linnaeus, C.

Nansen, F.
White, G.
Yale University Press
Cooper, T.
Gibbs, J.W.
Lyell, C.
Malesherbes, C.G.
de L. de
Marsh, O.C.

Appendix C: Index of Series

Great naturalists series (Witherby): White
Great Nobel prizes (Heron Books): Röntgen; Rutherford
Great thinkers of India (Asia Publishing House): Ramanujan Iyengar
Great travellers (Faber & Faber): Bates; Ross
Great writers (Walter Scott): C.R. Darwin
Hall of fame books (Prentice-Hall): Eads
Harvard monographs in the history of science (Harvard University Press): Dalton
Harvard studies in English (Russell & Russell): Arbuthnot
Heinemann books on the history of science: Dalton
Heritage (Macdonald Futura): White
History of American science and technology series (University of Alabama Press): Featherstonhaugh
History of geology (Arno): Hall; Smith
History of medicine series (Scarecrow): Pasteur
History of modern physics (Tomash): Fermi
History, philosophy, and sociology of science (Arno): Banks
Hoover library on war, revolution, and peace (Stanford University Press): Ipatieff
Horizon Caravel books (American Heritage): C.R. Darwin
Immortals of mankind (Franklin Watts): C.R. Darwin
Immortals of science (Chatto & Windus): Davy
Immortals of science (Franklin Watts): Gibb; Volta
Indiana historical collections (Indiana Historical Bureau): Owen
Indiana-Michigan series in Russian and East European studies (Indiana University Press): Vernadskii
International archives of the history of ideas (Martinus Nijhoff): Duhem; Somerville
International series of monographs in history and philosophy of science (Pergamon): Frisch
Iowa State University Press series in the history of technology and science: Bessey
Johns Hopkins studies in the history of technology (Johns Hopkins University Press): Edison; Steinmetz
Kentucky bicentennial bookshelf (University Press of Kentucky): Morgan
Laurel great lives and thought (Dell): Pascal
Leaders in science (Putnam): Agassiz; C.R. Darwin; T.H. Huxley
Leaders of philosophy (Ernest Benn): Leibniz
Legends of our time (Edition Frontieres): Sakharov
Life of science library (Abelard/Schuman): Browne; Lavoisier; Leewenhoek; Newton; Silliman; Wallace
Life stories of famous men (Watts): C.R. Darwin; T.H. Huxley
Literature of photography (Arno): Niépce; Wedgwood
Lives of achievement (Longmans): Edison
Lives to remember (Putnam): M. Curie; Edison; Steinmetz; Von Braun
Loyalist library (Gregg Press): Thompson
Makers of America (Dodd, Mead): Fulton
Man, state and society series (Allied): Bose
Masters of medicine (T. Fisher Unwin): Helmholtz
Memoirs of the American Philosophical Society: Dawson; Smith; Young
Men of physics (Pergamon): Strutt
Men of Russian science (Foreign Languages Publishing House): Mendeléeff
Methuen's shilling library: T.H. Huxley
Modern English writers (Blackwood): T.H. Huxley
Modern masters (Viking): Einstein
Monographs and textbooks in pure and applied mathematics (Mariel Dekkek): Noether

Monographs on the history and philosophy of biology (Oxford University Press): Krebs
National biography series (National Book Trust): Ray
Natural history library (Doubleday): C.R. Darwin
Natural sciences in America (Arno): Merriam
Navies and men (Arno): Maury
Nieuwe Nederlandse bijdragen tot de geschiedenis der geneeskunde en der natuurweten-
  schappen (Rodopi): Leewenhoek
Outstanding Soviet scientists (Mir): Steklov; Vavilov; Vernadskii
Oxford English memoirs and travels (Oxford University Press): C.R. Darwin
Pathfinder biographies (Weidenfeld & Nicolson): C.R. Darwin; Faraday; Rutherford
Penguin modern masters: Einstein
Pennsylvania lives (University of Pennsylvania Press): Bache; Bartram; Brashear; Rit-
  tenhouse
Personal portraits (Max Parrish): Newton
Philosophical classics for English readers (Blackwood): Berkeley
Pickering masters: E. Darwin
Polish heritage series (American Institute of Polish Culture): M. Curie
Popular biographies (Partridge): Faraday
Portfolio: monographs on artistic subjects (Seeley): Wedgwood
Profile in science (Eriksson/Souvenir): Einstein; Fermi; Joliot; Pasteur; Teilhard de Chardin
Profiles of genius series (Boole Press): Boole; W.R. Hamilton
Profiles, pathways, and dreams: autobiographies of American chemists (American
  Chemical Society Press): Barton; Calvin; Cram; Dewar; Djerassi; Eliel; Havinga;
  Lemieux; Mark; Merrifield; Nakanishi; Nozoe; Roberts; Prelog; Stone
Riverside biographical series (Houghton Mifflin): Eads
Riverside library (Houghton Mifflin): Kropotkin
Roadmaker series (Small, Maynard): Faraday; Watt
Science study series (Doubleday): Dalton; Newton; Pasteur; Thompson
Scientific revolutionaries a biographical series (Science Tech Publishers): Bohr; Wegener
Scribners scientific memoirs: Shapley
Selborne in Hampshire series: (Nimrod): White
Select bibliographies reprint series (Books for Libraries Press): Bering; T.H. Huxley
Seventeenth and eighteenth century British philosophy (Routledge): Berkeley
Smithsonian history of aviation series (Smithsonian Institution Press): Karman
Society of Automotive Engineers historical series: Ricardo
Sources of Science (Johnson Reprint): Newton
South African biographical and historical studies (Balkema): Broom
Southern biography series (Louisiana State University Press): LeConte
Spectrum series (Mathematical Association of America): E.T. Bell
Star series (Garden City Publishing Co.): Edison
Story biographies (Methuen): Dodgson
Stratford library (Hutchinson): C.R. Darwin
Studia Kircheriana (Edizione del Mondo): Kircher
Studies in French civilization (Edwin Mellen Press): Bougainville
Studies in Jewish history (Oxford University Press): Weizmann
Studies in the history of mathematics and physical sciences (Springer-Verlag): Liouville
Studies in the history of modern science (D. Reidel): Peano
Studies in the libertarian and utopian tradition (Schocken): Kropotkin
Technology and society (Arno): Kettering
Telecommunications (Arno): Baird; Morse
Thinker's library (Watts): C.R. Darwin

Three centuries of science in America (Arno): Bond; Hare: Howard; Remsen; Rittenhouse; Woodhouse

Translations of mathematical monographs (American Mathematical Society): Cartan

True stories of great Americans (Macmillan): Edison

Wiley series in probability and mathematical statistics: Fisher Wisconsin Publications in the history of science and medicine (University of Wisconsin Press): Lavoisier

Works of the Cavendish Society: Dalton

World perspectives (Harper & Row): Heisenberg

World's epoch-makers (T. & T. Clark): Herschel

Yale University historical publications (Yale University Press): Cooper